W9-BUJ-648

SHAKESPEARE'S TRAGIC IMAGINATION

Also by Nicholas Grene

BERNARD SHAW: A CRITICAL VIEW
SHAKESPEARE, JONSON, MOLIÈRE: THE COMIC CONTRACT
SYNGE: A CRITICAL STUDY OF THE PLAYS
TRADITION AND INFLUENCE IN ANGLO-IRISH POETRY (*editor with Terence Brown*)
SHAW, LADY GREGORY AND THE ABBEY: A CORRESPONDENCE AND A RECORD (*editor with Dan H. Laurence*)
J.M. SYNGE: THE WELL OF THE SAINTS (*editor*)

Shakespeare's Tragic Imagination

Nicholas Grene
Associate Professor of English
Trinity College Dublin

St. Martin's Press   New York

First published in the United States of America in 1992

Printed in Hong Kong

ISBN 0–312–06218–4

Library of Congress Cataloging-in-Publication Data
Grene, Nicholas.
  Shakespeare's tragic imagination / Nicholas Grene.
    p. cm.
  Includes bibliographical references and index.
  ISBN 0–312–06218–4
  1. Shakespeare, William, 1564–1616—Tragedies.   2. Tragedy.
I. Title.
PR2983.G74   1992
822.3'3—dc20
                                        91–8155
                                           CIP

To
Sophia, Hannah, Jessica, Clement

Contents

Acknowledgements

I wish to acknowledge gratefully a year's leave of absence from Trinity College Dublin in 1988–9 and, equally gratefully, a Visiting Fellowship for that time at Clare Hall Cambridge where much of this book was written in most congenial conditions.

I owe a great deal to two friends (and former colleagues at the University of Liverpool). Hermione Lee was warmly encouraging at a crucial early stage of planning the book, and gave every line of my first draft the benefit of her wonderfully acute eye for flabby writing and fudged argument. Her critical comments made splendid reading. Philip Edwards, struggling heroically with an almost illegible typescript, offered both detailed and general advice which I found most helpful in revising the book. His generous and appreciative reaction was all the more heartening coming from someone whose own work on Shakespeare I so much admire. I gained also from the constructive criticisms of Lucy McDiarmid on the first chapter, though I am afraid she may not see much improvement as a result.

My wife Eleanor not only made useful editorial suggestions on the book, but put up patiently – and at times impatiently – with the endlessly repeated obsessions of the writer writing it. The book is dedicated, with dearest love, to my children.

Preface

My starting-point for this book was a sense of wonder at the contiguity of Shakespeare's last three tragedies. The world of *Macbeth*, so much the incarnation of a metaphysics of absolute good and evil, seemed extraordinarily remote from the shape-changing relativism of *Antony and Cleopatra* or the analytically observed psychological and political realities of *Coriolanus*. Yet there were similar thematic concerns, similar preoccupations, running through all three: the relation of power to legitimating authority, for instance, or of male and female roles in the imagination of (male) heroic endeavour. Looking back through the tragedies, I felt increasingly that this pattern of striking difference in imaginative milieu combined with thematic congruences was repeated in earlier pairs of companion plays: *King Lear* and *Timon of Athens*; *Othello* and *Troilus and Cressida*; *Hamlet* and *Julius Caesar*. There appeared to be a doubleness in Shakespeare's tragic imagination itself, which could be traced back eventually to different modes in the histories. The book that follows is my attempt to explore this doubleness.

It is worth exploring if only because it represents a way of looking at the full sweep of Shakespeare's work in the tragic form in the period from 1599 to 1608 when that was his main creative concern. As such it may be a means of avoiding the limiting effects of some previous critical approaches to the tragedies. The prescriptive/evaluative model of A.C. Bradley is still, at the opposite end of the twentieth century from *Shakespearean Tragedy*, immensely influential in isolating the four 'major' tragedies. After Bradley, *Hamlet*, *Othello*, *King Lear* and *Macbeth* came to constitute a sort of inner canon, the other tragedies defined as they variously fell short of, or were lesser in kind, than these. Even though the generic superiority of the Bradleyan 'big four' might not be universally accepted, a second tendency in modern criticism reinforced their special status. This was the establishment of separate categories corralling off some of the tragedies from *the* tragedies. The viewpoint of Vivian Thomas, in his recent book on *Shakespeare's Roman Worlds*, is representative: 'The substance and vision inherent in the Roman plays is such that the perspective of tragedy is inadequate to provide a thoroughgoing critical appreciation of them'.[1] *Troilus and Cressida*, also, has been removed into an indefinite class of 'problem plays', bracketed with *Measure for Measure* and *All's Well* outside the tragic form altogether. Kenneth Muir's statement, in *Shakespeare's Tragic Sequence*, was intended as an empiricist reaction against this isolation of Bradley's four tragedies from the others: 'There is no such thing as Shakespearian Tragedy: there are only Shakespearian tragedies'.[2] This is a sane corrective, but it has its own limitations in restricting the understanding of the tragedies to a 'sequence' only of one play after another.

It is perhaps impossible to see Shakespearean tragedy clearly and see it whole. This book is no exception in so far as, following through a view of Shakespeare's tragic imagination which grows out of the histories, it omits the two earlier tragedies *Titus Andronicus* and *Romeo and Juliet*. The design of its argument is to offer individual readings of the nine plays of the main tragic period which may help to illuminate their interrelationship. There *are* striking differences between the Bradleyan four and the other five, differences above all in mode and milieu. To see this, and yet to see also that all nine works are bound together by a pattern of themes and images mirrored from one to another, may take us some way towards a more comprehensive concept of Shakespeare's tragic drama. I hope at least that, by not quarantining some of the tragedies as 'Roman' or 'problem' plays, by looking at juxtaposed pairings both obvious (*Julius Caesar* and *Hamlet*) and less obvious (*Troilus and Cressida* and *Othello*) while observing differences, it may be possible to hold the plays together in relationship without reducing them to a monolithic one or to the sum of their various parts.

In writing about the tragedies, though I have not been primarily concerned with staging or with its interpretive variations, I have tried always to see the plays as texts for enactment. This is not a matter of analysing stagecraft or spotting actors' points, but of intuiting what the plays have to *say* dramatically. Just what they appear to say, and to whom they are speaking, necessarily changes depending on the age, the circumstances, and the medium of representation. Nevertheless, for all the unstable variables, there remains a strong sense when we watch or read the tragedies of Shakespeare that what we attend to are coherent, if elusive and almost infinitely multi-faceted, imaginative forms. The critical readings in this book constitute one attempt to define such forms.

As a means of embodying in my writing an awareness of the potentially shifting perspectives, I have worked with a conventional code of reference points. I have used the first person pronoun in the text to indicate where I as critical interpreter differ from others. I have referred to 'the audience', or 'the Elizabethan/ Jacobean audience', when the original reception of the plays is at issue. Most of the time, however, I have adopted the style 'we' for an audience implied within the text which is not merely the contingent assembly of customers for whom Shakespeare wrote, nor my book's readers grammatically inveigled into collusion with my opinions as critic, but the necessarily changing, yet not wholly subjective and unstable, collectivity to which the dramatic representation called for by the text reaches out.

A last prefatory note on scholarship. To write about Shakespeare is fully to discover the meaning of critical belatedness. Not only are there the incomparably great voices of the past on the subject, Johnson or Coleridge, but every available position seems to have been occupied, all the possible words used up. If I try to acknowledge even a representative sample of those who have gone before with whom I agree or disagree, the result is soon an argument intolerably fussy, tortuous and over-annotated. And yet how arrogant or naive it may appear to ignore so much that is subtle, relevant and illuminating in the scholarship and criticism of the past and present. What I have done in the face of this dilemma, is lay down certain rough ground-rules for myself. I have quoted from critics only where the quotation bears immediately on my argument. I have not referred to books and articles simply in order to demonstrate I have read them. I have provided references to material which I have found useful and which readers may want to look up. I have tried to be aware of textual issues where they affect my readings without involving myself in the full, and often compelling, complexities of Qs and Fs. I hope that the balance struck between a readable individual argument and the acknowledgement of critical context proves an acceptable one.

1
From the Histories to the Tragedies

In *Richard II*, at the moment when Bolingbroke proposes to ascend the throne, one voice is raised in opposition. The Bishop of Carlisle protests, and ends his indignant protest with an eloquent prophecy:

> My Lord of Hereford here, whom you call king,
> Is a foul traitor to proud Hereford's king;
> And if you crown him, let me prophesy –
> The blood of English shall manure the ground,
> And future ages groan for this foul act;
> Peace shall go sleep with Turks and infidels,
> And in this seat of peace tumultuous wars
> Shall kin with kin and kind with kind confound;
> Disorder, horror, fear, and mutiny,
> Shall here inhabit, and this land be call'd
> The field of Golgotha and dead men's skulls.
> O, if you raise this house against this house,
> It will the woefullest division prove
> That ever fell upon this cursed earth.
> Prevent it, resist it, let it not be so,
> Lest child, child's children, cry against you woe.
>   IV.i.134–49[1]

Carlisle's warning projects an audience forward in historical time to the Wars of the Roses in the next century which, in the orthodox political view of the Tudor period, were God's punishment on England for the deposition of Richard II which is here being dramatised. In terms of Shakespeare's theatre, however, it would have worked retrospectively to supply a cause for the whole dire cycle of 'tumultuous wars' which the playwright had already so vividly staged in the *Henry VI–Richard III* tetralogy. Within those four plays themselves, such was the bloody tangle of violence and counter violence, it was often hard to see more than local cause

1

and effect. Here in *Richard II*, a primary historical source is provided to give the mess of civil war the overarching meaning of the Tudor myth. Carlisle's argument is based upon the divine right of kings, the inalienable position of Richard as monarch, his subjects' lack of the right to judge him. The country that permits 'so heinous, black, obscene a deed' as the usurpation will be plagued by the just wrath of God with wars appropriate to 'Turks and infidels' in place of the Christian peace of England.

Carlisle's speech has often been picked out as a key statement not only for *Richard II*, but for the complete sequence of the history plays. But, curiously, in context it appears to make very little impact. Northumberland, Bolingbroke's henchman, makes a response which is swift and to the point:

> Well have you argued, sir; and, for your pains,
> Of capital treason we arrest you here.
>
> IV.i.150–1

Bolingbroke himself, brisk and businesslike as always, brushes the intervention aside without even acknowledging that it has happened:

> Fetch hither Richard, that in common view
> He may surrender
>
> IV.i.155–6

There is a striking disjunction here between the language and attitudes of Carlisle, and those of Bolingbroke's new court. For Northumberland, Carlisle's eloquence affords a welcome and unexpected pretext to dispose of an opponent; in 'well have you argued, sir' there is nothing but contemptuous irony for the political foolishness of the outburst. For Bolingbroke it only underlines the need to have King Richard abdicate publicly – 'so we shall proceed without suspicion' (IV.i.156–7). The emotional charge of Carlisle's words spends itself in an atmosphere of cool incomprehension. The Bishop's rhetoric is made to seem out of place, almost embarrassing, in the low-key functional world which Bolingbroke creates and controls. Carlisle's apocalyptic vision sounds strident and melodramatic against the shrewd purposefulness of the new *Realpolitik*.

Bolingbroke and Northumberland are not conventionally characterised as usurper and traitor. The amplification of moral disapproval, ordinarily associated in Renaissance drama with the concepts of usurpation and treachery, seems to be missing. Northumberland, indeed, through *Richard II* and its two sequels, *Henry IV Parts I and II*, is developed into a thoroughly obnoxious character, in turns as sycophantic follower of Bolingbroke, as righteously indignant rebel against him, and then as the 'crafty-sick' fox who fails to support even his own son in the rebellion. Yet the very meanness of his instinct for survival, his self-deceiving hypocrisy, make for a dramatic reality which allows us to regard him with detachment. Bolingbroke's motivation in *Richard II* is notoriously opaque; we are never given the inner evidence to decide how far he is deliberate Machiavel or mere lucky opportunist with greatness thrust upon him. Even when, as the king in the *Henry IV* plays, he does reveal to his son the deliberateness of his political calculations, they are discussed with a pragmatism which invites a morally neutral attitude. Henry may have notions of atonement for the deposition and murder of King Richard, notions represented symbolically in his recurrent project for a crusade which is always deferred by one more piece of domestic trouble. But guilt hardly grips him as we might expect it to beset a Renaissance stage usurper. This is no Richard III, much less a Macbeth. His tiredness and discouragement as his reign ends, the contraction of his dreams of a redeeming death in the Holy Land to the Jerusalem chamber, neither of these seem a very spectacular nemesis for the man who committed the primal crime of a hundred years of English history. The portrait of Henry seems instead an understanding, if not particularly sympathetic, study of a man who has limited his life to the manipulation of power.

Richard II may be read as the dramatised movement from one historical epoch to another, from the hieratic kingship of Richard II to the management monarchy of Bolingbroke. In this view, Carlisle's speech is an old guard stand against the all but complete takeover by Henry's Lancastrian *apparat*. In a broader context of Shakespeare's drama, however, the scene has a rather different significance. There are here juxtaposed two radically contrasting ways of apprehending history and politics. Carlisle's is mythic and mystical. The Bishop speaks with an authority that outweighs his relatively lowly social rank:

> Worst in this royal presence may I speak,
> Yet best beseeming me to speak the truth.
>   IV.i.115–16

He is raised to the role of seer, with a visionary sense of the
consequences of what is going forward:

> I speak to subjects, and a subject speaks,
> Stirr'd up by God, thus boldly for his king.
>   IV.i.132–3

His warning of civil war to come is not merely cautionary, enforcing the dangers of disrupting an accepted political order; it is
intended to have the full impact of divine sanction. For Carlisle the
events of here and now live within a sacred order of things.
Northumberland and Bolingbroke ignore this order of things, as
they ignore the rhetorical afflatus of Carlisle's speech. Their concern with political consequences never touches upon the supernatural or providential; Bolingbroke's ever-postponed plans for a
crusade are somewhere between a public relations exercise and an
insurance policy against the possibility of divine retribution. Henry
and Northumberland operate within a secular system governed
entirely by the balance of power which is aptly represented elsewhere in the play in the image of a scales in which Richard and
Bolingbroke are weighed.

What emerges in *Richard II* (and the later history plays) is a
contrast between two different imaginations of the world. Richard
himself tries to sustain the unexamined role of God-appointed
king, and takes literally the metaphors associated with the part:

> For every man that Bolingbroke hath press'd
> To lift shrewd steel against our golden crown,
> God for his Richard hath in heavenly pay
> A glorious angel. Then, if angels fight,
> Weak men must fall, for heaven still guards the right.
>   III.ii.58–62

But, as Richard is immediately made to realise, it ain't necessarily
so; the angels don't always appear, and 'shrewd steel', though
baser than gold in a metaphorical hierarchy, is yet a tougher metal.
It is after Richard has lost, when he histrionically submits to his

successful cousin, that he contrives partly to validate and substantiate the sacred idea of kingship which he has so signally failed to embody. He makes of the supposed abdication a ceremony of self-sacrilege:

> With mine own tears I wash away my balm,
> With mine own hands I give away my crown,
> With mine own tongue deny my sacred state,
> With mine own breath release all duteous oaths
> IV.i.207–10

The abdication scene is perfectly poised between a sense of Richard's self-pitying antics – as in Bolingbroke's dry comment on his play with the mirror, 'The shadow of your sorrow hath destroy'd The shadow of your face' (IV.i.292–3) – and an imaginatively authentic identification of Richard's betrayal with the betrayal of Christ. Even as Richard displays the qualities which made him unfit to be king, he transforms his deposition into a martyrdom.

The Tudor myth was not only political propaganda: built into it were archetypal images of a lost era of Paradisal peace,[2] of a country visited by God's anger, of the long-promised return of divine favour to England. But in the *Henry VI* trilogy, the suggestiveness of these images was limited by the rhetorical mode in which the plays were conceived and executed. The development from the first to the second tetralogy was largely a stylistic one. In the first tetralogy it is rhetoric which gives the drama its shape, both locally in set speeches, and comprehensively in form and structure. The rhetorical strategies employed serve as ends in themselves. The confrontation between Richard, Duke of York and Queen Margaret, at the beginning of *3 Henry VI*, is a useful illustration. That scene (I.iv) provokes horror at the cruelty of Margaret and compassion for York even in some of his Lancastrian enemies; it is designed as the culmination of the process of increasing savagery which is the underlying pattern of the three *Henry VI* plays. It has its theatrical logic: nemesis for the ambitious Duke, the final expression of the aggressiveness which has always been the Queen's dominant characteristic. Yet the dramatic significance of the scene is restricted by its means of presentation. If the great set speech of vituperation by York against Margaret (I.iv.111–68) is a measure of the extremity of the situation, its hyperboles appropriate enough, it has little moral or spiritual impact beyond its context. It is a, in a sense deserved, portrait of the Queen as a denatured woman, as in the famous parodied line, 'O tiger's heart wrapp'd in a woman's hide!' (I.iv.137); yet, coming as it does from the mouth of her tortured adversary, it is no more than the set speech to be expected from him. Though the crowning with a paper crown, the bloody napkin, the elevation on a molehill, all make for ritual mockery, the stylised rhetoric seems to preclude an echo of the mockery of the Passion, close as some of the images are. Its form of rhetorical theatricality cuts the scene off from the fullest resonance of myth and symbol.

Shakespeare had to develop away from the formal rhetoric of the early plays before he could find the great poetic style of the tragedies. He learned, first of all, to exploit the gap between the rhetorical style and lower, more colloquial and more fluent styles. This appears already in *Richard III*, where Richard consciously manipulates the techniques of rhetoric while taking the audience into his confidence in a sharp and bathetic vernacular. 'I am determined to prove a villain', he says with a wink. Still in *Richard III*, though, the main mode of the play is rhetorical, its structure dependent on the rhetorical forms of premonition, prophecy and nemesis, so that Richard's own alienated style is not ultimately dominant. In *King John*, often placed chronologically between the two tetralogies, Shakespeare introduces the character of the Bastard Faulconbridge as satiric commentator on the unreality of the main characters' high style, and makes the plot itself point up the meaninglessness of the high-sounding purposes of the kings and princes. The culmination of this technique comes in *Troilus and Cressida*.

Another development, however, in the diversification of the rhetorical mode was the cultivation of a 'mean' style – a flexible blank verse which was dignified but undecorated. This appears first in *Richard II* as the speech of Bolingbroke and his associates. It is a style in conflict with the lyrical/rhetorical speech of Richard himself and some others of the characters such as the Bishop of Carlisle. It becomes the staple of the verse sections of the two parts of *Henry IV*. It is sufficiently strong and substantial, for instance, to withstand the pre-emptive parody represented by Falstaff and

Hal's mimic versions of the scene between Hal and his father (*1 Henry IV*, II.iv). When we come to the scene itself (III.ii), it strikes us as serious and life-like, not pompous and bombastic as the parodies have suggested it will be. It is a style which is susceptible to the variation of character necessary, for example, to distinguish Hotspur from the other courtiers. It can at times be almost non-descript, neutral and translucent. It can move easily up into a more lyrical mode – Vernon's description of Hal vaulting on to his horse (*1 Henry IV* IV.i.104–10) – or down to the satiric – Hotspur on Glendower (III.i.146–64).

It was not until Shakespeare had so mastered the rhetorical style, learned to laugh at it constructively, to break it down and discipline it to the whole range of dramatic purposes which the later histories demanded, made it capable of co-existing comfort-ably with the world of prose, that he was able to exploit the deepest levels of meaning which rhetorical figures potentially offered in the densely metaphoric style of the mature tragedies. In his two earliest tragedies, *Titus Andronicus* and *Romeo and Juliet*, rhetoric was as much his master as in the early histories. The contrast with *Hamlet* is particularly striking here. For *Hamlet* is in its way as rhetorical as any of the histories or tragedies of the early period. The Ghost, with its Senecan associations of blood-curdling menace, speaks in a conventionally rhetorical style and shapes our apprehension of the action ahead. But the Ghost shares a dramatic habitat with very real – and very cold – midnight sentries, with a diplomatic court where we learn to read between the lines of the King's supple and cleverly controlled speech. And in this context the rhetorical horrors of which the Ghost tells Hamlet (and us) do more than merely chill the blood and make the hairs to stand an end like quills upon the fretful porpentine. They mimic what has happened and is to happen to the play, the spreading of a deep taint of evil through the community as the deadly poison cor-rupted the body of the murdered king. Through the Ghost and the impact it has on Hamlet's imagination, we are made aware of a world beneath and beyond the solid and often complacent realities of Elsinore.

In the later histories the visionary sense of king and kingdom appears only intermittently and is registered as much by its absence as its presence. Henry IV never does lead his crusade, never does make it to Jerusalem. The England he presides over so uneasily is dramatised as a much broader, more heterogeneous, and more demotic place than the lost 'other Eden' glimpsed in *Richard II*. In *King John* we have a satirically observed world of political expediency in which royal claims and counterclaims of right and truth are reduced to black farce. Yet the idea of the true king remains a powerful one, even though the true king is lost or hidden.[3] Hence, for example, the sudden soar of the Bastard's verse as he watches Hubert pick up the dead body of Arthur:

> How easy dost thou take all England up!
> From forth this morsel of dead royalty
> The life, the right, and truth of all this realm
> Is fled to heaven; and England now is left
> To tug and scamble, and to part by th' teeth
> The unowed interest of proud-swelling state.
>
> IV.iii.142–7

Within Shakespeare's English history plays, kingship could never be wholly divested of its sacred and symbolic significance. Power and political action could never be wholly secularised.

The point is underlined if the Bastard's words on Arthur are contrasted with a moment in *Antony and Cleopatra*. Enobarbus in that play is a character not unlike the Bastard, a semi-choric commentator, a blunt and cynical soldier whose loyalty is constantly qualified by his cynicism. In the splendidly satiric scene when all three of the triumvirs get drunk on Pompey's galley, Enobarbus is as usual an onlooker. As the feeble Lepidus is carried off far gone in drink, Enobarbus makes a characteristic joke:

ENOBARBUS: There's a strong fellow, Menas.
> [*Pointing to the Servant who carries off Lepidus.*]
MENAS: Why?
ENOBARBUS: 'A bears the third part of the world, man
> II.vii.87–9

Here is the exact antithesis of the Bastard's wondering awe at the disparity between the light body of the boy and its immense meaning. Instead Enobarbus reduces to absurdity the metaphoric claims of the triumvirate to be 'triple pillars of the world'; one of the three pillars is dead drunk, but the world hardly totters. In *Antony and Cleopatra* where there is no extra-human source of authority or legitimacy, the idea of greatness must be sustained by individual personality or an imagination of magnificence which is always liable to exposure as the mere delusion of grandeur.

In writing the later history plays Shakespeare developed his interest in the complex interrelation of character and action, of private personality and public role. In place of the sequence of great men rising and falling which made up the first tetralogy, there emerges in the later histories, and in the *Henry IV* plays in particular, an analysis of politics which is much more subtle and diffuse. All the same, the English chronicles bound the dramatist to certain shaping pieties, to orthodoxies built into the nature of the material. The histories are by no means merely a pious dramatisation of the Tudor myth, as critics such as E.M.W. Tillyard used to make out.[4] Yet certain Elizabethan political tenets – the sacred status of the true monarch, the wickedness of rebellion, the ultimate horror of civil war – could not help but be postulates of any Shakespearean play about English history.

The discovery of Plutarch, the switch from an English to a Roman milieu, allowed Shakespeare to develop fully the more neutral, the secularised exploration of power and human purpose which are there intermittently in *Richard II* and the *Henry IV* plays. There were, of course, received attitudes towards Roman history in the Renaissance, but they were more complex and ambiguous, besides being politically less sensitive, than those represented in the English chronicles. The period of transition from Republic to Empire which concerned Shakespeare in *Julius Caesar* and *Antony and Cleopatra* could be viewed as an inevitable and desirable progression towards centralised monarchical government; equally, however, it could be regarded as a sad decline from the ideal state of Cato and Cicero. Brutus and Cassius could be either regicides, the ultimate traitors consigned as they had been by Dante to the lowest circle of Hell, or tyrannicides, martyrs to an ideal of liberty. The very plurality of these perspectives gave Shakespeare the opportunity for a shifting and uncommitted imagination of the historical events. The Roman plays did not need to be either king-centred or God-centred, as the English histories more or less had to be. In a context without unchallenged absolutes of faith or feeling, it was possible to stand back from myth and see the part it played within a historical pattern of human cause and event.

What is suggested here is a bifurcation in Shakespeare's imaginative development at the turn of the sixteenth century, when he shifted his creative concentration from the histories to the tragedies. In *Henry V*, dated 1599, he came to the end of the set of history plays which had been one of his major concerns over the first decade of his career in the theatre. In 1599, also, he discovered in *Julius Caesar* a new secular historical setting. And within a year of that (if the date of 1600 is accepted for *Hamlet*) he went on to the first of the tragedies dominated by the sacred, the mythic, the visionary. The relation between the king and the country is a metaphysical one in *Hamlet, King Lear* and *Macbeth*, as it is in the histories; but it is not, as in the histories, a matter of the political orthodoxy of divine right. The nature of the identity between the monarch and the society which he represents is explored as something primal and archetypal. In such a line of development from the histories to the tragedies, *Othello* may seem to have little place, *Othello* traditionally classed as Shakespeare's only 'domestic tragedy', concerned with a private and circumscribed rather than public world. But in *Othello* too, image and action constantly open out into a visionary world, a universe of good and evil. In *Othello*, as in *Hamlet, Lear* and *Macbeth*, the situation of the tragic hero, as it is realised dramatically, figures significance which cannot be analysed merely as the interaction of character and event. In all four of these tragedies, the providential and the demonic are felt to be real or potential powers which shape the apprehension of reality.

By contrast with these plays, the secular world of *Julius Caesar, Troilus and Cressida, Antony and Cleopatra* and *Coriolanus* is one in which principles and ideas are seen in a predominantly human context. It is a world which is relativist in its values and yet determinist in its causality; if it does not have the doomed inevitability of the other tragedies, it has instead its own historical determinism. The plays often involve a situation in which one older, more idealistic code is being destroyed by a newer, more ruthless and pragmatic one: in *Julius Caesar* it is the republican values of the conspirators which are being eliminated by the rule of Caesarism, in *Troilus and Cressida* the ideals of chivalry of the Trojans are going down before the brutality of Greek warfare, in *Coriolanus* patrician principles are compromised, at least from the hero's point of view, by grubby deals with proletarian politicians. In *Antony and Cleopatra* it is a clash between two cultures, the imperial asceticism of Rome and its complementary opposite in the hedonism of Egypt. Shakespeare accords to each of the codes and cultures meeting defeat a measure of sympathy and respect, but at the same time analyses with clear-eyed detachment the sources of their destruction in inner origins or in historical laws of cause and effect. Within this secular world, good and evil, such as they are, can be no more than variable man-made categories. This is in striking contrast with the other tragedies where those who adopt such a secular view of things – Iago or Edmund – are seen to be evil, and the secularity of their outlook is itself a mark of their evil natures.

The lack of a spiritual or visionary dimension within the Roman plays is what has been commonly used to differentiate them from the 'major' tragedies and reduce them to minor status by comparison. This was the evaluative judgement of Bradley's original selection and it is implied also in the attitude of a later twentieth-century critic such as Arthur Sewell. 'The great tragic heroes', Sewell says, 'are the only characters who address themselves to a metaphysical world in such a way that we feel them to be citizens of that world as much as of this.' This is in contrast with the protagonists of the Roman plays who are 'none of them men for whose souls there is competition between the forces of good and the forces of evil'.[5] Such a contrast can be seen as part of the essential design of the Roman plays. J.L. Simmons, in *Shakespeare's Pagan World*, argues that throughout the Roman plays there is an awareness of a missing Christian perspective, missing for the pagan characters but constantly present for Shakespeare's audience. Shakespeare, according to Simmons, would have been drawing on an Augustinian tradition of historical interpretation turning on an implicit contrast between the city of man and the city of god.[6]

There *are* fundamental differences in the dramatic worlds of the Roman and the non-Roman tragedies. Yet it will not do, with Bradley or Sewell, to relegate the Roman plays to some lesser second order, lacking in the spiritual depth which makes the 'great' tragedies great. And Simmons's basic assumption that Shakespeare's pagans are viewed always with Christian principles in mind is not ultimately convincing. Indeed what often seems remarkable about the Roman plays is their degree of imaginative autonomy from the Christian culture in which they were conceived. The antithesis of Christian and pagan, used by Simmons and so many other of Shakespeare's critics, belies the complexity of the issue. A broader view is necessary to come to terms with the capacity of Shakespeare's tragic imagination to shift from a milieu where the human and the spiritual, the individual and the universal, constantly interpenetrate, to an ethos very specifically rooted in the play of human action and consciousness.

In the tragedies from 1599 on there appears to be a dialectic between these two modes of tragic imagination. Cognate themes, related situations and dramatic images, are pursued alternately in sequent plays, now in one mode, now in another. When Shakespeare wrote *Hamlet*, he evidently still had *Julius Caesar* in mind. The similarities between Brutus and Hamlet have often been commented on: they are both isolated by their idealism and their speculative cast of mind from the theatre of action in which they must play their parts. But the questioning of Hamlet resonates out into metaphysical space – 'what should such fellows as I do crawling between earth and heaven?' – whereas Brutus in *Julius Caesar* articulates and embodies problems specific and immediate to Rome. In *Troilus and Cressida* Shakespeare demythologised the Trojan war, turning the legendary events and characters into a satirically observed reality; Troilus and Cressida themselves and their love share in the demythologising. In *Othello*, by contrast, the next tragedy after *Troilus and Cressida*, Shakespeare made from a contemporary Italian *novella* with a routine narrative of love and jealousy a play in which love and its failure took on fundamental spiritual significance. Problems about the date, text and authorship of *Timon of Athens* make it hard to know how it relates to *King Lear* in Shakespeare's creative development. If, however, *Timon* is placed immediately before *King Lear*,[7] it can be seen as an only partially successful expression of ideas and images later realised in *King Lear*. The primitive and consciously archaic setting of *King Lear* made for a fully mythic treatment of the themes of loyalty and ingratitude, whereas the Plutarchan source and rather ill-defined Athenian setting turned *Timon* into something more like a moral fable. *Macbeth*, *Antony and Cleopatra* and *Coriolanus* are all three studies in the heroic temperament; in all three the tragedy relates to the efforts of the protagonist to expand, transcend or escape from the role of soldier hero; all three are also concerned with the relationship between the heroes and the women that dominate them as wife, mistress, mother. But the damned heroism of Macbeth is totally different from the histrionic persona of Antony or the all but psychotic ego of Coriolanus.

The nine plays, in the order of their composition, can be read thus as a continuing dialogue between the contrasting modes of Shakespeare's tragic imagination. The pattern of interrelated divergence outlined here is to be explored in detail in what follows. The aim is to try to define how the distinctive imaginative territory of the several tragedies is created through language, tone and dramatic design, echoing and contrasting from play to juxtaposed play. Although each tragedy is given its own chapter, the individual readings are designed to work with the awareness of their next-door neighbours: the analysis of *Julius Caesar* informing that of *Hamlet*, the discussion of *Troilus and Cressida* counterpointed by the following critique of *Othello*, the treatment of *King Lear* expanding out from the limitations of *Timon, Antony and Cleopatra* and *Coriolanus* seen in a perspective which takes in *Macbeth*. The object throughout is to resist homogenising the plays, bending them to a single model of 'Shakespearean Tragedy', while recognising the one quite extraordinary imaginative enterprise which they collectively represent.

2

Julius Caesar

Ambivalence in literature is a much cherished modern virtue, but many of the ambiguities of *Julius Caesar* Shakespeare inherited from his classical and Renaissance sources. There was no single tradition of interpreting the events leading up to and following the assassination of Caesar, no one orthodox evaluation, moral or political. Scholars have documented in detail the varying attitude towards Caesar himself, Brutus, Cassius and the rest of the conspirators.[1] In Shakespeare's main source, Plutarch, the movement from Republic to Empire is regarded with very mixed feelings. It is seen as inevitable – 'the state of Rome . . . could no more abide to be governed by many Lordes, but required one only absolute Governor' – and Caesar is described at one point as 'a mercifull Phisition, whom God had ordeyned of special grace to be Governor of the Empire of Rome' (Bullough, V, 127, 133). Yet Plutarch can also be markedly anti-Caesarian, moralising on his death,

> So he reaped no other frute of all his raigne and dominion, which he had so vehemently desired all his life, and pursued with such extreme daunger: but a vaine name only, and a superficial glory, that procured him the envy and hatred of his contrie.

> (Bullough, V, 88)

Bernard Shaw, in the Preface to his *Caesar and Cleopatra* complained that Shakespeare wrote 'Caesar down for the merely technical purpose of writing Brutus up'.[2] But Plutarch had done something very similar in his near exemplary *Life of Brutus*. Ernest Schanzer's conclusion seems well justified:

> In a sense, all that Shakespeare does is to dramatize the views of Caesar and the conspirators which he found in his 'sources', and especially Plutarch, distributing what are the divided and contradictory responses of a single writer among several characters

who take different sides, so that what is a mental conflict in
Plutarch and others becomes a dramatic conflict in his play.[3]

There is, though, more to *Julius Caesar* than merely animated
Plutarch; and it is not a matter only of varying approval or disapproval of Caesar and the conspirators, their political purposes or
moral characters. There is a much more radical ambivalence in the
dramatic images which make up *Julius Caesar*. Shakespeare seems
to adopt, and lend to his audience, an attitude of studied detachment from the constructions and misconstructions the characters
put upon the events in which they are involved. *Julius Caesar* is no
world of appearance and reality conjuring tricks, now you see it,
now you don't. It is realised with extraordinary clarity, definition
and substance, a milieu remote from the radical instability of being
in *Hamlet*. But in the very transparent lucidity of its style, we are
allowed to watch the varying human process of creating and
interpreting reality through language, sign and gesture.

The little opening scene between the tribunes, Flavius and
Marullus, and the plebs serves as key-note. 'Hence! home, you idle
creatures, get you home' is the silence-compelling opening line, no
doubt necessary in Shakespeare's public theatre, even after the
knocking on the stage signalling the start of a performance. For a
moment the audience are the 'idle creatures' and can be expected
to enjoy the citizens' good-humoured recalcitrance to the imperi-
ous earnestness of Flavius and Marullus. At the name of Caesar,
however, when the first rhetorical tirade takes off –

> You blocks, you stones, you worse than senseless things!
> O you hard hearts, you cruel men of Rome,
> Knew you not Pompey?
>
> I.i.36–8

– the rhetoric has its effect. We watch language do its work, not
moved as the citizens are, yet not unmoved either. Here, as with
the much more elaborate rhetorical strategies of Antony's funeral
orations, we respond directly to the emotional appeal of the
words, while remaining acutely conscious of the manipulative
purposes of the speaker. It is no surprise to hear the drop in tone
when Flavius and Marullus have cleared the stage of commoners:

> These growing feathers pluck'd from Caesar's wing
> Will make him fly an ordinary pitch,

> Who else would soar above the view of men,
> And keep us all in servile fearfulness.
>
> I.i.73–6

A consistent concern of the opponents of Caesar, whether the Pompeyan Flavius and Marullus here, or the conspirators later, is to cut Caesar down to size. But it remains uncertain in the play just what size or shape Caesar really is. Flavius' image of him as soaring falcon leaves the tribunes as feeble would-be prey looking up into the sky. Cassius' ironic hyperbole –

> Why, man, he doth bestride the narrow world
> Like a Colossus, and we petty men
> Walk under his huge legs, and peep about
> To find ourselves dishonourable graves.
>
> I.ii.135–8

– in its very vividness risks authenticating the image it purports to deride. Shakespeare, with his iconoclastic use of Caesar's invented deafness and his rendering of Caesar's fatuous self-apotheosis, seems at times to be conspiring with the conspirators to do the would-be emperor down. Yet Caesar's name and image continue to fill the play, as much after his death as before it, as a living presence of power and authority, not a hollow or inflated idol.

Caesar, of course, is not seen in isolation from the movement of political process. If we come in on the high-tide of Caesar's triumph, it is with an awareness of a slight remaining backwash from Pompey the Great. The brief ascendancy of Brutus and Cassius is to be replaced by the rule of the triumvirate and, by the end of the play, the signs are already there that this is to be whittled down to a principate at last. Shakespeare hardly demonstrates in this process the Providential pattern driving towards Empire which he found in Plutarch, much less the object-lesson in monarchism which some critics have detected. 'In *Julius Caesar*', J.E. Phillips tells us, 'we see, in the successful government of the title figure, the advantages of monarchy, and in the disastrous consequences of his assassination the evils of multiple sovereignty.'[4] It might well be expected that, in a play written at the end of Elizabeth's reign, such a dominant political orthodoxy of the time would be there to be found. In fact, the evidence of Caesar's 'successful government' is scrappy and inconclusive. Although

Brutus allows that 'I have not known when his affections sway'd
More than his reason' (II.i.20–1), and Caesar shows himself firm in
refusing to repeal the banishment of Publius Cimber, there are
signs of the tyrant in his nervous distrust of Cassius, and in the
news that Flavius and Marullus, sinisterly if appropriately for
those eloquent tribunes, have been 'put to silence'. (In Plutarch
they are merely deprived of their tribuneships.) The consequences
of Caesar's assassination are disastrous indeed, but largely for the
conspirators. For Rome it is merely a return to those civil wars from
which Caesar entered victorious at the beginning of the play. It
cannot be compared with the spiralling disintegration which leads
out from the murder of old Hamlet or of Duncan, or even from the
voluntary abdication of Lear.

In *Julius Caesar* Shakespeare allows us to watch with an uncommitted detachment, which is often sceptical but never simply cynical,
the deeply complicated play and interplay of image, action and
event. The encounter between Brutus and Cassius in I.i is often
spoken of as a seduction-scene, with the wily Cassius tempting the
upright but gullible Brutus into the toils of conspiracy. It is as such
that Cassius himself regards it in his concluding soliloquy:

> Well, Brutus, thou art noble; yet, I see,
> Thy honourable mettle may be wrought
> From that it is dispos'd. Therefore it is meet
> That noble minds keep ever with their likes;
> For who so firm that cannot be seduc'd?
>
> I.ii.307–11

This is the familiar Renaissance stage convention of the villain
moralising on the effects of his own villainy – as Webster's Bosola
puts it, 'sometimes the devil doth preach'. Yet it is also in its way,
as hypocrisy is supposed to be, a tribute paid by vice to virtue. In a
very odd comment, Cassius adds:

> Caesar doth bear me hard; but he loves Brutus.
> If I were Brutus now and he were Cassius,
> He should not humour me.
>
> I.ii.312–14

This is contorted enough to have left commentators uncertain of its meaning; but if the 'he' of line 313 is taken to refer to Brutus rather than Caesar, Cassius seems to be saying that he would not be /deceived by Cassius-like flattery, if he were Brutus. If he were not the self-interested Cassius, however, he would not feel the need to persuade the disinterested Brutus on to his side. The scene demonstrates a relationship between Brutus and Cassius which is by no means just a matter of one 'humouring' the other to his will.

The Brutus of this scene is a man disturbed within himself, who is only half listening to what Cassius says to him. Much of his attention is directed towards the noises off indicating what is happening in the Forum:

> What means this shouting? I do fear the people
> Choose Caesar for their king.
>
> I.ii.79–80

He is reserved with Cassius, holding him at arm's length, even though what Cassius is saying jibes with what he himself is thinking. He is aware of Cassius as tempter – 'Into what dangers would you lead me, Cassius . . .?' (I.ii.63) – and is guarded against him. When he finally turns and gives Cassius his whole attention, it is courteously to place him, and the conversation they have had, with a fully conscious authority:

> That you do love me, I am nothing jealous;
> What you would work me to, I have some aim;
> How I have thought of this, and of these times,
> I shall recount hereafter. For this present,
> I would not, so with love I might entreat you,
> Be any further mov'd.
>
> I.ii.162–7

The verbs, 'work me to', 'mov'd', and later retrospectively, 'whet' – 'Since Cassius first did *whet* me against Caesar' (II.i.61) – pinpoint Brutus' firm knowledge of what Cassius is about.

Taking their cue from Antony's 'All the conspirators save only he', critics have often portrayed Brutus as the good man fallen among rogues, the idealist who cannot perceive the unidealistic motives of his collaborators. This is to misjudge the relationship between them. Cassius, Casca, and the rest want Brutus as co-

conspirator because his presence can transform them and their
conspiracy. As Casca says:

> O, he sits high in all the people's hearts;
> And that which would appear offence in us
> His countenance, like richest alchemy,
> Will change to virtue and to worthiness.
>
> I.iii.158–60

Casca is talking here partly about public political perceptions, the
need to have an incorruptible on the platform. But the alchemy
image suggests more, that the involvement of Brutus will actually
metamorphose the base metals of the conspirators. It is this which
accounts for Brutus' extraordinary moral ascendancy over his
fellows, turning them into a bunch of yes-men, however ill-
advised and politically unwary his attitudes may be. Of course,
Cicero with his 'silver hairs' should be included in the conspiracy,
until Brutus says no – 'Then leave him out', 'Indeed he is not fit'
(II.i.152–3). Certainly it would be wise for Antony to be murdered
along with Caesar, until Brutus 'proves' the opposite. A word from
Brutus convinces more than the shrewdest arguments of Cassius,
as even Cassius accepts.

Brutus' task is to transform the conspiracy, and he knows it. The
words 'conspiracy' and 'conspirator' evidently had full pejorative
loading in Shakespeare's time, and a line in North's Plutarch
seems to express doubt as to whether this was the proper term for
the Caesaricides – 'the conspirators (if so they should be called)'
(Bullough, V, 101). In the original Greek the word used means
literally 'those joined together by an oath', and the parenthesis
refers back to the fact that, as Plutarch has told us, they had not
taken an oath. Shakespeare attributes this lack of an oath to
Brutus, and makes it part of his attempt to change the face of
conspiracy. When Lucius tells him that men with their 'hats . . .
pluck'd about their ears And half their faces buried in their cloaks'
are at the door, Brutus can immediately identify them: 'They are
the faction' (II.i.73–7). The word was used at this time, as OED
notes, 'always with opprobrious sense, conveying the imputation
of selfish or mischievous ends or turbulent or unscrupulous
methods'. A full Renaissance horror of such factions is apparent in
the speech of Brutus that follows:

                    O conspiracy,
Sham'st thou to show thy dang'rous brow by night,
When evils are most free? O, then by day
Where wilt thou find a cavern dark enough
To mask thy monstrous visage? Seek none, conspiracy;
Hide it in smiles and affability!
For if thou path, thy native semblance on,
Not Erebus itself were dim enough
To hide thee from prevention.

                                        II.i.77–85

Yet Brutus, with full awareness of the underworld of images which the idea of conspiracy releases, resolves to join it and bring it out into the daylight.

   Is Brutus here deceiving himself? The crucial soliloquy 'It must be by his death', suspiciously scrutinised as a piece of ill-argued sophistry, can be seen as Brutus' attempt to rationalise a decision for which there is no rationale. This is the view of Ernest Schanzer, for example: Brutus' 'gentle, frank, and generous nature is in revolt not only against the deed itself, but against the whole conspiracy, with all the secrecy and deceitfulness it entails'. On the apostrophe to conspiracy just quoted, he comments, 'To save himself from these nightmare realizations he plunges headlong into self-delusion'.[5] A similar drive towards self-deception has been detected in Brutus' efforts to sanitise the murder, in his refusal to accept a secret society oath, above all in his imagery of the assassination as a ritual sacrifice:

                 Let's be sacrificers, but not butchers, Caius.
                 We all stand up against the spirit of Caesar,
                 And in the spirit of men there is no blood.
                 O that we then could come by Caesar's spirit,
                 And not dismember Caesar! But, alas,
                 Caesar must bleed for it! And, gentle friends,
                 Let's kill him boldly, but not wrathfully;
                 Let's carve him as a dish fit for the gods,
                 Not hew him as a carcase fit for hounds;
                 And let our hearts, as subtle masters do,
                 Stir up their servants to an act of rage,
                 And after seem to chide 'em. This shall make
                 Our purpose necessary, and not envious;

> Which so appearing to the common eyes,
> We shall be call'd purgers, not murderers.
>
> II.i.166–80

Commentators, in arguing that this is an ironically observed attempt to make murder aesthetic, have pounced on the hypocrisy of the image of the 'subtle masters'. The whole speech is seen as a self-deceiving exercise in disguising a horrific reality.

It is difficult to make good a charge of self-deception against a character in a Shakespeare play. We used to be told, for instance, that Hamlet in the speech, 'Now might I do it pat' was deceiving himself as to his motives for not killing Claudius then and there: he could not actually mean what he says. That reading is now commonly thought to show a squeamish lack of understanding of the Renaissance revenge ethos. To chart the implied movements of an unconscious 'real' self beneath the apparent self in a drama as rhetorically overt as Shakespeare's is a doubtful proceeding. In the case of Brutus, though, what is remarkable is that the doubts and self-divisions, which we are explicitly shown in the character in his first two appearances, vanish completely from the moment he commits himself to joining the conspiracy. His soliloquy in II.i gives us an insight into a tortured mind which obviously anticipates that of Macbeth:

> Since Cassius first did whet me against Caesar,
> I have not slept.
> Between the acting of a dreadful thing
> And the first motion, all the interim is
> Like a phantasma or a hideous dream.
> The Genius and the mortal instruments
> Are then in council; and the state of man,
> Like to a little kingdom, suffers then
> The nature of an insurrection.
>
> II.i.61–9

Macbeth moves from this state ever deeper into a disordered inner world alienated from the outer world of experience, an inner world which provides the substance of the drama. By contrast, once Brutus has engaged himself in a public role, we are never again allowed to see a divided self within. To some the stoic self-mastery of the later Brutus is a weakness, and intended to be seen as such.

But to detect a silenced self in the actions and attitudes of Brutus throughout may be to mistake the nature of the play Shakespeare has created.

The idealising of the assassination by Brutus cannot be simply defined as self-deluding falsification, both because of its effect on his co-conspirators, and because of the strength and significance of the images used. Brutus proposes that the conspirators should be sacrificers not butchers and, in the most extraordinary of Shakespeare's invented scenes in the play, he initiates the blood-ritual which follows the assassination:

> Stoop, Romans, stoop,
> And.let us bathe our hands in Caesar's blood
> Up to the elbows, and besmear our swords.
> Then walk we forth, even to the market-place,
> And waving our red weapons o'er our heads,
> Let's all cry 'Peace, freedom, and liberty!'
> III.i.106–11

The ceremony enacted here reaches down to what is, arguably, an archetypal myth of violence and regeneration, the king/father who must be sacrificed to give his sons/country life. If the thesis of René Girard is accepted that ritual sacrifice had, in origin, the object of restraining and canalising violence within the community,[6] then the paradox of the bloody-handed assassins crying 'Peace, freedom, and liberty' goes beyond irony. Cassius, joining in, makes of the blood-bath a sacrament to be re-enacted:

> Stoop then, and wash. How many ages hence
> Shall this our lofty scene be acted over
> In states unborn and accents yet unknown!
> III.i.112–14

There is more here than a metadramatic gesture towards the play in action, the 1599 audience watching 'Caesar bleed in sport'. It makes even of the real violence which has just taken place the mimic violence of sacrificial ceremony.

In a curious sense what this process of ritualisation does is to grant to Caesar the kingly status which it is the object of the assassination to deny him. It is, within the mythic pattern, the king who must die in order to restore health and prosperity to his people. The conspirators strenuously resist Caesar's pretensions to be more than another Roman citizen, his claim to absolute pre-eminence. Cassius harps on his physical weakness, Casca derides his histrionic carry-on in the market-place, for Brutus the menace is that 'he would be crowned'. Yet in planning his murder as sacrifice and enacting it as ritual, they imagine him in death the life-giving source which, in a patriarchal imagination of things, only a king/patriarch could be. There is a real ambiguity in the play, deriving from Plutarch, as to how tyrannical Caesar's rule actually is. Brutus' lines, already quoted, 'I have not known when his affections sway'd More than his reason', have often been used as evidence that Caesar's tyranny is only a conspiratorial pretext. But the formal exculpation here is consistent also with Brutus' desire to make of Caesar an almost innocent victim, to make of the assassination something like an act of love. Once again we are close to the idea of the scapegoat/king who is not actually guilty of the burden of sins which he must carry and, in dying, expiate.

Brutus' aim is not just to idealise, but to mythologise the murder of Caesar. His great value to the conspiracy is that he can impose his view of the event on the conspirators so that they can believe in themselves as 'the men that gave their country liberty'. He can impose that view upon the conspirators, but not on Mark Antony and only doubtfully on an audience in the theatre. There are varying positions on the stage impact of the murder of Caesar, on how an audience may be intended to react to the would-be myth and the reality.[7] A good deal here depends on the decisions of theatrical production. But Caesar so acts out godhead, is so literally statuesque in the attitudes he adopts, that we may not experience the full pathos of a human death when he is stabbed. It may be even that an audience could be carried with the Brutus-led conspirators' sense of the event as a ritual or myth, at least up to the point of the entrance of Antony.

Brents Stirling has written convincingly of the 'counterceremony' which Antony opposes to the supposed ceremony of Caesar's death.[8] Antony's performance is a brilliant improvisation, disrupting and undermining the ritual play which the conspirators have staged. He appears to collaborate with their self-images – 'the choice and master spirits of this age' (III.i.164) – and even with their sacramental metaphors – 'your swords, made rich With the most noble blood of all this world' (III.i.156–7) – but it is only the more effectively to subvert them. Brutus continues to respond at a fully rhetorical level, but Cassius shifts uneasily towards straight political bargaining:

> Your voice shall be as strong as any man's
> In the disposing of new dignities.
>
> III.i.178–9

The dominant feeling of the conspirators, as Antony names them and shakes them by the 'bloody hand' one by one, must surely be that of disoriented embarrassment. It is all very well to join in a communal rite in which the group is anointed with the blood of the victim, but to have a suspect enemy clasp you individually by that anointed hand must be extremely disquieting. There is more than a hint of threat in Antony's action. Even as it ostensibly signals solemn friendship and forgiveness, it shadows an equally solemn vow of vengeance against each one of them as they are named. Above all in this scene, what Antony does with his constantly shifting language and his controlled outbursts of feeling is to break up the conspirators' act, to destroy the atmosphere of high mimesis which they have tried to sustain.

Significantly, when Antony is left alone with the body of Caesar, the sentimental/sacramental view of that body is brutally discarded:

> O, pardon me, thou bleeding piece of earth,
> That I am meek and gentle with these butchers!
>
> III.i.255–6

The speech is strictly pathetic fallacy; the corpse is no more than a 'bleeding piece of earth', 'the *ruins* of the noblest man', literally, as newspaper funeral notices put it, the 'remains'. Antony animates the dead Caesar only as a spirit to invoke vengeance upon his killers. His speech here has obvious resemblances to the Bishop of Carlisle's prophecies of civil war considered in the previous chapter. It has been argued that such resemblances mean that 'it is to be taken seriously as a choric interpretation of Caesar's death'.[9] But the contexts are quite different. Carlisle's prophecy is sustained by the conventional interpretation of English history, and lent sacred authority by his episcopal status. In an overview of Roman history, Caesar's murder occupied no such crucial place as the deposition of Richard II, but rather was one more episode, albeit the most dramatic one, in the long history of civil wars which eventually transformed the Roman Republic into the Empire. With Antony's unquestionably partisan point of view, the speech is something more like a Senecan invocation to revenge. The sacred or symbolic interpretation of history, represented by Carlisle's speech, is opposed in context by the pragmatic politics of Bolingbroke's court, as we have seen. Yet that dimension of the sacred never loses its place within the English history plays. In *Julius Caesar* it is Antony more than any other character who invalidates and destroys history as sacred drama, and makes of it instead an opportunistic exploitation of events as they arise. His grief for Caesar may be real; there is authentic feeling in his emotional arias. But when he comes to speak at Caesar's funeral, he exploits the body as *pieta* with a purely knowing manipulation which turns Brutus' attempted ritual of the assassination into grotesque and tear-jerking melodrama.

The world of Roman history, as Shakespeare imagined it, is without a fully mythic vision. For J.L. Simmons, this is specifically because it is a pagan world, and 'the ideals that the tragic heroes envision, representing a humanistic and heroic desire for perfection, cannot be requited within the confines of the Earthly City'.[10] But the treatment of ideal and reality, of image and event in *Julius Caesar*, is less pointedly didactic than this Augustinian reading would suggest. Nicholas Brooke seems closer to the mark: 'Roman society lacked a divine sanction, or at least it seemed to the Christian tradition to have done so; it was therefore a fit ground in which to explore the political behaviour of men empirically, freed from the assumption of a providence shaping their ends'.[11] The tragedy of Brutus does not function as an object-lesson in the futility of the idealistic urge towards transcendence without the proper transcendental perspective of Christianity. The failure of his mythic view of the murder of Caesar must be related to a whole range of views of that action, which are presented with a relativism not bound to a single moralising vision. In shaping images, both before and after the death, we are given repeated interpretations of its significance. Shakespeare lends to such images a deliberately limited resonance, and by setting one interpretation against another, constantly reinforces the neutrality of a sceptical detachment.

Calphurnia's dream, as Caesar recounts it in II.ii, is a set-piece of such multiple significance. It is, on the face of it, a very sinister portent, and a quite precise prevision of what is to happen:

> She dreamt tonight she saw my statua,
> Which, like a fountain with an hundred spouts,
> Did run pure blood; and many lusty Romans
> Came smiling and did bathe their hands in it.
>
> II.ii.76–9

There is a basic theatrical pleasure in the matching of prophetic image to its fulfilment. As an audience sees the conspirators wash in the blood of Caesar, they will recall the details of Calphurnia's dream. Even the statue is to be there, only it is the statue of Caesar's arch-enemy Pompey, which, as Antony says later, 'all the while ran blood'. Misinterpretation of prophecy, however, is just as common a dramatic ploy as its fulfilment. Decius Brutus supplies a specious alternative reading of Calphurnia's nightmare:

> This dream is all amiss interpreted:
> It was a vision fair and fortunate.
> Your statue spouting blood in many pipes,
> In which so many smiling Romans bath'd,
> Signifies that from you great Rome shall suck
> Reviving blood, and that great men shall press
> For tinctures, stains, relics, and cognizance.
>
> II.ii.83–9

The smart-talking flattery of Decius is enough to bamboozle Caesar; his easy credulity, together with his wilful disregard of the Soothsayer's warnings, mark him out as a blind victim of the fate to come. But beyond the evident irony of Caesar's blindness, is the closeness of the reinterpreted dream to Brutus' redemptive vision of the assassination, or to Antony's later imagination of the grateful Roman people, if allowed to read Caesar's will:

> they would go and kiss dead Caesar's wounds
> And dip their napkins in his sacred blood;
> Yea, beg a hair of him for memory
>
> III.ii.132–4

We are cautioned into scepticism of the sacramental view of Caesar's murder by its association with the devious Decius Brutus, on the one hand, and the meretricious rhetoric of Antony on the other.

In I.iii Shakespeare makes a key issue of the interpretation of omens. We are told at length by a breathless and terrified Casca of the sights he has seen, natural and unnatural – the storm, the slave with the burning hand, the lion near the Capitol, the owl hooting at midday. Casca, so unlike the railing cynic of the previous scene that some scholars have argued for an uncompleted Shakespearean revision, is convinced of the ominousness of what he has seen.

> When these prodigies
> Do so conjointly meet, let not men say
> 'These are their reasons – they are natural',
> For I believe they are portentous things
> Unto the climate that they point upon.
>
> I.iii.28–32

It is an attitude which is to be later adopted by Gloucester in *King Lear*, shaking his head over what 'these late eclipses in the sun and moon' may portend. In this context, however, such belief is not countered with the scornful iconoclasm of an Edmund, but with Cicero's cautious comment:

> Indeed, it is a strange-disposed time;
> But men may construe things after their fashion,
> Clean from the purpose of the things themselves.
>
> I.iii.33–5

Cassius then enters, to put an entirely different construction on the night and its visions. It is to him 'a very pleasing night to honest men', and he has proved himself of that category by baring his 'bosom to the thunder-stone' (I.iii.43, 49). He reinterprets the omens as 'instruments of fear and warning Unto some monstrous state':

> Now could I, Casca, name to thee a man
> Most like this dreadful night
> That thunders, lightens, opens graves, and roars
> As doth the lion in the Capitol;
> A man no mightier than thyself or me
> In personal action, yet prodigious grown,
> And fearful, as these strange eruptions are.
>
> I.iii.70–8

The portents, by Cassius' reading, are not the signs of the death of Caesar to come, as Calphurnia will see them – 'The heavens themselves blaze forth the death of princes' (II.ii.31). Instead they bespeak the corrupt state of Rome under Caesar's tyranny. We can see what is tendentious, even perverse, in Cassius' interpretation, like Decius Brutus' gloss on Calphurnia's dream, and we can identify the element of bravado in his gestures. The scene contrasts the superstitious fear of Casca with the bold resolution of Cassius, using Cicero's laconic agnosticism as a pivotal point of rest between the two.

How far does the external world reflect the life of human actions, to what extent are men's affairs governed by forces beyond their control, what are the connections between projected patterns and eventual outcome? To none of these questions does *Julius Caesar* give definitive answers. Cassius speaks to Brutus for a rationalist philosophy of will:

> Men at some time are masters of their fates:
> The fault, dear Brutus, is not in our stars,
> But in ourselves, that we are underlings.
>
> I.ii.139–41

For Ernest Schanzer this is the Shakespearean mark of a villain: 'Shakespeare's noblest characters generally affirm their belief in man's dependence on an ulterior power, while it is his villains, such as Iago and Edmund . . . who insist on men's mastery of their fates'.[12] But generalisations which run from plays with a Christian to those with a non-Christian milieu may not be valid. Within the context of *Othello* or *King Lear*, the rationalism of an Iago

or an Edmund may be judged and found wanting. Yet within the
Roman context, there is more room for respect for varying sorts of
independence of mind. Brutus' famous image before Philippi is an
elaboration of Cassius' 'Men at some time are masters of their
fates':

> There is a tide in the affairs of men
> Which, taken at the flood, leads on to fortune
> IV.iii.216–17

The fact that Brutus' practical judgement in this instance proves
disastrously wrong does not destroy the imaginative and intellectual credibility of the position.

From initial attitudes of scepticism or reserve, there is a drift
rather than a drive towards belief in fate in *Julius Caesar*. Caesar
brushes aside the warning of the Soothsayer: 'He is a dreamer; let
us leave him. Pass' (I.ii.24). Yet Cassius tells us that Caesar

> is superstitious grown of late,
> Quite from the main opinion he held
> Of fantasy, of dreams, and ceremonies.
> II.i.195–7

Calphurnia uses the same word to comprehend all types of omens
and auguries, and she too has moved away from dismissing them:
'Caesar, I never stood on ceremonies, Yet now they fright me'
(II.ii.13–14). Decius Brutus not only reinterprets Calphurnia's
dream but, to persuade Caesar not to stay at home, he reduces it
once again to meaningless fantasy:

> it were a mock
> Apt to be render'd, for some one to say
> 'Break up the Senate till another time,
> When Caesar's wife shall meet with better dreams'.
> II.ii.96–9

We know dramatically that Calphurnia has good reason for her
fears, and that Caesar would do well to listen to them. Yet Calphurnia's is not a Cassandra-like role, nor is Caesar presented as a
figure of *hubris* defying supernatural warning. The scene works as a
psychological study of the wife's protective anxieties, the husband's

oscillation between a superstition he is afraid to confess, and a
susceptibility to flattery which plays upon his fear.

Brutus and Cassius before Philippi shift in significant ways from
attitudes of stoic self-sufficiency. The Ghost of Caesar visits Brutus
in his tent with signs such as the dimming of the candle which, for
Shakespeare's audience, would have authenticated it as a 'real'
apparition. Brutus, like Hamlet after him, is aware of the range of
explanations, natural and supernatural, which could be given for
such a phenomenon:

> How ill this taper burns! Ha! who comes here?
> I think it is the weakness of mine eyes
> That shapes this monstrous apparition.
> It comes upon me. Art thou any thing?
> Art thou some god, some angel, or some devil,
> That mak'st my blood cold and my hair to stare?
> Speak to me what thou art.
>
> IV.iii. 273–9

The Ghost may be a hallucination 'shaped' by the weakness of the
eyes, or a supernatural being, good or ill. Brutus is momentarily
panicked, yet he can respond to the Ghost's threat to reappear at
Philippi with a blank courage which is without swagger – 'Why, I
will see thee at Philippi, then' (IV.iii.284). We do not see the
second appearance of the Ghost, but we hear of it and Brutus'
conclusion from it, as he faces suicide:

> The ghost of Caesar hath appear'd to me
> Two several times by night – at Sardis once,
> And this last night here in Philippi fields.
> I know my hour is come.
>
> V.v.17–20

Brutus 'lays' the Ghost with his dying words, 'Caesar, now be still.
I kill'd not thee with half so good a will' (V.v.50–1). Yet at no point
does he acknowledge that the killing of Caesar was a crime for
which he is haunted by the Ghost, or that a cycle of vengeance is
being executed. The apparition belongs for him at some more
neutral level of causality, as merely the sure sign of his death to
come, a death which he accepts with resignation but without
remorse.

In V.i, both Cassius and Brutus speak of changes of doctrine, Cassius from his Epicureanism, Brutus from his Platonism. Cassius reflects to Messala on the fact that the day of battle is his birthday.

> You know that I held Epicurus strong,
> And his opinion; now I change my mind,
> And partly credit things that do presage.
> Coming from Sardis, on our former ensign
> Two mighty eagles fell; and there they perch'd,
> Gorging and feeding from our soldiers' hands,
> Who to Philippi here consorted us.
> This morning are they fled away and gone,
> And in their steads do ravens, crows, and kites,
> Fly o'er our heads and downward look on us
> As we were sickly prey. Their shadows seem
> A canopy most fatal, under which
> Our army lies, ready to give up the ghost.
>
> V.i.76–88

Cassius' speech moves from the omen of the eagles replaced by the ignoble carrion birds to a much more vivid and urgent vision of coming disaster, a whole army of corpses-to-be. Yet he can respond to Messala's stiffening 'Believe not so':

> I but believe it partly;
> For I am very fresh of spirit and resolv'd
> To meet all perils very constantly.
>
> V.i.89–91

Cassius' Epicurean belief, that there is no influence of the supernatural on the sublunary world, is consistent with his earlier attitude – 'The fault, dear Brutus, is not in our stars, But in ourselves' – and the partial change is all the more effective as a result.

With Brutus' views on suicide, as with Cassius' attitude to omens, Shakespeare was dependent on Plutarch, though Plutarch as confusingly misrepresented by North. Where Plutarch had Brutus explain that when he was young he condemned suicide but had now changed his mind, Shakespeare's character, following North, gives both views, for and against suicide, as present, and

therefore apparently contradictory.[13] At first when Cassius asks
him what he intends to do if they are defeated, he resolves to act

> Even by the rule of that philosophy
> By which I did blame Cato for the death
> Which he did give himself
>
> V.i.100–2

But when Cassius presses him as to whether he is prepared to 'be
led in triumph Through the streets of Rome', he replies proudly

> No, Cassius, no. Think not, thou noble Roman,
> That ever Brutus will go bound to Rome;
> He bears too great a mind.
>
> V.i.110–12

In a sense this is the opposite change from that experienced by
Cassius: Brutus goes from a Platonist belief of waiting on destiny –

> arming myself with patience
> To stay the providence of some high powers
> That govern us below.
>
> V.i.105–7

– to the stoic self-mastery of great-minded suicide. Beyond these
variations in philosophical attitude, what emerges from the second
half of *Julius Caesar* is an impression of the indefiniteness, the
moral and political neutrality of the 'high powers that govern us
below', in so far as they can be made out at all. For Brutus and
Cassius they are accepted as irresistible, and the choice is how
most nobly to meet them.

From the fourth act on, there is a new sympathy for the republicans which is more than merely a facile pity for the underdogs. It is
noticeable that we see no more of all the other assassins, the shady
and shadowy crowd of Casca, Cinna, Metellus Cimber and the
rest, who are associated with secret night meetings and murderous
intentions. Instead in the army of Brutus and Cassius we meet
what amounts virtually to a whole new cast of supporting players ,
Messala, Titinius, young Cato, Dardanius, Strato. These are
staunch soldiers, lieutenants loyal to death, figures who enhance

the reputation of the republican camp. It is true that in this change
of personnel, and to some extent in the shift of sympathy, Shakespeare follows Plutarch, who also fails to mention the presence of
any of the conspirators besides Brutus and Cassius on the field of
Philippi. But the dramatic effect is to ennoble the two leaders and,
by implication, their cause. This is the more striking in the case of
Cassius who, by his knowing comment on Brutus in the first act –
'Well, Brutus, thou art noble . . .' – clearly marked himself as less
than noble. Cassius grows in stature even as his weaknesses, his
impulsiveness, his tendency to bluster, his somewhat shop-soiled
principles of honour, are dramatised in the quarrel-scene. In that
scene our understanding of both the leaders is enlarged and
enriched, and they take on a new grace.

In the nobility of the later Brutus and Cassius, preparedness for
death is central. Cassius from the start is much given to threats of
suicide. If Caesar is crowned, 'I know where I will wear this dagger
then; Cassius from bondage will deliver Cassius' (I.iii.89–90). If
Casca informs on him, 'I am armed, And dangers are to me
indifferent' (I.iii.114–15). When it looks as though the conspiracy is
betrayed, 'Cassius or Caesar never shall turn back, For I will slay
myself' (III.i.21–2). The tone of these threats seems to vary between boasting and panic, and nothing marks the superiority of
Brutus over the earlier Cassius more than his contrasting calm
constancy. It is, in fact, in a moment of mistaken despair that
Cassius finally kills himself. But his death is gathered into the
attitude of noble defiance of life which is the dominant trait of the
republicans at the end. The bodies of Titinius and Cassius, post-
humously crowned with laurel, become a twin icon of *Romanitas*:
'Are yet two Romans living such as these?' (V.iii.98). The conspirators originally sought liberty or death; by the end, death itself is the
liberty they seek and find.

In *The Rape of Lucrece*, the heroine has to argue out the case for
suicide against what appears to be an anachronistically Christian
opposing attitude:

> 'To kill myself,' quoth she 'alack, what were it,
> But with my body my poor soul's pollution?
> They that lose half with greater patience bear it
> That they whose whole is swallowed in confusion.
>   1156–9

But in *Julius Caesar* there is no hint that the Almighty has set his canon 'gainst self-slaughter; suicide is regarded with a purely Roman approval. Cassius' apostrophe is typical:

> Therein, ye gods, you make the weak most strong;
> Therein, ye gods, you tyrants do defeat.
> Nor stony tower, nor walls of beaten brass,
> Nor airless dungeon, nor strong links of iron,
> Can be retentive to the strength of spirit;
> But life, being weary of these worldly bars,
> Never lacks power to dismiss itself.
>
> I.iii.91–7

The idea of the life of the body as a prison from which death provides release is, of course, fully assimilated into Christian thought, but the glorification of suicide as the capacity for self-liberation is not. In this Shakespeare goes out imaginatively to what is conceived as a specifically Roman ethos and, although the element of rodomontade in Cassius' speech at this point may make us critical, our sympathy is engaged for the attitude which it represents.

Renaissance playwrights on the whole had very little difficulty in reconciling themselves and their audiences to the sin of suicide, when it was proudly accomplished by their heroes.[14] The influence here of Seneca, both as tragedian and stoic moralist, is well-known. But in *Julius Caesar* the leaders of the conspiracy seem more than half in love with easeful death, and it comes in the end as a desired consummation. For Brutus it is victory in defeat:

> I shall have glory by this losing day,
> More than Octavius and Mark Antony
> By this vile conquest shall attain unto.
>
> V.v.36–8

Both Brutus and Cassius maintain to the last the integrity of their cause, and offer their deaths to authenticate their honour. In the context of the play over all it is hard to know how we are to evaluate or interpret this attitude. In Jonson's *Sejanus*, the Germanicans meet death one after another with a proud defiance which has the unequivocal political approval of the author. Jonson's inexorable tragedy is a study in the systematic destruction of liberty by the tyrant Tiberius. The end of Brutus and Cassius, though, can hardly be used to point such a definite pattern.

The conclusion of the play and the deaths of what are by now its joint protagonists seem, in fact, to elude the various interpretations of them available. Their defeat might, for example, be taken to represent the inevitable triumph of Caesarism, the futility of their attempt to resist monarchical government. Yet, curiously, the impetus towards one-man rule does not seem a specially strong driving-force; though it is there, relatively little is made of the coming rivalry between Antony and Octavius. Alternatively, there is the view of the action represented by Antony's valediction – 'This was the noblest Roman of them all' – isolating Brutus as the single misguided idealist misled into conspiracy. But the final acts have so closely identified Brutus with Cassius, and have so detached them from the original conspiracy, that Antony's judgement hardly sums up the experience of the end of the play. Brutus and Cassius die as martyrs to an imagined cause which Shakespeare allows us to see as being without political substance. Yet they die according to some sort of truth of the spirit which transcends and ennobles the insubstantiality of their ideals.

Julius Caesar was the first full attempt by Shakespeare self-consciously to evoke a milieu distinct from his own Renaissance Christian culture, and to find a distinctive mode of dramatic representation for it. This is reflected in its language which, as Maurice Charney suggests, represents 'a stylistic experiment on Shakespeare's part. He appears to be attempting a special "Roman" style for the play, one that can express the clarity of thought and forthrightness of action in the Roman subject matter'.[15] This is well observed. Certain habits of language – the much discussed 'illeism', for example, characters referring to themselves in the third person – are marked enough in *Julius Caesar* to seem deliberately 'Roman'. The dramatic 'experiment', however, went well beyond the development of a rhetorical style suitable for the public figures of Roman history, and involved the deliberate exclusion of an inner life of the self. As Reuben Brower puts it, commenting on Brutus' soliloquy 'Between the acting of a dreadful thing And its first motion', 'Shakespeare glances at the possibility of another kind of play, and as certainly puts it behind him'.[16] The inwardness which was to be so much a part of the tragic realisation of a Hamlet, Lear or Macbeth, is finally excluded from the character of Brutus. This was not to make of the Romans of *Julius Caesar* public figures only, hollow men playing out self-created roles or roles created for them by history. Shakespeare, often with tiny deft touches, lends to his main characters the specificity and authenticity of individual life. Such individuality, however, is established within the context of a limited world of social and political reality. In so far as images and ideals in the play aspire to transcend that limited world, they are regarded with a studied neutrality or a carefully poised ambivalence. In his next tragedy, Shakespeare was to return to many of the concerns of *Julius Caesar* – the relations between the life of the state and the life of its ruler, the interpretation of omens, the movement from thought to action. But in *Hamlet* those dimensions of inner consciousness and outer absolutes which were so rigorously restricted in the Roman play were to become the very essence of the drama.

3

Hamlet

The writing of *Julius Caesar* left a rich deposit in *Hamlet*. The two plays may well have been written within a year of one another and have been in the Globe repertoire together in the period 1599–1600.[1] At times in *Hamlet* Shakespeare deliberately recalls the earlier play, as in the speech of Horatio –

> In the most high and palmy state of Rome,
> A little ere the mightiest Julius fell
>   I.i.113*ff*.

– where the omens recounted recapitulate the scene before the assassination enacted in *Julius Caesar*. At one point, there even appears to be a theatrical in-joke turning on the casting of the two plays. The exchange between Hamlet and Polonius about the latter's amateur theatrical past, which seems a little gratuitous and irrelevant, had significance in the original production if the actors, Burbage and Heminges, who had played Brutus and Caesar, were now playing Hamlet and Polonius. So, when Polonius reminisces, 'I did enact Julius Caesar; I was kill'd i' th' Capitol; Brutus killed me', and Hamlet wisecracks back, 'It was a brute part of him to kill so capital a calf there' (III.ii.100–3), the audience would have read an allusion to Burbage/Brutus' recent assassination of Heminges/Caesar.[2] Elsewhere, also, there are signs that Shakespeare used some of the spoil from researching *Julius Caesar* in writing *Hamlet*. An occasional word such as 'hugger-mugger' – Claudius regretting the private nature of Polonius' funeral: 'we have done but greenly In hugger-mugger to inter him' (IV.v.80–1) – derives from the *Life of Brutus* in North's Plutarch, where it is used in a similar context. One of the prominent episodes of Caesar's early life in Plutarch which Shakespeare did not use in *Julius Caesar* was his capture by pirates and their release of him on terms; in *Hamlet* the incident became the means of aborting Hamlet's English voyage and getting him back to Denmark.

The general and specific similarities between *Julius Caesar* and

37

Hamlet are well-known. Analogies can be drawn between Hamlet and Brutus, both reflective men who take on their roles in action with reluctance. Both plays have at their centre the (supposed) need for the death of the king/head of state as a means of political renewal. Philip Edwards sums it up succinctly: '*Hamlet* is a re-working of the basic underlying theme of *Julius Caesar*, namely the commitment of the philosopher-hero to violent action in order to remove an intruder from the government of the state and restore an ideal condition belonging to former times'.[3] Yet to identify this common theme with such clarity is to highlight all the more the fundamental differences in the political, moral and spiritual atmos-phere of the two plays. The term 'philosopher-hero' applied to Brutus and Hamlet, though perfectly just, pinpoints the radically diverse sorts of both philosophy and heroism involved. Claudius and Caesar can both be identified as 'intruders' to be 'removed from the government of the state', but the usurping regicide is an intruder of a quite different order from the ambiguous would-be king-dictator. Brutus unquestionably has as his aim the restoration of the Roman republic to 'an ideal condition belonging to former times', however politically unrealistic that may be. But Hamlet moves in a post-heroic world of loss in which there seems little formed prospect of an issue from the fallen state of degeneracy that is Denmark. *Hamlet* arises out of *Julius Caesar* as the inchoate other to its counterpart's splendid objectivity, exploring at once areas of the subjective and the transcendent which Shakespeare had delib-erately set outside the limits of his Roman play.

The Ghost provides a point of entry – the Ghost with which *Hamlet* begins, and with which *Julius Caesar* all but ends. Caesar's ghost is the most undemonstrative, the most supernaturally unspectacular of spectres. We only see it once, though Brutus tells us of its second appearance, accepted without histrionics as the sure sign of his coming defeat and death. By contrast the Ghost in *Hamlet* is, notoriously, the most characterised apparition in Elizabethan drama, generating a whole critical literature on whether it is a Protestant or Catholic ghost, really Hamlet's father or just a devil tricked up to deceive. The opening scene certainly provokes doubt, both in the stage watchers and the theatre audience, as to the nature and significance of the Ghost. It is referred to throughout as

an indeterminate 'thing'; its resemblance to the dead king does not
move Horatio beyond the cautious assumption that old Hamlet's
form is only borrowed:

> What art thou that usurp'st this time of night
> Together with that fair and warlike form
> In which the majesty of buried Denmark
> Did sometimes march?
>
> I.i.46–9

Yet, in spite of such caution, the awe the Ghost arouses is partly a
sense of reverence for the dead king it may not be. It *has* 'the
majesty of buried Denmark', if only by usurping it. It draws to
itself the heroic standing of the warrior-king Hamlet, evoked in
Horatio's recollections:

> Such was the very armour he had on
> When he the ambitious Norway combated;
> So frown'd he once when, in an angry parle,
> He smote the sledded Polacks on the ice.
>
> I.i.60–4

The attempt of the sentries to strike at it is felt as indecorum, if not
lese-majesty:

> We do it wrong, being so majestical,
> To offer it the show of violence
>
> I.i.143–4

The Ghost may be an illusion, but if so there remains a strong
sense of the substance of which it is an illusion.

Horatio has been invited to address the Ghost as he is a 'scholar'
and, in spite of his initial scepticism, he shows himself well-
informed on the folklore of apparitions and their possible reasons
for appearing. He charges the Ghost to speak:

> If there be any good thing to be done,
> That may to thee do ease and grace to me,
> Speak to me.
> If thou art privy to thy country's fate,
> Which happily foreknowing may avoid,

> O, speak!
> Or if thou hast uphoarded in thy life
> Extorted treasure in the womb of earth,
> For which, they say, you spirits oft walk in death,
> Speak of it.
>
>   I.i.130–9

Horatio here gives three common explanations for the return of revenants. For much of the opening scene speculation on the motive for the Ghost's appearance centres on the second of the three. When Horatio tells Marcellus and Bernardo of the reasons for the current military mobilisation in Denmark, the possible renewal of the Dano-Norwegian conflict of a generation ago, it seems to them a plausible explanation of the Ghost's walking:

> Well may it sort, that this portentous figure
> Comes armed through our watch; so like the King
> That was and is the question of these wars.
>
>   I.i.109–11

Whether he comes like the legendary warrior-king of the past to defend his country in time of war, or being 'privy to [his] country's fate' to forewarn against it, the armed Ghost is considered to augur coming disturbance to the state. It is in this context that Horatio makes the analogy with the omens which preceded the death of Caesar, and interprets the appearance of the Ghost as

>   the like precurse of fear'd events,
>   As harbingers preceding still the fates
>   And prologue to the omen coming on
>   I.i.121–3

The emphasis falls throughout on what the omen may signify for the future – 'precurse', 'harbingers', 'prologue'. The invoked memory of *Julius Caesar*, the suggestion of a war to come with Norway, the interpretation of the watch, would all combine to suggest a climactic and catastrophic coming event in the life of the state of Denmark.

The omens before the death of Caesar were susceptible to alternative interpretations depending on the viewpoint of the interpreter – the awed credulousness of Casca, the self-righteous bravado of Cassius, the measured scepticism of Cicero (not unlike the caution of Horatio). We were in a position to see these several constructions and misconstructions for what they were. In *Hamlet* the vantage-point of ironic awareness is replaced by an awed uncertainty; the Ghost represents for us, as for the stage audience, a mystery as to what it means, and draws us with them into doubtful conjecture. The misconception that the Ghost may come to prophesy war to come, an outer action in the future, serves to heighten our subsequent awareness that it is something inward, something in the past, which is 'rotten in the state of Denmark'. The ominousness of the Ghost can not be pinned down as a supernatural sign with a single significance. Horatio, understating as always, calls it 'a mote . . . to trouble the mind's eye' (I.i.112); Hamlet, however, is hardly overstating when he describes its capacity 'to shake our disposition With thoughts beyond the reaches of our souls' (I.iii.55–6).

Critical controversy over the Ghost has tended to be concerned with defining its nature, according to the signs conventionally used for judging or classifying spirits in Shakespeare's time. Hence John Dover Wilson's important pioneering work on the various theological positions concerning the spirit-world.[4] The very dubious nature of the Ghost, in Renaissance demonological terms, has now been amply demonstrated. But the efforts by, outstandingly, Eleanor Prosser to prove that the Ghost would unquestionably have been regarded as a devil by the Elizabethan audience are misguided.[5] Such an approach seeks to reduce the doubleness of what the Ghost is doing in the play to the singleness of a defined moral status.[6] For the Ghost is both the murdered hero-king, protesting the outrage of his killing, demanding restitution of the order of which he is emblem, and the sinister portent of what must flow from his murder. Horatio and the others were not entirely wrong. The Ghost does prefigure catastrophe for Denmark in the death of its king, prince, and most of its court. But it is not the instrument or agent of that catastrophe; it is rather the symbolic projection of a past which in its violent disruption will lead inexorably to the spreading eruptions of the future. Its moral standing, or its exact demonological classification, are less important than its significance as the representative of a spiritual order beyond the dichotomies of good and evil, crime and punishment.

In the first scene of the play we see the past king of Denmark or a spectral image of him; in the second scene we see the reigning king. The contrast between the two brothers is emphasised again and again in the most lurid rhetorical terms by Hamlet and the Ghost himself – 'Hyperion to a satyr', 'no more like my father than I to Hercules', 'a wretch whose natural gifts were poor to those of mine'. Yet what we see initially in Claudius is by no means an obviously inadequate 'king of shreds and patches'. Wilson Knight's famous apologia for Claudius has not attracted much support from later critics of *Hamlet*, yet his praise is not mere devil's advocacy. It is true, as Wilson Knight claims, that in I.ii 'Claudius shows every sign of being an excellent diplomatist and king'.[7] And it is his skill in diplomacy which epitomises his difference from old Hamlet. Where the past reign is recalled in terms of lands won from Norway in hand-to-hand combat, Polacks (or pole-axe) smitten on the ice, what we see under Claudius is the, admittedly swift and efficient, dispatch of a diplomatic mission. In the first scene we hear a great deal of Denmark being placed on a war-footing, but the only guns actually fired off in the play before the final cortège are salutes to the King's drinking bouts. Claudius' is a peace-time court. The League of Nations type approval that Wilson Knight accords the diplomatic solution achieved in the Dano-Norwegian crisis is surely misplaced. 'Tact has found an easy settlement where arms and opposition might have wasted the strength of Denmark.'[8] The contrast between the warrior-king of the past and the politician/diplomat king of the present, even if it is not registered as the absolutely degenerate falling-off which it represents for Hamlet or, *a fortiori*, the Ghost, can hardly be regarded as progress towards an era of peace and civilisation.

Wilson Knight's eulogy of Claudius may take him too far – 'the typical kindly uncle', 'a good and gentle king'[9] – but his analysis usefully illuminates how little the King in fact resembles the monster he is made out to be by Hamlet and his Ghost-father. There may well be an unpleasant unctuousness in Claudius' opening speech, 'Though yet of Hamlet our dear brother's death . . .' (I.ii.1ff.), the signs of emotional duplicity, but the effect is more one of worldly urbanity than of evil. In the order of Shakespeare's usurpers, he is a Bolingbroke rather than a Richard III or Macbeth. He tries to ingratiate himself with his spiky cousin-son and to keep him home from Wittenberg, no doubt partly out of political self-interest, but also possibly out of a genuine step-fatherly desire to cement his uncertain place in the family. His relationship with Gertrude is always characterised by Hamlet and the Ghost in terms of a perverse and repulsive lubriciousness on her part as well as his:

> O, most wicked speed, to post
> With such dexterity to incestuous sheets!
>
> I.ii.156–7

> lust, though to a radiant angel link'd,
> Will sate itself in a celestial bed
> And prey on garbage.
>
> I.v.55–7

Yet throughout the play the King and Queen seem bound by a stable, mutual and genuine affection. The irony of Claudius' role is that his quite ordinary human crookedness makes him an inadequate representative of evil. It is this perhaps which gives force to Hamlet's otherwise unnecessary discovery 'that one may smile, and smile, and be a villain' (I.v.108).

For both Hamlet and the Ghost, Claudius and Gertrude are guilty of one of the most heinous and forbidden sins. They are 'incestuous sheets' to which the Queen posted with such dexterity. The Ghost names the marriage as an outrage of national pollution:

> Let not the royal bed of Denmark be
> A couch for luxury and damned incest.
>
> I.v.82–3

Yet it is remarkable that no-one else in the play ever so much as glances at this view of the matter. Of course we could hardly expect the tactful and flattering courtiers of King Claudius to refer to the dubious propriety of his marrying his deceased brother's wife. But neither Gertrude nor Claudius themselves, even in moments of regret or penitence, face up to a charge of incest. The Queen admits the marriage was 'o'erhasty', not that it was of its nature sinful. Her guilt under the lash of Hamlet's tongue in the closet-scene appears to be for the lust which drove her to adultery, not the blacker crime of incest. Claudius prays for forgiveness for his 'rank' offence of fratricide; his marriage to the queen is only one more of the fruits of murder, not a separate compounding sin. The horror of incest which so obsesses Hamlet and the Ghost is as though invisible to the other characters in the play, and the anomaly helps to highlight the gap between the father and son's vision and that of the rest.

Part of Hamlet's difficulty in executing his father's commands is the very banality of the world in which he finds himself, the gap between the visionary night of the Ghost on the battlements and the court of spies and surfaces that is Elsinore. The Players, Rosencrantz and Guildenstern, the grave-diggers, Osric, people Denmark with a heterogeneous life independent of the Prince and his preoccupations. Above all the Polonius family, as they appear for the first time in I.iii, belong to an order of existence quite distinct from the moral and spiritual imperatives introduced by the Ghost. Laertes and Polonius, with their father–son resemblance, their myopic moralising and men-of-the-world cunning, only emerging a bit more coarsely and crudely in the father than the son, are characterised with a solidity marvellously poised between satiric caricature and social realism. Whether Ophelia is played as mere passive victim of these two egregiously complacent male egos (a characterisation becoming less common than it used to be), or as a contained person capable of some measure of self-assertion, she lives appropriately enough within the dramatic dimensions of her father and brother. *Hamlet* I.iii could quite easily be moved into the realistic serio-comic milieu of the middle comedies without changing its mode of representation.

The world of *Hamlet* is an ordinary world, a world of the morally second-rate, overtaken, invaded, metamorphosed by a visionary world of the extraordinary. What this means to Hamlet, and how it affects him, emerge in his encounter with the Ghost. Hamlet's disenchanted distance from the court atmosphere, marked even in his mourning isolation in I.ii, is further accentuated by his bitter reflections on the sounds of revelry heard from the cold and dark castle walls – reflections all the more bitter because the celebrations are supposed to be in honour of his own 'gentle and unforc'd accord' in staying home in Denmark. The Ghost enters at the end of Hamlet's meditations on the national vice of drunkenness, on the suggestive (though textually muddled) lines,

> The dram of eale
> Doth all the noble substance of a doubt
> To his own scandal.
>
> I.ii.33–6

In Hamlet's dramatic response to the Ghost's appearance we see
the range and complexity of its significance:

> Angels and ministers of grace defend us!
> Be thou a spirit of health or goblin damn'd,
> Bring with thee airs from heaven or blasts from hell,
> Be thy intents wicked or charitable,
> Thou com'st in such a questionable shape
> That I will speak to thee. I'll call thee Hamlet,
> King, father, royal Dane.
>
>   I.iv.39–45

The address in its context crystallises all that the Ghost comes to
represent in the play.

For Hamlet, still living with the aching loss of grief, the chance of
talking again to his beloved father is a wish-fulfilment dream
which makes any risk worth taking. The idealisation of the father,
the blank recognition that he was gone for ever, were apparent in
the earlier scene –

> 'A was a man, take him for all in all,
> I shall not look upon his like again.
>   I.ii.187–8

– and there is an awed joy at 'looking upon his like again' against
all the odds. He is, however, not only 'Hamlet . . . father', but also
'King . . . royal Dane'. The Ghost is that figure of royal majesty
and martial dignity which so intimidated and impressed the
watchers in the first scene, and for Hamlet too he is more than the
father as superego. As the remembered king he stands as the
source of power, of monarchic authority and heroic action. King
Hamlet only died two months before the beginning of the play,
and his most famous military action against the older Fortinbras
was thirty years before, but already his reign is made to seem a
pristine era of long ago, separated by a gulf in time from a fallen
present. From the start there are hints of Hamlet's sense of self-
inadequacy in relation to his father, that the Prince feels inescapably of the latter-day here and now. The contrast of his father with
Claudius – 'no more like his brother than I to Hercules' (I.ii.152–3)
– carries an implied suggestion of his own puniness by heroic
standards.

Hamlet has not Horatio's cautiousness: he *will* call the Ghost what it appears to be, rather than assuming that it is merely usurping its apparent shape. Yet he too is aware that it is necessarily something other than the dead king his father. It may be 'a spirit of health or goblin damn'd', from heaven or hell, with 'intents wicked or charitable'. Although these are posed as sets of alternatives, ostensibly mutually exclusive, their effect is of 'both . . . and' rather than 'either . . . or'. Hamlet is not at this stage expressing real uncertainty as to the Ghost's spiritual standing; he is not, at least here, raising as a question the issue which modern *Hamlet* scholars have debated so fully. Rather what is suggested is the whole realm of the supernatural world from which the Ghost emanates, whether it comes from one part or another. Heaven and Hell seem to lose their spiritually polarised separation both here and later. After the Ghost leaves in I.v, there is Hamlet's strange exclamation:

> O all you host of heaven! O earth! What else?
> And shall I couple hell?
>
> I.v.92–3

Harold Jenkins comments, 'Uncertainty about the Ghost's provenance (cf. I.iv.40–1), quieted during its presence, returns when it is gone'.[10] A possible reading. But in the flood-tide of emotion on which Hamlet is here borne along, it would seem unlikely that there is a real pause for doubt about the Ghost's nature. Here, as again in the third soliloquy where he speaks of being 'prompted to my revenge by heaven and hell' (II.ii.580), he is invoking the whole spiritual universe in which he finds himself, and in which he must find his way.

The speech 'So, oft it chances in particular men', which precedes the Ghost's entrance in I.iv is one of the passages which appears only in Q2 and not in F, and which it has been suggested Shakespeare marked for cutting.[11] However, it does include the idea of a spreading taint, of good things 'taking corruption', which is a *leit-motif* not only throughout the play, but very specifically in the scenes between Hamlet and the Ghost. Towards the end of the Ghost's long and appallingly vivid account of his own murder, moving Hamlet to revenge, there comes the solemn injunction, 'Taint not thy mind' (I.v.85). The impossibility of the command is obvious: what, after all, has the Ghost been doing throughout the speech, throughout the scene, but tainting the mind of Hamlet,

filling it with the most horrific images? It is hard to do justice to the
complexity of the dramatic effect here. The key-note of the Ghost's
speeches is one of sinister and perverted natural energies: the
'juice of cursed hebona' which 'swift as quicksilver . . . courses
through the natural gates and alleys of the body', and clots 'like
eager droppings into milk', leaving the 'smooth body' 'bark'd
about . . . with vile and loathsome crust' (I.v.62–73). The later
phrase 'blossoms of my sins' suggests the tone; it is a speech of
fleurs du mal. In its combination of the visionary and the visceral,
this is language which stands out in exceptionally pointed contrast
to the concrete abstractness, the clarity and definition, which are
the prevailing qualities of style in *Julius Caesar*.

What the Ghost here evokes is simultaneously what happened
to its body, what is happening to Denmark, and what will happen
to Hamlet. Those commentators who are suspicious of the Ghost
are, therefore, in a sense right to place it as a precipitating source of
corruption in the play and in the mind of Hamlet, but only in so far
as it represents a dynamic process which is already at work in the
action. Even before he knows of the Ghost's existence, Hamlet's
view of the world as an 'unweeded garden' anticipates the Ghost's
images of corrupt fecundity – 'the fat weed That roots itself in ease
on Lethe wharf' (I.v.32–3). Denmark is poisoned, and the magis-
terial command to Hamlet to purge the country of its pollution
comes from a figure which itself illustrates the poisoning process,
is itself a carrier of disease. When Hamlet cries out

> The time is out of joint. O cursed spite,
> That ever I was born to set it right!
> I.v.189–90

he recognises the universal malaise he has been assigned to cure
and his unfitness for the part, both as he senses his incapacity for
the action his father would expect, and his entanglement in the
corrupt world to be redeemed.

Hamlet is given a task like that of Brutus: he is to restore the 'time'
to the ideal state associated with a heroic predecessor and name-
sake – the Brutus who drove out the Tarquins, the Hamlet who
defeated Fortinbras in single combat. The thought of that mission

moves both Brutus and Hamlet in on themselves, as reflected in
Brutus' guarded reticence to Cassius:

> If I have veil'd my look,
> I turn the trouble of my countenance
> Merely upon myself.
>
> I.ii.37–9

But, as pointed out in the previous chapter, after the Gethsemane
of Brutus' meditations in the orchard, he emerges to take a public
role which he never subsequently relinquishes, almost totally
repressing the private inner self. For Brutus the state of internal
turmoil precipitated by the call to action is strictly limited:

> Between the acting of a dreadful thing
> And the first motion, all the interim is
> Like a phantasma or a hideous dream.
>
> II.i.63–5

By contrast, virtually all *Hamlet* is 'interim', concerned with the
insurgent dislocations of the inward world. Brutus commits himself to action, and insists upon imposing on outer reality his vision
of what that action means. For Hamlet the continuing disparities
between his inner consciousness and the world without are dis-
abling impediments to action. Brutus and Hamlet are complementary and antithetical idealists. Brutus, against considerable evidence, persists in petrifying his dubiously honourable friends into
a frieze of Roman honour; Hamlet, under the shock of ideals
shattered by murder and incest, will take nothing and nobody
(save Horatio) at face value.

This contrast is most strikingly illustrated in the attitudes of the
two towards acting and action. Brutus advises the conspirators to
disguise their intentions:

> Let not our looks put on our purposes,
> But bear it as our Roman actors do,
> With untir'd spirits and formal constancy.
>
> II.i.225–7

In context, with the load of approval that 'Roman' always carries in
the play, the stoical associations of 'bear', 'untir'd', and 'con-

stancy', this is less a figure for deceit than an image of exemplary truth and dignity. So too with the ritual blooding after the assassination; this is intended as an act of theatre which in its repetition down the ages will symbolise sacramentally the liberating death of Caesar. Brutus has full confidence in the power of acting to manifest the moral-political truth of action – a confidence which Antony's meretricious histrionics at Caesar's funeral rapidly reveals as misplaced.

Hamlet, on the other hand, for all his interest in theatre and his implicit belief that it can potentially 'hold the mirror up to nature', is from the start distrustful of acting. In his haughty rebuke to his mother – 'I know not seems' – he dismisses the various outward tokens of his grief as inadequate expressions of his true feeling:

> These, indeed, seem;
> For they are actions that a man might play
> I.ii.83–4

He is moved to wonder that the player could feel so much 'in a fiction, in a dream of passion . . . and all for nothing' (II.ii.545–50). Yet action itself feels as futile and unreal as acting to Hamlet. The example of Fortinbras in Act IV parallels and complements the example of the Player in Act II. Though in both cases there are elements of envious admiration, for the actor who can truly feel and the soldier who can unhesitatingly act, his admiration is blended with scepticism. Fortinbras and his Polish expedition are 'examples gross as earth' which 'exhort' Hamlet because they are instances of action meaningless, motiveless, in comparison with the action he has in hand.[12]

Hamlet finds himself imprisoned in a Denmark where he cannot act because it is a world of acting merely, of seeming and stratagems. He is haunted by other worlds – the heroic world of the past, the supernatural universe of the Ghost, the bad dreams which visit him even bounded in the nutshell of the self. Partly out of a need to distract himself from these haunting obsessions, partly out of a satiric contempt for the obvious crudity of the performances going on around him, Hamlet decides to play out a part in the court comedy. It is impossible to tell from Ophelia's report of his visit to her closet (II.i.77ff.) if this was a set-piece of the assumed antic disposition, as some interpreters have argued, or a real and anguished silent farewell. But the cruel games that Hamlet plays with Ophelia in the nunnery-scene and the play-scene can be explained (if not excused) by his feeling that she too has been cast as an actress in his enemies' charades. There is no need to adopt Dover Wilson's elaborate hypothesis of Hamlet's overhearing the eavesdropping plan for the nunnery-scene, or the common theatrical practice of having him spot the eavesdroppers. The constraints that must necessarily appear in Ophelia's behaviour under Polonius' tutelage would be quite enough to convince Hamlet, the geigercounter of inauthenticity, that she is no longer merely herself. In the first encounter with Claudius' bit-players, Rosencrantz and Guildenstern, we see Hamlet's initial, somewhat guarded, camaraderie turn into a sour and satiric watchfulness which ultimately costs the luckless stooges their lives. In his games of sense and nonsense with Polonius, there is both pleasure and exasperation. 'They fool me to the top of my bent' (III.iii. 374–5), the aside following the episode of the camel/weasel/whale-like cloud, expresses at once Hamlet's pride in his own mischievous acting, and his indignation that he should be taken for the madman he seems to be.

The key commitment to acting in place of action is the decision to stage *The Mousetrap*. The Player's tears for Hecuba drive Hamlet to a fury of self-execration in the third soliloquy, and the attempt to convert self-hatred into hatred of Claudius only arouses more revulsion at his own violent rhetoric: 'Why, what an ass am I!' (II.ii.578). It is in flight from this inward spiralling self-disgust that Hamlet turns to the play – 'About, my brains' (II.ii.584). In deciding to set his trap for the King, Hamlet here for the first time explicitly questions the authenticity of the Ghost:

> The spirit that I have seen
> May be a devil; and the devil hath power
> T' assume a pleasing shape; yea, and perhaps
> Out of my weakness and my melancholy,
> As he is very potent with such spirits,
> Abuses me to damn me. I'll have grounds
> More relative than this.

II.ii.594–600

It will not do to read this simply as Hamlet finding excuses for his delay, or to underestimate the questionableness of a Renaissance ghost. Yet it is noticeable that all of the earlier part of this soliloquy

rests on the assumption that his father *had* been murdered by his
uncle. There is, moreover, an air of *ad hoc* rationalising in the
speech, particularly in the improvisatory movement of a phrase
such as 'Yea, and perhaps . . .'. What Hamlet is doing here is not
merely procrastinating; he is putting behind him the world of the
Ghost which, in its challenge to his selfhood, is proving an intolerable anguish, and plunging instead into the ethos of Elsinore
where indirections are used to 'find directions out'. In looking for
'grounds more relative[13] than' the Ghost's word, Hamlet is seeking
the sort of proof Polonius wanted of Laertes' Parisian misdemean-
ours, or that the King wants of the motives behind the Prince's
madness, and he is using the same means. He is hunting 'the trail
of policy', devising stratagems to penetrate masks, to detect people
unawares:

> The play's the thing
> Wherein I'll catch the conscience of the king.
> II.ii.600–1

The Mousetrap re-enacts not once but twice, first in the icon of the
dumb-show, then in the aborted performance of *The Murder of
Gonzago*, the primal crime which is the source of Denmark's pollution. As such it has all but ritual significance. Yet to Hamlet it is
just play, show, poisoning in jest, treated to the sort of derisive
and illusion-shattering commentary which the courtier/lovers of
the comedies give to the Nine Worthies or Pyramus and Thisbe. (If
these are any indication of Elizabethan court behaviour at plays,
one does not envy the Lord Chamberlain's Men their many royal
command performances.) The play has become for Hamlet mere
instrument in his verbal vendetta against Claudius, against his
mother, and by extension against Ophelia. He is completely unmoved by the mirror image of his mother's faithlessness, his
uncle's treachery, his father's murder, except in sardonic mockery
of the emotions they arouse in his audience. Hence the exhilar-
ated, all but hysterical, glee in the 'success' of the play, as he
celebrates with Horatio:

> Would not this, sir, and a forest of feathers – if the rest of my
> fortunes turn Turk with me – with two Provincial roses on my
> raz'd shoes, get me a fellowship in a cry of players, sir?
> III.ii.269–72

Though Horatio, with his effectively sobering reticence, will grant him only 'half a share' in the cry of players, Hamlet here constitutes himself actor–manager extraordinary.

Hamlet's sceptical indulgence in acting blends into the sceptical attitude towards action. He is constantly aware of the possibility of action as acting, both in himself and in others, as we see in his reflections on Fortinbras, and in his crocodile-eating contest with Laertes in the graveyard. If *The Murder of Gonzago* becomes no more than a travesty of his father's murder, then his own role as avenger runs the risk of reverting to stage stock too. The corrosive suspicion of seeming, the conviction that he has 'that within which passes show', makes it increasingly hard to imagine, much less accomplish, any action which will adequately express what is unshown within. He uses the avenger's mood music to fit himself for the part:

> 'Tis now the very witching time of night,
> When churchyards yawn, and hell itself breathes out
> Contagion to this world. Now could I drink hot blood,
> And do such bitter business as the day
> Would quake to look on.
>
> III.ii.378–82

But when the opportunity to do 'bitter business' arises in the following prayer-scene, it is not bitter enough for him. The actual killing of the King seems 'hire and salary, not revenge' (III.iii.79), and his imagination must strain on to the monstrous hyperbole of a death ensuring eternal damnation. The conception of action turns it always into a form of acting inadequate to what it should represent. Ironically, Hamlet is often left posturing histrionically in the effort to avoid action which might merely seem.

It has often been pointed out that Hamlet's delay would not be a problem for an audience, if Hamlet himself did not think of it as such. The paradox is that Hamlet is far from inactive and *Hamlet* is an action-packed play, yet the common impression is of a meditative, procrastinating hero and a drama of disconnected non-events. This duality is aptly symbolised in Hamlet's fitness/unfitness for the final duel: the man who has 'forgone all custom of exercises' (II.ii.296–7) has nonetheless been 'in continual practice'

(V.ii.202–3) at his fencing; for all that he is 'fat and scant of breath' (V.ii.279), the champion swordsman Laertes can gain no advantage over him in fair fight. Such a bifocal effect is achieved by the split-level at which we experience the play. On the surface, we attend to an action which is overloaded with plot, bustling with business; but below, the consciousness of Hamlet expressed in the soliloquies is standing water. The soliloquies still the flow of dramatic development, to reveal the depths of a Hamlet within that remains largely disengaged from the plots and counterplots. The movement of moods in this inner underworld corresponds to no fixed pattern; the prevailing themes – thoughts of suicide, *taedium vitae*, self-nausea, and a circling obsession with failure – recur in an intricate series of variations which bears no demonstrable relation to what is going on immediately around the Prince. The most notorious instance of this disjunction between soliloquy and action is the uncertain placing of 'To be or not to be'. Even though the joint authority of Q2 and F leave no justification for moving it from III.i, it is easy to understand why the theatrical production reflected in Q1 (the 'bad' Quarto) inserted it in the second act instead. It has apparently no continuity with the surrounding action, and in it Hamlet does not even mention the subject of revenge directly, much less allude to *The Mousetrap* which we last saw him gleefully setting.

The purpose of the 'antic disposition' is at once to defend and to extend the inner life represented in the soliloquies. In the source-story of Saxo Grammaticus, the madness of Amleth is functional, a means of ensuring the hero's survival in a hostile environment until he is in a position to accomplish his revenge. This function remains to some extent in Shakespeare's play, in so far as Hamlet uses his antics as a barrier to the crude intrusions and interrogations of the likes of Polonius, Rosencrantz and Guildenstern. As a mode of strategic defence, however, in the Amleth line, it is worse than useless; indeed Hamlet in his mad persona seems to take pleasure in teasing and exacerbating the King's suspicions, rather than trying to allay them. To the traditional old question – is Hamlet mad or only pretending? – all that can be offered is the apparently evasive answer: both. The 'antic disposition' is the expression of an ego genuinely fragmented and disturbed, the assertion of an alienation which Hamlet really feels. But in so far as it is alienation from a world which he despises and derides, it is a controlled assertion of superiority.

The complexity of Hamlet's inner life, its interaction and lack of interaction with the outer life of social behaviour, have attracted psychoanalysis and diagnosis. Ernest Jones's Oedipal model allowed him to account for many of Hamlet's 'symptoms' – his preoccupation with his mother's sexuality, his violent hatred of Claudius together with his paralysed inability to kill him.[14] Without necessarily accepting the Freudian analysis, many other critics have seen Hamlet's character in terms of psychological or moral deviation. The clinical question to be answered has been 'what is wrong with Hamlet', and there has been no shortage of answers. Against a hypothetical model of mature behaviour, it is easy to point to the mental characteristics by which Hamlet would be classified as immature, 'a man who in the face of life and death can make no affirmation'.[15] There is his prurient disgust with sex, which has its roots in an idealisation of his parents' relationship as asexual, and the horror of having to recognise his mother's continuing sexual life. There is his ruthless egotism, his self-righteous and self-justifying cruelty in his onslaught on Ophelia and on Gertrude, in his murders of Polonius, Rosencrantz and Guildenstern. Above all there is his obsession with death; he is, in Wilson Knight's famous phrase, 'the ambassador of death walking amid life'.[16]

There is much that is persuasive in the varying accounts of Hamlet as a more or less psychopathological case. Yet they hardly represent accurately the experience of the play, for two reasons. One is that we live through *Hamlet* so much with Hamlet himself, that it is difficult to attain the detachment from which to judge him and find him wanting. In *Julius Caesar* we can identify the workings of Brutus' mind, and see where he is misguided or mistaken; again and again in the play, Cassius' pragmatic clear sight is used to point up Brutus' delusions. The images of events which Brutus projects are sharply defined, and as sharply distinguished from the reality on to which they are projected. In *Hamlet*, also, there is a recognisable world which exists independently of the Prince's vision. Claudius is not the goatish 'satyr' of Hamlet's imagining, Polonius is not (quite) the buffoon he is made to appear, Ophelia is certainly not the dishonest coquette of Hamlet's nunnery-scene vituperations. But Hamlet's domination of the play is such that his vision, however prejudiced and distorted it may be, does impose itself upon us. We are subsumed within Hamlet's ego, drawn into the inner life of the soliloquies, imprisoned with him as centre of consciousness, whether we like it or not.

The second limitation in the diagnostic view of Hamlet is that it tends to separate him from the situation of which he is part, to place as individual psychological disorder what is in fact the larger disorder of his world. Here once again the ambience of *Julius Caesar* may be differentiated from that of *Hamlet*. In *Julius Caesar* there is a progression from a humanist confidence in man's mastering control –

> The fault, dear Brutus, is not in our stars,
> But in ourselves, that we are underlings.
> I.ii.140–1

– to a stoic acceptance in which suicide remains as a defiant assertion of the integrity of the self. Neither humanist optimism, nor stoic acceptance are possible as such in *Hamlet* because self and world are too deeply interpenetrated. Suicide in Roman terms set a proud spirit free, fixing its identity in ideal form for ever. Hamlet, longing for death as dissolution, is forced to live not only in the imprisoning body, but within transcendent constrictions which forbid escape:

> O, that this too too solid flesh would melt,
> Thaw, and resolve itself into a dew!
> Or that the Everlasting had not fix'd
> His canon 'gainst self-slaughter!
> I.ii.129–32

The fear of the 'To be or not to be' soliloquy is that the nightmare of being in the world may, after death, be extended infinitely into an eternal nightmare of consciousness. The dreams that may come 'when we have shuffled off this mortal coil' may be a terrible continuation of the bad dreams that haunt him in Denmark.

In *Julius Caesar* Shakespeare's historical imagination allowed him to enter in to the Roman republican horror of kingship as tyranny, while the play as a whole is profoundly ambiguous as to whether that view of monarchy is correct within the context. The assassination is attended by the supernatural signs which might prefigure the death of a prince, the murder of Caesar certainly creates a power vacuum into which Caesar's heirs, Antony and Octavius, rapidly move. But, in preventing Caesar from attaining kingship, were the conspirators interfering with a natural and desirable political evolution, or merely deferring temporarily the onset of imperial dictatorship? The play does not allow us to make a decisive judgement. In *Hamlet*, for all Denmark's special form of elective kingship, the monarchy has a sacred status with roots much deeper than the orthodox Tudor political theory which the play at several points affirms.[17] The fact that the true king has been killed, and that a usurping simulacrum of the king sits on the throne, defiles and distorts the whole country. Among other things, it makes it impossible for the true Prince of Denmark to be true prince. This is part of the force behind Ophelia's moving lines:

> O, what a noble mind is here o'erthrown!
> The courtier's, soldier's, scholar's, eye, tongue, sword;
> Th' expectancy and rose of the fair state,
> The glass of fashion and the mould of form,
> Th' observed of all observers – quite, quite down!
>
> III.i.150–4

This is not just a loving, and perhaps a biassed, eulogy of the character of Hamlet; it is the elegy for the Prince that was, the epitome of what a prince and heir could be to a state. It is the complement to Hamlet's portrait of his dead father as ideal king:

> 'A was a man, take him for all in all,
> I shall not look upon his like again.
>
> I.ii.187–8

The melancholy-mad Hamlet is the deformation of princeliness consequent on the desecration of kingship in his father's murder.

Hamlet's task is that of Orestes, a connection made long ago by Gilbert Murray.[18] For each of them it is mission impossible: each must restore the kingdom and come into his inheritance by avenging his father's death, though to do so is to take on the curse under which the kingdom lies. In the case of Orestes it involves matricide, and all the polluting guilt which flows from that crime. The Ghost's charge to Hamlet is just as difficult, although it is specifically *not* to follow Orestes' example:

> Taint not thy mind, nor let thy soul contrive
> Against thy mother aught
>
> I.v.85–6

In fact matricide, at one point, is as much a temptation to Hamlet as it is a duty to Orestes:

> O heart, lose not thy nature; let not ever
> The soul of Nero enter this firm bosom.
> III.ii.383–4

The pollution which Hamlet must inevitably take on is not the outward guilt of an Orestes, but the inward taint of the mind. It is not merely, as so many critics have maintained, that the task of avenger corrupts Hamlet by contagion, that brooding on death turns him into a death-consciousness. The tainted state of mind is already there in the first soliloquy, before he has been given the task of revenge. It is by taking it within his own mind that he must bear the burden of his country's curse, must carry it as a disease which he transmits as well as endeavouring finally to cure.

And is it a cure in the end? Is Hamlet in death at last the agent of his own and his country's redemption? Answers to the question depend very much on how we read Hamlet's attitude of mind in the last act, and how we interpret the effect of the final scene in which revenge is at last accomplished. The Hamlet who returns from his shortened voyage is often seen as a changed man, someone who has achieved the mental state necessary for his role. This change has been detected in the graveyard-scene: there, Hamlet has 'an air of self-possession greater than at any time in the play';[19] he is 'a Hamlet now royally master of himself'.[20] The alteration in the graveyard-scene tends to be related to the new belief in Providence in the scene that follows:

> There's a divinity that shapes our ends,
> Rough-hew them how we will.
> V.ii.10–11

there is a special providence in the fall of a sparrow. If it be now, 'tis not to come; if it be not to come, it will be now; if it be not now, yet it will come – the readiness is all.
> V.ii.211–15

This has been construed as a decisively different spiritual attitude in Hamlet, a willingness to put himself into the hands of Providence and be used as its agent/instrument. Hamlet in the final act becomes 'a passively active figure',[21] waiting in readiness on events.

This is an attractive view, but there are weaknesses in it as an argument.[22] Apart from anything else, there are far too many similarities between the supposedly changed figure of the final act and the unrehabilitated Hamlet of the previous four. The preoccupation with death in the graveyard has been variously differentiated from his earlier obsession with the subject; it is seen as less morbid, more mature. Yet the fantasias on Alexander and Caesar – 'may not imagination trace the noble dust of Alexander till 'a find it stopping a bung-hole' (V.i.197–9) – are surely closely akin to the *danse macabre* demonstration of 'how a king may go a progress through the guts of a beggar' (IV.iii.29–31). The attempt to establish the mood of Hamlet in the graveyard-scene as one of calm self-possession is blown apart by the towering rage in which he appears to Laertes – 'This is I Hamlet the Dane' (V.i.251–2). Even if he does not actually leap into the grave, according to the time-honoured stage practice, his violent show of feeling is hardly that of a man serenely waiting on Providence. His sardonic exit-couplet –

> Let Hercules himself do what he may,
> The cat will mew, and dog will have his day.
>   V.i.285–6

– sounds remarkably like the old, satiric, 'antic' Hamlet.

Hamlet is not, then, a totally transformed character in the final act; he can take as much pleasure in satiric cat-and-mouse games with Osric as ever he did with Polonius. Nor perhaps is it a new attitude to Providence which is significantly changed. What makes us feel that Hamlet is different in Act V is that we are cut off from the sense of his inner life. The soliloquies are so important in the creation of the depth and intimacy of our understanding of Hamlet, that the lack of soliloquy in the final act brings a distancing alienation. The endlessly self-scrutinising and self-examining character now stands aloof and alone, giving to Horatio only limited glimpses of his feeling. The isolation and the loss of inwardness are in part linked to a preparation towards death. For the Hamlet of Act V may be construed as a man who has given himself over to death, rather than holding himself ready as an instrument of Providence. The contempt for living which was there from the beginning – 'I do not set my life at a pin's fee' (I.iv.65) – has settled into something different: 'a man's life's no more than to say "one"' (V.ii.74). This expectation of death has the premonitory signs

which we would expect in the theatre, 'thou wouldst not think
how ill all's here about my heart' (V.ii.203–5). This is the sort of
premonition which had led him earlier to his shipboard discovery
of the mischief intended him by the King: 'in my heart there was a
kind of fighting That would not let me sleep' (V.ii.4–5).[23] But the
positive reliance on Providence here seems to be limited to something like a quiescent fatalism. Hamlet rather has answered his
own key question and decided not to be, to abandon the struggle
in the mind and accept self-extinction. The escape from the burden
of consciousness, the sense of mystery as he moves towards the
darkness of death, create within the stage figure a dignity, a
glamour almost, giving weight and beauty to his last words, 'The
rest is silence'.

V.ii re-creates I.ii. In each the full court assembles with due pomp
and ceremony, in each there is the same configuration of central
characters. In the opening court scene the King dealt in turn with
Fortinbras (who at that stage was only a rumour of war offstage)
and with the two university students on leave, Laertes and
Hamlet. There is a symmetry in the ending, with the duel to the
death between the Prince and courtier, followed by the entrance of
the potential invader. Claudius in both scenes does his best to
ritualise and ceremonialise events, with the cannons used to salute
Hamlet's points in the fencing-bouts as they had been earlier to
celebrate his decision to stay home in Denmark. Yet by the end of
the play the deadly realities beneath the formal superficialities are
all too evident. The duel has the theatrical irony of the so-called
'murderous masque' which was to become such a standard ending
for Jacobean tragedy. The fencing-match, like the masque, is intended as the proper peace-time entertainment of a court. The
masque is the emblem of the noble virtues and order which the
monarch and court collectively epitomise; the fencing-bout, like a
tournament, is the mimic display of the warrior powers appropriate to an aristocratic caste. But in each case what is working
beneath these illusions of hieratic play is real hatred and violence.
The symbols of order, of contained and ritualised combat, are
made the instruments of a devastating and anarchic destruction.
   This is partly why the final scene of *Hamlet* makes such a double
impression. On the one hand, looking at the litter of bodies on

stage, we see murder and mayhem. Horatio sums it up well when he talks of 'carnal, bloody, and unnatural acts; . . . accidental judgments, casual slaughters' (V.ii.373–4). If Hamlet has finally killed the King, and thus avenged his father's death, it is only very messily, after the Queen has died of poison intended for him, Laertes of the 'anointed' rapier, and he himself is mortally wounded. It is certainly hard to see this as a very clear-cut victory, the act of vengeance which was to heal the ills of Denmark. It has even been argued that in leaving the throne to a foreigner, to the son of the man whom his father defeated, Hamlet's mission must be seen as a signal failure.[24] For those who interpret it in this way there can only be irony in Fortinbras' funeral eulogy:

> Let four captains
> Bear Hamlet like a soldier to the stage;
> For he was likely, had he been put on,
> To have prov'd most royal
>
> V.ii.387–90.

Hamlet's actions in the play have hardly been soldier-like, nor such as to make us sure that he would 'have prov'd most royal' given the chance.

Yet the 'soldiers' music and the rite of war' which end the play need not seem ironically inappropriate, nor the solemn words of Fortinbras merely empty rhetoric. It is surely a mistake to see Fortinbras as a foreign opportunist taking over the Danish kingdom, with the sardonic ironies of some modern productions.[25] It is true that when we hear of him first he has 'shark'd up a list of lawless resolutes' (I.i.98) against Denmark, and that Hamlet's reflections on his Polish expedition make it seem a piece of futile adventuring. But audiences commonly have short memories for minor characters, and they need not remember all this against Fortinbras when he enters in the final scene. What is important about his appearance here is that he comes from without, from the field of war, and that, together with the ambassadors from England, he can make up an international audience before whom Hamlet's story will be told. In the first act he may have been seen as a dangerous firebrand, but here he can be a convincing order-figure, reinstating something like normality in the kingdom and providing formal closure to the play. If he has not the personal heroic standing of the old King Hamlet, he comes from the outward world of military conflict associated with the former king (and his own father). And coming from that world, he marks the hideous indecorum of the intestine violence which has consumed Denmark:

> Such a sight as this
> Becomes the field, but here shows much amiss.
> V.ii.393–4

If it is not wholly fitting that Hamlet should be given honorary soldier status in death, Fortinbras' salute seems right in that we feel something has been completed, has taken its course, in which Hamlet had a hero's part; not perhaps the hero of epic, but the tragic hero who must take upon himself the ills of the world and by opposing end them.

Brutus tried and failed to make sacred drama of the assassination of Julius Caesar; his imagination did not succeed in imposing itself on the event. Instead the play allows us to see the situation (and Brutus' imagination of it) as products of that complex interaction of character and circumstance, idea and action, which is human history. The drama is determined not only as it is known to be historical, of central importance in the authenticated chronicle of Rome. Shakespeare's tragedy is shaped around the contingencies of causes both local and universal, the still potent ideal of Republican Rome, the mixed motives of conspiracy, the dynamics of the creation and destruction of the one great man in a state. Brutus, outwitted and defeated by history, can only occupy the hero's role by living out to the death his commitment to a self-validated integrity of the self.

In *Hamlet*, sacred drama is visited on a world which seems intractable and resistant to it. It is a play far fuller of a variegated and heterogenous dramatic life than the consistently public stage of *Julius Caesar*. Its astounding richness of different styles, different modes of being, makes it nearly impossible to hold all of it in the mind at once. Hamlet himself suffers constantly from its multifariousness, as he loses himself in the diversions of Danish drunkenness, the War of the Theatres, the art of acting, militarist adventuring and its causes. Yet below it all is the poisoned body of the dead king, and haunting it always as correlative image is the insistent figure of the Ghost. From these and what they signify of a tragic action beyond human control, neither Hamlet nor *Hamlet* can escape. The distractions – of the actors, of the court intrigues, of the comedy of Polonius or the gravediggers – are felt to be distractions only. The tragedy moves in and through all these from origins and towards ends beyond their imaginative reach.

Brutus' (largely self-appointed) task is to renew the Romans' vision of Rome. There is a splendid constancy both in that vision and in Brutus' truth to it, though at every stage we are shown how much it leaves out of account, how far it opposes the very nature of things as they are. In *Hamlet* there is no such stable perception of an untransfigured reality as against the hero's imagination of it. We must struggle with Hamlet's phantasmagoria as he does himself, isolated and alienated from any set of shared social values, caught between the intimations of the Ghost's metaphysical universe and the inward stagnancies of the self.

> The time is out of joint. O cursed spite,
> That ever I was born to set it right!
> I.v.189–90

> What should such fellows as I do crawling between earth and heaven?
> III.i.127–8

This is the cosmic context, such is the dislocation of self and world, from which Hamlet must attempt to wrest meaning. The tragedy is in the anguish that struggle involves, and the doomed necessity to go through with it to the end without any sustaining certainties.

Hamlet has been commonly seen in the twentieth century as a characteristically early modern work, 'the detailed image, the elaborately wrought symbol' of the 'unresolved distress of modernity'.[26] It represents a historical moment of transition; it appeals to us as it stands at the beginning of what is identifiably our era. Hence C.S. Lewis's statement that the play's true hero is 'man – haunted man – man with his mind on the frontier of two worlds, man unable either quite to reject or quite to accept the supernatural'.[27] This view of *Hamlet* as a characteristically Renaissance work, poised between an accepted system of Christian belief inherited from the Middle Ages, and the rationalist scepticism of modernity, helps to define the play's historical context and may partly account for its imaginative resonance for us. But *Hamlet* dramatises also still older, more atavistic, and primitive patterns of meaning. The spreading pollution, expressed in the fitful and convulsive action, acts as an informing principle, interconnecting inner and outer being in a way which makes the rational analysis of cause and effect, guilt and responsibility, all but impossible. We watch a chain of events which bears away totally innocent victims such as Ophelia, 'wretched, rash, intruding fools' like Polonius, those unfortunates such as Rosencrantz and Guildenstern (and even Laertes) who come 'between the . . . fell incensed points of mighty opposites', Gertrude, the King himself, human figures too small for the terrible criminal parts they are cast to play. It is a world in which primal crime originates a contagious evil, mediated through the figure of the Ghost and the consciousness of Hamlet which are at once the symptoms of its sickness and the agents of its reform. Against the imaginative historicity of *Julius Caesar* it reaches back through metaphor towards myth.

4

Troilus and Cressida

Twice, before writing *Troilus and Cressida*, Shakespeare had inset extended scenes of the Trojan War into works distant from it in setting. In *The Rape of Lucrece*, Lucrece contemplates 'a piece of skilful painting, made for Priam's Troy' (ll. 1366–67); in *Hamlet*, the Player, at the Prince's request, declaims his favourite part of Aeneas' speech to Dido evoking the fall of Troy and the death of Priam. In both cases, the emphasis is on the remoteness of the original events, and the extraordinary skills of painter and actor which can make them live as though in a dramatic present. Lucrece is only calling the painting to mind, not actually looking at it, but even so the besieged Trojans peering out from the battlements come vividly before her (and us the readers):

> Such sweet observance in this work was had
> That one might see those far-off eyes look sad.
>   ll. 1385–6

Hamlet's Player is re-enacting, as an impromptu performance, a tale told long after the event, and yet can move himself to tears with the immediacy of fellow feeling. How can it be done, demands the emotionally paralysed Hamlet, 'What's Hecuba to him, or he to Hecuba, That he should weep for her?'

Within such insets, Shakespeare could concentrate on the continuing imaginative potency of the legendary Trojan War, the type of all tragedies in European literature, stressing at once its mediated distance from the fictional present of his work and the directness of its impact. In the case of *Hamlet*, there was also a heightened epic style to mark off the inset from the dramatic fabric surrounding it. When, however, Shakespeare decided to make the Trojan War itself the subject and setting for a play, the mediating distance was removed. How then was an audience to regard these mythical figures on stage before them? With what language could they convincingly speak? Could they live a life independent of the sequence of sources which had transmitted them through time to the present?

Whatever Shakespeare's purpose in his characterisation of the Greeks and Trojans in *Troilus and Cressida*, it was certainly no naive and unmediated dramatisation of the siege of Troy. Bringing an audience into the play by means of an alienating chorus much more characteristic of the histories than the tragedies, he constantly altered the angle of vision, the focal length at which the action is seen, making a knowing and eclectic use of his sources. G.K. Hunter has argued persuasively that it may have been the encounter with Chapman's Homer (the first part of which was published in 1598) acting upon the familiar received medieval versions of the Trojan material which catalysed the creation of the play.[1] *Troilus and Cressida* undoubtedly works by means of bouncing different recensions of the Troy story off one another, and the opening scenes suggest an awareness of the Chaucer–Caxton–Lydgate–Henryson tradition as a medievalisation grafted on to the Homeric original.

The first two scenes, concerned with Troilus, Cressida and Pandarus, the medieval additions to the Homeric story, start like a leisurely comic interlude on the periphery of the serious business of the siege. The symmetrical role of Pandarus in both scenes, in colloquy first with Troilus and then with Cressida, seems to be preparing us for a sharply observed comedy of love, the tone almost that of *Much Ado*, with love-making the light-hearted relaxation from an offstage war. Pandarus' hyperbolic attempts to make Cressida out as more beautiful than Helen, Troilus more heroic than Hector, are self-discrediting; in their implied ludicrousness, they reduce the lovers to a different order of existence from the very types of beauty and heroism with which they are compared. Chaucer describes Criseyde's beauty at great and eloquent length, and the medieval versions generally saw Troilus as indeed second only to Hector, Troy's chief defender after Hector's death. Here such claims are no more than the fatuous and transparent ploys of the protopandar to boost the images of the lovers one to the other. We are prepared for a dramatic rhythm of contrast by which we will move from this light-hearted chamberworld of comedy into the sombre narrative of Homer as into a different order of things.

There is certainly a change of tone, a change up in style, when in I.iii we meet the Homeric heroes of the Greek camp, Agamemnon, Nestor and Ulysses, for the first time. Yet here is where it begins to be difficult to understand what mode of representation Shakespeare is using. For the Greek leaders are given a rhetoric as heightened as the Player's Pyrrhus speech in *Hamlet* (although very different), a rhetoric somehow dislocated from the surrounding human reality. Critics have been quick to scent parody, though the degree and nature of the parody remain elusive.[2] The sense of strain in the language, the disproportion between speech and action, are hardly enough to warrant a caricature or burlesque interpretation. Yet Ulysses seems to go out of his way to introduce the idea of burlesque in his account of Patroclus' 'pageanting' the Greek commanders for the benefit of Achilles; and the incident in which Aeneas elaborately fails to recognise Agamemnon, 'that god in office, guiding men', comes dangerously close to farce.

The peculiarity of the tone, here, is made more obvious if we compare the figure of Agamemnon with that of Julius Caesar. The ambiguous status of Caesar is central to the play that bears his name, but the language he is given makes that a humanly credible ambiguity. Caesar is prone to a magniloquence punctured from time to time with lapses which betray his more ordinary weaknesses. There is a sonorous authority in his speech, if at times a little overamplified by the self-consciousness of the public image. The aging great man, who has come to live out the legend of his own greatness, is easy enough to portray convincingly on stage. But how is an actor to play the part of Agamemnon? What is an audience intended to make of his opening speech which appears to says so little in such an ostentatiously elaborate way?

> The ample proposition that hope makes
> In all designs begun on earth below
> Fails in the promis'd largeness; checks and disasters
> Grow in the veins of actions highest rear'd,
> As knots, by the conflux of meeting sap,
> Infects the sound pine, and diverts his grain
> Tortive and errant from his course of growth.
>
> I.iii.3–9

The image of the knotted pine seems to embody the action of

Agamemnon's speech which, in its muscle-bound syntax and opaque vocabulary, does often sound 'tortive and errant from his course of growth'. It is hard to be sure if this should be played up as pomposity, or accepted as the high style appropriate to the great commander-in-chief opening the council of war.

In *Julius Caesar*, Shakespeare had cultivated a special Roman language, serious, dignified and substantial. It is a style rich in abstractions but with the clarity and semi-concretised force of Latin abstract nouns. 'Honour', 'virtue', 'glory', ring loud and true in the mouths and minds of these Romans. Shakespeare's success in *Julius Caesar* was to shape a speech clear and vivid enough for living characters, which yet had a rhetorical formality felt to be right for the classical subject and setting. In *Troilus and Cressida* there is no such stable integrity of style; instead we are given the puzzling disjunctions of language and reality, jarring indecorums, which prevent us from ever settling into an assured dramatic world representing the Trojan War. Where the opening scenes might have led us to expect a modulated contrast between a 'high', Homeric war-plot, and a mutedly comic love-plot derived from Chaucer and the medieval tradition, no such simple and intelligible generic division survives for long. We are unable to make out where we are or what we are watching, whether Homer's epic heroes, their medievalised knightly counterparts with the customary English Renaissance pro-Trojan, anti-Greek bias, or some knowing contemporary send-up of these venerated figures of antiquity.

This theatrical estrangement is represented most strikingly in the key moment in III.ii, at the exact centre of the play, in which Troilus, Cressida and Pandarus freeze themselves in the proverbial roles they are to acquire. This compares significantly with an equivalently metadramatic scene in *Julius Caesar*, where the conspirators foresee the repeated replaying of the assassination. In both plays the actors project forward to a hypothetical future time which is the audience's present. Brutus and Cassius imagine the blooding in which they are engaged as a rite inaugurating year one of the revolution:

How many ages hence
Shall this our lofty scene be acted over

In states unborn and accents yet unknown!
III.i.112–14

Troilus and Cressida affirm their love with oaths which become
prophecies, in Cressida's case a curse:

> TROILUS: . . . True swains in love shall in the world to come
> Approve their truth by Troilus, when their rhymes,
> Full of protest, of oath, and big compare,
> Want similes, truth tir'd with iteration –
> As true as steel, as plantage to the moon,
> As sun to day, as turtle to her mate,
> As iron to adamant, as earth to th' centre –
> Yet, after all comparisons of truth,
> As truth's authentic author to be cited,
> 'As true as Troilus' shall crown up the verse
> And sanctify the numbers.
> CRESSIDA: Prophet may you be!
> If I be false, or swerve a hair from truth,
> When time is old and hath forgot itself,
> When waterdrops have worn the stones of Troy,
> And blind oblivion swallow'd cities up,
> And mighty states characterless are grated
> To dusty nothing – yet let memory
> From false to false, among false maids in love,
> Upbraid my falsehood when th' have said 'As false
> As air, as water, wind, or sandy earth,
> As fox to lamb, or wolf to heifer's calf,
> Pard to the hind, or stepdame to her son' –
> Yea, let them say, to stick the heart of falsehood,
> 'As false as Cressid'.

III.ii.169–92

In *Julius Caesar* the irony turns on the disparity between the
mode in which the assassination scene will be re-enacted, *is* being
here re-enacted before the Globe audience, and the ritual which
the conspirators envisage. They are right in thinking they are
engaging in a historical moment important enough to be remembered and dramatised in 'states unborn and accents yet unknown',
wrong only in the spirit of the dramatisation. The metadrama here
does not undermine the illusion of the characters' reality, if any-

thing it reinforces it. The conspirators remain wholly engaged in their own action, while the scene gives us a perspective on their misinterpretation of the course history will take. Troilus and Cressida were legendary, where Brutus and Cassius were historical, and the effect of their speeches here is therefore very different. They do not reach forward, like Brutus and Cassius, to some future point in the continuum of time when they will have become history; instead they imagine an impossible void beyond time and history in which they will stand as types of lovers true and false. In so far as this is what they have become in the time of the audience that watches them make their declaration, then distinctions between past and present are collapsed and the status of the scene as a moment of 'authentic' human reality is subverted.

Troilus and Cressida strain towards Platonic ideas of themselves, set themselves up as marks of ultimate truth and falsehood. Yet their hyperbolic strategy runs the risk of making them rather the ultimate clichés. As Troilus conjures up the rhyming lovers with their hackneyed similes, he takes his place, not as 'truth's authentic author', but as merely one last standard of comparison for 'truth tir'd with iteration'. 'As false as Cressid', here coined 'to stick the heart of falsehood', was already for the original audience as well-worn as the commonplaces of treachery against which it is set. And Pandarus weighing in to christen all future pandars by his name is a further alienation. This, the moment just before the consummation of Troilus and Cressida's love, should be the emotional climax of the play. But Shakespeare does not allow us to give ourselves up to the scene, or the lovers to give themselves to one another; instead he reduces them to distancing attitudes of language.

One of the features of *Troilus and Cressida* most frequently commented upon is the way in which it opens up gaps between language and its referents, calls in question value-systems which language claims to embody.[3] The parallel council scenes of Greeks and Trojans centre on issues of value in language, abstract enough to have inspired the theory that the play was designed for a special Inns of Court audience.[4] Notoriously, however, what we actually see in action bears little relation to the conceptual positions adopted by the speakers in the debate and, even more notoriously, debate is divorced from practical consequence. Ulysses produces by way of diagnosis of the ills in the Greek camp one of the greatest ever statements of the Renaissance vision of order in the universe (I.iii.75–137). But the strategy he proposes to remedy these ills is a merely opportunistic piece of tactics which, as Thersites croaks with malignant pleasure in due course, 'is prov'd not worth a blackberry'. Hector's contribution to the Trojan argument on whether or not to give back Helen to the Greeks appears decisive:

> these moral
> Laws of nature and of nations speak aloud
> To have her back return'd.
>
> II.ii.184–6

— an unanswerable argument in Shakespeare's time.[5] Yet it turns out this is only Hector's 'opinion . . . in way of truth'; in spite of it he 'propends' to his brothers 'in resolution to keep Helen still'.

Such disjunctions between word and action can be seen as pointedly anti-climactic, totally subverting the principles which the speeches serve to advance. But they may also represent a less completely destructive sceptical relativism. Ulysses' vision of order is also a vision of its antithetical disorder, culminating in the terrible images of anarchy:

> Then everything includes itself in power,
> Power into will, will into appetite;
> And appetite, an universal wolf,
> So doubly seconded with will and power,
> Must make perforce an universal prey,
> And last eat up himself.
>
> I.iii.119–24

Ulysses offers this as hypothetical threat, turning on the conditional imperative, 'Take but degree away, untune that string'. His speech moves between the local partial instance, the Greek camp where the 'specialty of rule hath been neglected' and the broad principles in which universal chaos is polar opposite of hierarchically arranged universal harmony. Yet the image of the wolf, power/appetite, as one of a series of images of self-devouring in the play, takes on an ominous strength beyond the bogey-man effect which is its intended rhetorical purpose here.

This speech of Ulysses is one of his two great set-pieces in the play, the other his speech on time to Achilles (III.iii.145–89). The two represent opposed, almost self-cancelling visions of the world. The degree speech implies an eternal and absolute order of things, the only alternative to which is chaos and apocalypse. The time speech, by contrast, sees the whole world as flux, to which the only possible counter is the ardour of energy. And the force of the language is such as to make it doubtful how much even the most ardent energy can achieve.

> For beauty, wit,
> High birth, vigour of bone, desert in service,
> Love, friendship, charity, are subjects all
> To envious and calumniating Time.
>
> III.iii.171–4

In this catalogue, one by one, all human sources of pride and value are snuffed out by the power of time. The main purpose of the speech is to force Achilles back on to the track in the race of emulation by bringing home to him the relentlessness of time. Yet it equally suggests the futility of any sort of race, when time will always be the winner.

A transcendent order of things is adumbrated at several points in the play, but always in conflict with other conceptual frameworks and always ultimately to be distinguished from things as they are. In the Trojan debate, the arguments of Troilus for the relative nature of value – 'What's aught but as 'tis valued?' – are not evidently specious, though Hector's counterargument is more authoritative:

> value dwells not in particular will:
> It holds his estimate and dignity
> As well wherein 'tis precious of itself
> As in the prizer.
>
> II.ii.53–6

Hector speaks for real value, for objective 'laws of nature and of nations' by which true justice can be established. Yet only 'in way of truth', which is not the way the actual world works. Instead, at best, it lives by Troilus' code of honour, a commitment to a coherent if arbitrary currency of valuing. At worst, it slips down to the level of mindless appetite and even more mindless aggression, summed up in Thersites' bottom line: 'Lechery, lechery! Still wars and lechery! Nothing else holds fashion' (V.ii.194–5).

By exposing to doubt the certainty of fixed and absolute systems of value, whether Ulysses' 'degree' or Hector's 'laws of nature and of nations', Shakespeare removes the validating guarantee of meaning in the world. This can be interpreted as the removal of a providential deity, or of a transcendent reality underpinning the truths of language.[6] Its effect in the play, however, seems oddly neutral, a case not of a tendentious presence of absence, like the Augustinian sense of the failure of pagan values against the perspective of revealed religion, posited by J.L. Simmons in the Roman plays, but merely of absence, an omnipresent ironic scepticism. Such scepticism, though, leaves the characters and their actions liable to a reductiveness of which Thersites' is the extreme expression. The most striking form that this reductiveness takes is the reduction of human beings to human bodies.

Troilus and Cressida is a play to put you off your food. The eating images that are everywhere in the play combine ideas of rampant, predatory appetite, with the sordid associations of satiety. Ravenous hunger and the sick after-effects of overeating coalesce. Time is personified with 'a wallet at his back' in which he throws great men's deeds as beggars' scraps, 'alms for oblivion'. Elsewhere, too, time is linked with the mess left after eating:

> What's past and what's to come is strew'd with husks
> And formless ruins of oblivion
>
> IV.v.166–7.

Troilus, in arguing for retaining Helen, makes a distinction between left-overs and scraps:

> the remainder viands
> We do not throw in unrespective sieve
> Because we now are full.
>
> II.ii.70–2

The image is hardly flattering to Helen, even if she is a half-carved joint, rather than the pieces of gristle from the side of the plate to be thrown into the slop-bowl. It is to this same idea that Troilus returns to evoke Cressida's infidelity:

> The fractions of her faith, orts of her love,
> The fragments, scraps, the bits and greasy relics
> Of her o'er-eaten faith, are bound to Diomed.
>
> V.ii.156–8

There is a consumerism of war as of love in the play, and the two are linked as physical needs. Achilles has a 'woman's longing, An appetite that I am sick withal, To see great Hector in his weeds of peace' (III.iii.237–9). Achilles' is not the longing of desire, but the craving for strange foods proverbial in pregnant women. When he does meet with Hector during the truce, it is with the hungry love of the butcher for the beast:

> Now, Hector, I have fed mine eyes on thee;
> I have with exact view perus'd thee, Hector,
> And quoted joint by joint.
>
> IV.v.231–3

The most horrifying eating image in the play also comes from Achilles, after the death of Hector:

> My half-supp'd sword, that frankly would have fed,
> Pleas'd with this dainty bait, thus goes to bed.
>
> V.viii.19–20

The sadistic appetite of Achilles' sword is only half-satisfied because the great hero has been too cowardly to fight Hector himself, and has had him dispatched unarmed by his Myrmidons. In the earlier scene, Hector mocked Achilles' huntsmanlike anatomy of his body:

> O, like a book of sport thou'lt read me o'er;
> But there's more in me than thou understand'st.
>
> IV.v.239–40

Yet he too uses the metaphor of the chase as he pursues the splendidly armed soldier that leads him to his death:

> Wilt thou not, beast, abide?
> Why then, fly on; I'll hunt thee for thy hide.
>
> V.vi.30–1

Troilus and Cressida is concerned with love and war: is that just another way of saying sex and violence? This is the question that the play forces us to ask, and does not answer simply with Thersites' 'yes'. The two activities are constantly linked, not only through the interweaving of the love-plot with the war-plot, but by the motivation of the warriors. Both Hector and Achilles fight, or do not fight, most unHomerically, for love. Hector's challenge, as announced by Aeneas, is a piece of medieval chivalry:

> Hector, in view of Troyans and of Greeks,
> Shall make it good or do his best to do it:
> He hath a lady wiser, fairer, truer,
> Than ever Greek did couple in his arms
>
> I.iii.273–6

It is not the dispute with Agamemnon, as in Homer, which motivates Achilles' refusal to fight, but his love for Priam's daughter Polyxena. Throughout the play, Helen as the *casus belli* is kept continually before us, from Troilus' dismissive comment on the war in the first scene –

> Fools on both sides! Helen must needs be fair,
> When with your blood you daily paint her thus.
>
> I.i.89–90

– to Diomedes' even more bitter misogyny:

> For every false drop in her bawdy veins
> A Grecian's life hath sunk; for every scruple
> Of her contaminated carrion weight
> A Troyan hath been slain
>
> IV.i.71–4

It is generally remarked how inconsistent Troilus' remark is with his later championship of keeping Helen at all costs, yet his apparently contradictory attitudes have some sort of materialist valuation in common. In his later positive mood, he argues that

Paris made a good bargain when he won Helen in exchange for Hesione:

> for an old aunt whom the Greeks held captive
> He brought a Grecian queen, whose youth and freshness
> Wrinkles Apollo's, and makes stale the morning.
> II.ii.77–9

New women for old. Nothing illustrates better than Troilus' own shifting point of view his principle, 'What's aught but as 'tis valued'.

The traditional chivalric code made of love and war complementary ideals, the viewpoint expressed by Agamemnon as he responds to Hector's challenge on behalf of the Greeks:

> we are soldiers;
> And may that soldier a mere recreant prove,
> That means not, hath not, or is not in love.
> I.iii.286–8

In Chaucer Troilus blossoms as a warrior after the consummation of his love with Criseyde, and as a result of it:

> And this encrees of hardynesse and might
> Com hym of love, his ladies thank to wynne,
> That altered his spirit so withinne.[7]

But in *Troilus and Cressida* the interrelationship of love and war is more often seen as antithetical. Troilus' love, admittedly at its unrequited stage, unmans him:

> I am weaker than a woman's tear,
> Tamer than sleep, fonder than ignorance,
> Less valiant than the virgin in the night
> I.i.9–11

Ulysses puts the opposition of sex and fighting in crude terms to Achilles:

> better would it fit Achilles much
> To throw down Hector than Polyxena.
> III.iii.207–8

Yet for all Ulysses' wily scheming, Achilles' commitment to Polyxena continues to keep him out of battle, until rage at the death of Patroclus drives him from his tent. Similarly it is a black vengefulness after the disillusionment of Cressida's infidelity which enables Troilus to do 'mad and fantastic execution' on the battlefield.

Making love, making war are physical activities – they may be something more; the play tests that 'may', looks sceptically at what more they are claimed to be. Yet the scepticism constantly stops short of complete reductivism. Hector throughout the play (with the single dubious example of the pursuit of the armoured warrior for his hide) represents a normative view of chivalry and its principle: his challenge in defense of his lady's supreme beauty, his reluctance to boast (IV.v.256–7), his refusal to take unfair advantage over his enemy, all of these make up a code which ennobles war and the warrior. Troilus, in his fierce and disillusioned mood, cuts sharply into Hector's attitudes of magnanimity:

> TROILUS: Brother, you have a vice of mercy in you
> Which better fits a lion than a man.
> HECTOR: What vice is that, good Troilus?
> Chide me for it.
> TROILUS: When many times the captive Grecian falls,
> Even in the fan and wind of your fair sword,
> You bid them rise and live.
> HECTOR: O, 'tis fair play!
> TROILUS: Fool's play, by heaven, Hector.
> V.iii.37–43

The lion may be able to afford the luxury of courage and nobility for which it has traditionally stood, but, Troilus sardonically implies, a man can not. The principle of 'fair play', apparently a phrase only beginning to gain currency, which was to animate the public school ethos, is here given short shrift. Troilus goes on to a celebration of pure aggression which sorts with his mood:

>   For th' love of all the gods,
> Let's leave the hermit Pity with our mother;
> And when we have our armours buckled on,
> The venom'd vengeance ride upon our swords,
> Spur them to ruthful work, rein them from ruth!

HECTOR: Fie, savage, fie!
TROILUS: Hector, then 'tis wars.
                                              V.iii.44–9

The intensity of Troilus' feeling here tends to leave Hector looking ineptly *pukka*, and indeed Troilus is to be proved objectively correct when Achilles, whom Hector has spared, does not scruple to take unHectorlike unfair advantage over him in his turn. Yet, given what we know of the particular reasons for Troilus' current black mood, and hearing the exaggerated macho edge of 'Let's leave the hermit Pity with our mother', who is to say that Troilus is here right and Hector wrong?

In relation to love, the play's poised ambiguity is even more striking. The treatment of Troilus and Cressida's love is remarkable, in terms of the normal conventions of Renaissance drama, for its lack of moral milieu or social sanctions. In the Shakespearean theatre, sexuality, whether within or out of marriage, was almost always placed within some sort of moral field, however conventional. A Rosalind, Beatrice or Portia might make bawdy jokes, but only in play, a play which strengthened their commitment to an ultimate monogamous union. The animal spirits of a Bertram or Proteus might move them to seduction or even rape, but a comic Providence channelled such illicit energies towards the socially wholesome end of matrimony. Romeo and Juliet, for all their ardour, required the blessing (albeit clandestine) of Friar Lawrence before consummating their love. Polonius and Laertes suspect that, given the disparity in their social rank, Hamlet's advances to Ophelia may prove 'springes to catch woodcock', a tragically short-sighted suspicion, as we discover at Ophelia's graveside with Gertrude's elegiac farewell: 'I hop'd thou shouldst have been my Hamlet's wife'.

Why does Troilus not marry Cressida? Why is there never any question of Troilus marrying Cressida (who appears in Shakespeare to be an unmarried virgin, rather than a widow like Chaucer's Criseyde)? He opens his speech in support of keeping Helen with a hypothetical analogy:

> I take to-day a wife, and my election
> Is led on in the conduct of my will
>   II.ii.61–2

It is literally the day on which he will go to bed with Cressida, yet his language here lives entirely in the dimension of hypothesis, unshadowed by any suggestion that he might or ought to take Cressida to wife. There is, of course, a simple explanation as to why marriage is excluded as a possibility. Shakespeare has inherited the story of Troilus and Cressida from the medieval courtly love tradition in which the central passion was virtually always extramarital. In Chaucer, no more than in Shakespeare, is there any question of Troilus marrying Criseyde. But in Chaucer there is the whole alternative code of courtly love, as solemn, as serious, as coherent as the social and moral ethic in which marriage is central. Without the deep perspective represented by courtly love in Chaucer's poem, the lovers stand anomalously foregrounded against nothing, without social or moral co-ordinates by which their love may be judged.

As a result, Chaucer's lovers give the impression of being more responsible than Shakespeare's. In *Troilus and Criseyde* when the news comes that Criseyde must be handed over to the Greeks, they consider the possibility of running away together but reject it because it would be a double breach of the code by which they live, Troilus losing his honour by deserting Troy at need, Criseyde her 'honeste' by the staining of her reputation. High principles, deeply apprehended, shape the tragedy of Troilus and Criseyde. In *Troilus and Cressida*, by contrast, as A.J. Smith puts it, the lovers' 'love meets no tragic fate; rather, the mere alteration of circumstances brings on a casual temporizing to decay and the all-but-incidental leaking away of the bright vision'.[8] Even allowing for the foreshortening made necessary by the change from leisurely poetic narrative to drama, the catastrophe of the parting of Troilus and Cressida does appear strangely unemphatic in its treatment, a blankly arbitrary contingency.

Still more striking as a contrast between Chaucer and Shakespeare is the lack of secrecy about the love affair in the latter. Criseyde's 'honeste' is a prime consideration throughout Chaucer's poem. Within the conventions of courtly love the lover's discretion, the protection of his lady's honour, was all-important. Pandarus goes to enormous lengths to smuggle Troilus into his house, Criseyde's bed, without anyone else knowing. Alibis are set up with the care of a detective story murderer. When the question of Criseyde being exchanged for Antenor is debated, Troilus is present, but

> he no word to it seyde,
> Lest men shoulde his affeccioun espye;
> With mannes herte he gan his sorwes drye.[9]

From start to finish, no-one but Diomedes (Pandarus always excepted) even guesses at Troilus' love; his fellow-Trojans take his sudden illnesses and despondencies at face value.

In Shakespeare, the affair between Troilus and Cressida is the casual talk of the town. When Pandarus, with a 'discretion' worthy of Congreve's Tattle, presents Troilus' excuses for absence at supper, Paris and Helen make no heavy weather of establishing his whereabouts:

> HELEN: You must not know where he sups.
> PARIS: I'll lay my life, with my disposer Cressida.
> III.i.80–1

Aeneas is sent ahead of the Trojan party to fetch Cressida so that he can forewarn Troilus to disappear before they arrive. He disposes briskly of Pandarus' feeble pretence that Troilus is not there, and meets Troilus' request for concealment with man-of-the-world confidence:

> TROILUS: . . .   my lord Aeneas,
> We met by chance; you did not find me here.
> AENEAS: Good, good, my lord, the secrets of neighbour Pandar
> Have not more gift in taciturnity.
> IV.ii.70–3

Hardly the most reassuring assurance. Where Chaucer's lovers exist in a privacy closeted away from the public world, Shakespeare's seem as exposed as the characters of a bedroom farce.

Coming to *Troilus and Cressida* from *Troilus and Criseyde*, the strong sense is of a loss of dignity, of depth, of tragic feeling. This has often provoked the view that Shakespeare deliberately trivialised and vulgarised the love-plot derived from Chaucer, as he satirically undercut the epic war-plot inherited from Homer. An

older generation of critics tended to be disapproving of Troilus and
Cressida's love. Oscar J. Campbell pursed his lips particularly
tightly, calling Troilus a 'sexual gourmet' and describing the conversation of Troilus and Cressida after their night of love as 'the
fretful dialogue of two sated sensualists'.[10] Suspicion falls on
Troilus' language before the encounter also, as he waits for
Pandarus to bring him to Cressida:

> I stalk about her door
> Like a strange soul upon the Stygian banks
> Staying for waftage. O, be thou my Charon,
> And give me swift transportance to these fields
> Where I may wallow in the lily beds
> Propos'd for the deserver.
>
> III.ii.8–13

The dominant idea here is that of ecstasy, of the soul separated
from the body as after death. The Elysian fields to which Troilus
imagines himself 'transported', in both senses, literal and metaphorical, were 'propos'd' for deserving lovers as well as heroic
warriors. 'Wallow', however, appears an indecorous word in context. Kenneth Muir quotes T.W. Baldwin on Troilus 'befouling his
Elysium with porcine lust', only to suggest by a Shakespearean
counter example that the word did not necessarily have its degrading associations of mudbaths at the time.[11] But even if we take
it in OED senses 2, 'roll about . . . while lying down' or 3, 'roll
about or lie prostrate in or upon some . . . yielding substance',[12] it
still seems disconcertingly corporeal. Even if pigs are left out of it,
wallowing in the lily-beds surely carries a hint of bathos, like
taking a tumble in the asphodel.

Troilus struggles with reconciling body and soul in love. He
fears that he may not be able to sustain physically the rapture of
consummation:

> I am giddy; expectation whirls me round.
> Th' imaginary relish is so sweet
> That it enchants my sense; what will it be
> When that the wat'ry palate tastes indeed
> Love's thrice-repured nectar? Death, I fear me;
> Swooning destruction; or some joy too fine,

Too subtle-potent, tun'd too sharp in sweetness,
For the capacity of my ruder powers.

                                        III.ii.17–24

It is this speech which provoked Oscar Campbell's sternest censure of Troilus as showing 'the educated sensuality of an Italianate
English roué'.[13] Surely rather than a roué, Troilus' apprehensions
here are those of a novice, a virgin, afraid that his actual performance will not match up to his delirious imagination? It is to this gap
between promise and performance that he returns in the curiously
cool piece of prose dialogue with Cressida later in the scene:

> This is the monstruosity in love, lady, that the will is infinite,
> and the execution confin'd; that the desire is boundless, and the
> act a slave to limit.
>
>   III.ii.78–80

The pathos of the love between Troilus and Cressida dwells in this
sense of the inadequacy of life in the body which is nonetheless all
we have. Troilus resists such an embodied love, strains towards an
India, an Elysium, which is yet felt to be fiction.

Troilus and Cressida cannot escape from their bodies, nor from
the limitations of the temporal world in which they live. The most
moving moment in the play is the enforced farewell:

> We two, that with so many thousand sighs
> Did buy each other, must poorly sell ourselves
> With the rude brevity and discharge of one.
> Injurious time now with a robber's haste
> Crams his rich thievery up, he knows not how.
> As many farewells as be stars in heaven,
> With distinct breath and consign'd kisses to them,
> He fumbles up into a loose adieu,
> And scants us with a single famish'd kiss,
> Distasted with the salt of broken tears.
>
>   IV.iii.38–47

The brilliant elaboration on the traditional idea of time as thief casts
him as a burglar overtaken by morning, stuffing his swag in a sack
any old way. We are made to feel the wastefulness, the casual

callousness, the scattering untidiness of time's action. In place of
the infinite order commensurate with love's conception – 'as many
farewells as be stars in heaven' – there is the 'rude brevity' of the
single moment. The awkward ungainliness of fumbling is trans-
ferred from the burglar time to the lovers' kiss, denying the grace
and beauty which ought to be theirs. We end with the imagery of
taste which had dominated Troilus' speech of anticipation. Now in
place of 'love's thrice-repured nectar' which he feared would be
too much for his 'wat'ry palate', there is only the 'famish'd kiss,
Distasted with the salt of broken tears'. It is one of the most
poignant illustrations in Shakespeare of the way our very being in
the world thwarts our need to give meaning, depth, resonance to
our lives.

Cressida, even more than Troilus, has often been considered less
sympathetic, less defensible, than her Chaucerian counterpart, a
noticeably coarser character than Criseyde.[14] Against this, John
Bayley argues that there are essential similarities between them:
'The thing they chiefly have in common is that neither of them
knows what she wants, and so they become the victims of what
other people want. Social exigencies compel them to act in ways
society then condemns.'[15] In such a view, if Cressida is fickle and
inconsistent, it is because she is representative of a world without a
stable system of values, representative of it and more aware of it
than others.[16] This helps to make sense of what is otherwise very
hard to pin down, an elusive selfhood in the character which is
never quite what the others make her out to be. The tone of her
first soliloquy at the end of a scene of sharp-edged bantering with
Pandarus can be read more than one way:

> Yet hold I off. Women are angels, wooing:
> Things won are done; joy's soul lies in the doing.
> That she belov'd knows nought that knows not this:
> Men prize the thing ungain'd more than it is.
>
> I.ii.278–81

Do these rather formulaic couplets bespeak someone genuinely
hard-boiled playing hard to get, or a prototype of the Restoration
heroine who must defend her emotions as best she can in a
predatory male world?

Cressida is given a key speech when she tries to articulate her reasons for wanting to go away from Troilus at the very moment when she has at last confessed her love for him:

> TROILUS: What offends you, lady?
> CRESSIDA: Sir, mine own company.
> TROILUS: You cannot shun yourself.
> CRESSIDA: Let me go and try.
> I have a kind of self resides with you;
> But an unkind self, that it self will leave
> To be another's fool.
>
> III.ii.140–6

In the midst of the coquetry in this scene, the bashfulness both assumed and genuine, there emerges a feeling of real disturbance in the personality, someone who distrusts and even dislikes any self she may manifest, who cannot find a point of rest for a true self. This residual impression of a disturbed and muddied self-awareness makes of Cressida something other than Troilus' ideal love, but something other also than the 'daughter of the game' which Ulysses instantly diagnoses her to be, and his fellow-Greeks almost equally instantly reduce her to being.

The opacity of Cressida's motivation complicates the great set-piece scene of her infidelity and Troilus' disillusionment. It is typical of the way in which the inherited material is re-shaped in the play that, where Chaucer showed a credible erosion of Criseyde's loyalty over a period of weeks or even months in the Greek camp, with Troilus racked by uncertainty in Troy, Shakespeare stages her treachery on the very evening following her one night of love with Troilus, and before his own eyes. Here indeed we see the illustration in action of Cressida's earlier intuition of a self-fissuring self-betrayal quoted above:

> I have a kind of self resides with you;
> But an unkind self, that it self will leave
> To be another's fool.

Cressida in this scene is plainly becoming the fool of Diomedes: it is a word he turns against her when he ruthlessly dispatches the will I/won't I haverings which Troilus had taken so seriously – 'I do not like this fooling' (V.ii.100). Yet it is as difficult here as it was

earlier for an audience, or an actress playing the part, to be sure
how much of Cressida's 'fooling' is come-on coquetry, as Thersites
of course believes – 'Now she sharpens. Well said, whetstone'
(V.ii.74) – or how much she is genuinely torn by the memory of the
'kind of self' left with Troilus. The last lines we ever hear from her,
a six-line soliloquy, moralise on her own behaviour:

> Troilus, farewell! One eye yet looks on thee;
> But with my heart the other eye doth see.
> Ah poor our sex! this fault in us I find,
> The error of our eye directs our mind.
> What error leads must err; O, then conclude,
> Minds sway'd by eyes are full of turpitude.
>   V.ii.105–10

The moral effect here is that of Ovid's famous tag, 'video meliora
proboque; deteriora sequor'. The scheme of values by which the
better is distinguished from the worse is acknowleged even as the
worse is chosen.

   With 'Ah poor our sex' Cressida is made to collaborate with the
misogyny for which she is to become a signal example. Troilus, at
least initially, resists it:

> Let it be not believ'd for womanhood.
> Think, we had mothers; do not give advantage
> To stubborn critics, apt, without a theme,
> For depravation, to square the general sex
> By Cressid's rule. Rather think this not Cressid.
>   V.ii.127–31

But here, as in the swearing of oaths, 'as true as Troilus', 'as false
as Cressid', meaning is trapped within a self-invalidating fold of
time. Troilus, in the shocked moment of betrayal, fights what is
already a rearguard action against the 'stubborn critics' who ad-
duce Cressida as an instance of the general depravity of women.
For the misogynists have won insofar as, in Troilus' own language,
Cressida already is the byword of faithlessness which she is
proverbially to become. Like those who followed the legend that
Helen did not really go to Troy and the Trojan War was fought for
her phantom lookalike, Troilus wants to disbelieve that it is really
Cressida he has seen. Puncturing his rhetorical exclamation, 'Was

Cressid here?' comes Ulysses' laconic rebuttal, 'I cannot conjure, Troyan' (V.ii.123).

The scene of Cressida's disloyalty, and Troilus' anguished reaction to it, works within an echo-chamber of ironies. We watch the catch-as-catch-can encounter between Diomedes and Cressida watched by the flanking onlookers, on one side Troilus with Ulysses, on the other Thersites. The comments of the two Greeks counterpoint Troilus' great anguished aria of disbelief after Cressida has left the stage.

> This she? No; this is Diomed's Cressida.
> If beauty have a soul, this is not she;
> If souls guide vows, if vows be sanctimonies,
> If sanctimony be the god's delight,
> If there be rule in unity itself,
> This was not she.
>
> V.ii.135–40

Under threat here is the principle at stake in so much Jacobean drama, the principle most succinctly expressed in *Don Quixote*: 'Modesty and the virtues are the adornments of the soul, and without them, even if the body is beautiful, it ought not to appear so'.[17] The beautiful *must* be good or the moral universe fractures. It is such a moment of spiritual fission that Troilus here lives through:

> this is, and is not, Cressid.
> Within my soul there doth conduce a fight
> Of this strange nature, that a thing inseparate
> Divides more wider than the sky and earth;
> And yet the spacious breadth of this division
> Admits no orifex for a point as subtle
> As Ariachne's broken woof to enter.
>
> V.ii.144–50

Troilus' pain is vividly expressed, although in the style of tortured intellect so endemic in the play. However, the metaphysical implications of female infidelity, which were to be at the heart of *Othello*, are here limited by the ironic theatrical design of the scene.

In its use of multiple, criss-crossing ironies the scene resembles the first interview between Angelo and Isabella in *Measure for Measure*, also overlooked by two spectators, Lucio and the Provost.

The Provost is a sympathetic supporter of Isabella's mission of mercy – 'Heaven give thee moving graces' – while Lucio urges her on to a subsexual *ad hominem* attack – 'Kneel down before him, hang upon his gown' – which, as it turns out, succeeds only too well with Angelo. What both moments achieve in the theatre is the experience of the simultaneousness of different orders of truth. Our awareness of the pathological effect of Isabella's sexuality on Angelo does not undermine the high eloquence of her plea, nor yet is Troilus' trauma turned into hysterical neurosis by the shrewd pragmatism of Ulysses or the cynical jibes of Thersites. But there is a sane and necessary corrective in Ulysses' retort to Troilus' outraged idealism, 'Let it not be believ'd for womanhood. Think, we had mothers': 'What hath she done, Prince, that can soil our mothers?' (V.ii.132). This is a brake on the instant resort from the particular to the universal typified by Hamlet's 'Frailty thy name is woman'. Where Hamlet had the stage to himself, could turn his embittered feelings of betrayal by his mother into an absolute and compelling misogyny underwriting a vision of moral chaos, Troilus' vision must compete with deflating alternatives. His language is at risk, as Hamlet's, safe in soliloquy, is not. And thus there is an ironic piquancy in Thersites' laconic paraphrase of Troilus' rhetoric of vengeance:

> TROILUS: . . . Not the dreadful spout
> Which shipmen do the hurricano call,
> Constring'd in mass by the almighty sun,
> Shall dizzy with more clamour Neptune's ear
> In his descent than shall my prompted sword
> Falling on Diomed.
> THERSITES: He'll tickle it for his concupy.
> V.ii.169–75

The absolute antitheses of Troilus' speech are called in question by the other points of view which the scene incorporates. For Troilus, Cressida must be either his or Diomedes', and the fact that she appears to be both collapses the cosmos:

> Instance, O instance! strong as Pluto's gates:
> Cressid is mine, tied with the bonds of heaven.
> Instance, O instance! strong as heaven itself:
> The bonds of heaven are slipp'd, dissolv'd, and loos'd
> V.ii.151–4

This imaginative reach of moral upheaval, though, must live with
the polite incredulousness of Ulysses –

> May worthy Troilus be half-attach'd
> With that which here his passion doth express?
>   V.ii.159–60

– and the gloating contempt of Thersites: 'Will 'a swagger himself
out on's own eyes?' (V.ii.134). Perhaps most of all, what we see of
Cressida herself qualifies the binary logic/illogic of Troilus' 'This is,
and is not, Cressid'. For this was a version of Cressida, 'a kind of
self', not Troilus' Cressida but, in becoming Diomedes', not wholly
her opposite either. The hint of an inadequate person, aware of her
inadequacy, creature of the patriarchy which idealises or degrades
her, introduces a dimension of human relativism outside the
schema of moral extremes within which Troilus suffers. As a result
the scene does not simply validate any one of the stage spectators'
view of it, not the desperate disillusion it brings for Troilus, nor the
sceptical detachment of Ulysses, still less the delighted disgust of
Thersites. Rather it orchestrates all these with a compassionate
understanding of the bleak little drama of human brutality and
weakness which is actually there before us.

Shaw included *Troilus and Cressida* among the plays which showed
Shakespeare 'ready and willing to start at the twentieth century if
the seventeenth century would only let him'.[18] In the view of many
later critics and theatre directors, especially since the Second
World War, the seventeenth century did not stop Shakespeare
from writing a play remarkably in tune with the modern ethos.
Troilus and Cressida has continued to be celebrated as a modernist
work before its time. Its disenchantment with war, its iconoclasm,
its formal discontinuities of language and dramatic mode, all seem
to anticipate the mood and practice of the twentieth century. For
post-structuralists *Troilus and Cressida* is not (*pace* Shaw) Shakespeare trying to be modern against the impediment of the seventeenth century, but one outstanding example in their contemporary
project of re-reading the seventeenth century. Thus it is not surprising to find Jonathan Dollimore including the play as a crucial
instance of the emergence of what he sees as the characteristic
Jacobean mode of 'radical tragedy', calling in question the

ideological orthodoxies of the period.[19] Where for earlier critics the anomalousness of *Troilus and Cressida* served to reinforce generalisations about Shakespeare to which it was the exception, 'a limiting case in Shakespeare's work',[20] the tendency now is to see its dissonant formal self-consciousness and its questioning scepticism as typical rather than atypical.[21]

There is no doubt that *Troilus and Cressida* is sceptical in mood and formally self-conscious in mode as no other Shakespeare tragedy is. Whatever the conjectural local reasons, Inns of Court performance or involvement in the War of the Theatres (both theories which seem to be going out of fashion), the play is twisted towards satire and jolts an audience through the genres in what must be a deliberate strategy of indecorum. Its instability of dramatic representation of the Trojan War is all the more striking in contrast with the steadiness of focus in the historical imagination of Rome in *Julius Caesar*. It plays one form of inherited mode off another, Homer's epic heroes against Chaucer's romance knights, but never settles down to a stable stage reality of its own. It denies tragic catharsis as it denies comic resolution. Not only is Hector's death dedramatised, a lynching by Achilles' Myrmidons in place of Homer's great and terrible duel to the death, but its horror is experienced in advance, *Through the Looking-Glass* fashion, in Cassandra's prophecy, leaving Troilus bereft of adequate words, 'Hector is dead; there is no more to say' (V.x.22).

Yet in spite of the uniqueness of the play's mood and form, its startling pre-modernity, it may be possible to place *Troilus and Cressida* in relation to Shakespeare's other work in the tragic mode. It takes further, develops to some sort of extremity, a secularising and relativising perspective which is already there in *Julius Caesar*. The conspirators led by Brutus had some limited success in acting out ideals of Roman honour, for all their doubtful disinterestedness and the disastrous practical outcome of their action. Those ideals retained a hold on the moral imagination though without the sustaining absolutes of spiritual action. The characters in *Troilus and Cressida* often invoke gods and heavens, but the heavens they look up to seem even barer and more empty. As Jane Adamson puts it, in contrast with Chaucer and the 'eighthe spere' to which his Troilus ascends at the end of the poem, 'there is no sense here that the world is held in a providential hand, nor that losses can be redeemed, nor that there is some ultimate place of extratemporal reality in which we might stand and observe and evaluate all that happens'.[22] The Greeks and Trojans must make good their own systems of order and value; again and again the play exposes their failure to do so.

Yet this failure does not irrevocably discredit the ideals in question. Ulysses' vision of order, Hector's invocation of the 'moral law of nature and of nations', Troilus' belief in constancy in love, are standards which must command respect if only to measure their falling-off. The play is constantly haunted by orders of truth and forms of order that cannot be realised in its world, by languages ironised to the point of parody by their lack of purchase upon the perceived actions and experiences of the characters. Language as much as history is the nightmare from which the people of *Troilus and Cressida* struggle to awake. Yet the sense of struggle, the need to be something more than talking animals driven by animal needs of sex and aggression, provides a muted sympathy for characters so often alienated by irony. *Troilus and Cressida* did not initiate a new phase of disenchanted, dissident proto-Brechtian drama in Shakespeare. Instead it was followed closely by a tragedy in which the heroic potential of love and war are given fuller embodiment than anywhere else in the canon. We must read the nay-saying of *Troilus and Cressida* in dialogue with the affirmations of *Othello*, the scepticisms of the one play against the beliefs of the other.

5

Othello

Troilus and Cressida is concerned with love and war, *Othello* with love and a war that does not happen. The play opens in an atmosphere of public as well as private crisis: not only the night elopement and marriage of Desdemona, but the threat of Turkish attack which makes it so important to establish the whereabouts of Othello, Venice's most trusted general. Through the first act we see this as an imminently menacing threat, in the conventional stream of messengers bringing new news every twenty-five lines, in the efforts of the Senate to construe their apparently contradictory signals as to the movements of the Turks, in the speed with which the business of Othello's marriage is dispatched and he is shipped for Cyprus. It may have come as something of a surprise to the original audience when this war, so elaborately prepared for, disappears with a few casual lines from a nameless Third Gentleman at the beginning of Act II:

> News, lads! Your wars are done.
> The desperate tempest hath so bang'd the Turks
> That their designment halts. A noble ship of Venice
> Hath seen a grievous wreck and sufferance
> On most part of their fleet.
>
> II.i.20–4

Why did Shakespeare add this abortive Turkish war which was not to be found in his source Cinthio? Was it a means of updating Cinthio's narrative of events which supposedly took place in 1544 (published in 1565) by setting them in 1570, the year before the famous battle of Lepanto?[1] And did the accession of James I influence Shakespeare in choosing the background because James (long before G.K. Chesterton) had written a poem about Lepanto?[2] What difference did it make to the sense of the play that, before narrowing to the tragedy of Othello and Desdemona, it appeared to be launching itself towards the last great conflict in European memory 'Betwixt the baptiz'd race, And circumsised Turband Turkes'?[3]

The war to come established a partisan polarisation which was notably not there in *Troilus and Cressida*. Traditionally, the English of Shakespeare's time were pro-Trojan, anti-Greek, in their attitudes towards the Homeric story because of the supposed Trojan descent of Brutus, legendary founding-father of Britain. But there is little to be seen of this bias in Shakespeare's play. If the Trojans are treated somewhat more sympathetically, the Greeks satirised more harshly, no us-and-them commitment is demanded from the audience. By contrast, a play which shaped up as though it were going to be Christian versus Turk drew upon the broadest, the most deep-rooted, and most unwavering system of positive and negative values: West against East, the Cross against the Crescent, Faith against the Infidel. All European Christians were necessarily embattled in common cause against what the Duke in the play calls 'the general enemy Ottoman'.

Yet such a background also meant that the anomalous position of the race and religion of the Moor of Venice was bound to be emphasised. The Moorishness of Cinthio's Moor is not really an issue; he may possibly only have been identified as such because a real-life original was called Moro.[4] Disdemona's relatives are opposed to her marrying him, but without Brabantio's violent horror of miscegenation. It was Shakespeare who elected to make his hero more than incidentally a Moor, to explore not only the full tensions generated by an inter-racial marriage but the cultural paradox of having a black general to defend Christendom against the Turks. It would, presumably, have been assumed at the period that any Moor in the service of Venice must be nominally Christian. But Othello is more than merely nominally Christian and what may be tacitly implied in Cinthio is spelled out in Shakespeare. The strength of his convictions, the importance of his conversion, are registered in Iago's evidently slanderous hyperbole that Desdemona could

> win the Moor – were't to renounce his baptism,
> All seals and symbols of redeemed sin –
> His soul is so enfetter'd to her love
>
> II.iii.332–4

If the Christian forces at Lepanto were headed by what King James uncharitably called 'a forraine Papist bastard',[5] the Venetian troops mustered to defend Cyprus in Shakespeare are led by an even more alien and yet fully Christian soldier of Christ.

G.K. Hunter has brilliantly analysed the complex use made of Othello's blackness in the play, showing how Shakespeare drew upon the theological tradition of viewing all men as black with sin, to challenge the conventional negative stereotypes associated with the colour.[6] The strategy of the play is thus to portray Iago, the white man, exhibiting all the characteristics of the black man of Renaissance prejudice (including his associations with the devil), whereas it is the black Othello who corresponds to the approved model of white virtue. Iago's tactic is to reduce Othello to being in fact the stereotypical black man, sexually jealous and violent, which he is not at first, and which he is not, Hunter argues, at the end.

This vision of the play can be sustained and extended by a consideration of Othello's soldiership. What most typically characterises Othello as a soldier is his capacity for calm and calming. In the first half of the play we never see, we never hear of him, in aggressive action. When we first meet him he is cooling the simulated rage of Iago against Roderigo:

>   Nine or ten times
> I had thought to have yerk'd him here under the ribs.
> OTHELLO: 'Tis better as it is.
>
>   I.ii.4–6

He stills the brawl between the two troops who are fighting over him later in the scene with the famous single commanding line, 'Keep up your bright swords,for the dew will rust them' (I.ii.59). His secure strength disdains the possibility that the swords, though drawn in anger, might be wet with anything but the night dew. Similarly, his lines to Brabantio magnificently combine courtesy with assurance:

> Good signior, you shall more command with years
> Than with your weapons.
>
>   I.ii.60–1

Here and in the second act, no contrast between Iago and Othello is more striking than that between the trouble-maker stirring up arguments, intrigues, quarrels, and the order-figure re-imposing peace.

The virtues of the soldier have not been those most appreciated in the present century, at least in literary critical circles, and this is no doubt one of the reasons why the character of Othello has so often fallen under antagonistic scrutiny.[7] A recent and particularly polemic example is Terry Eagleton, who dismisses Othello's 'love' (his inverted commas) as the 'sheerest narcissism: he wins Desdemona by military boasting, and is agreeably flattered by her admiration for his skill as a professional butcher'.[8] It is, in fact, Iago not Othello who speaks as the professional butcher – 'in the trade of war I have slain men' (I.ii.1). By contrast, when Othello tells the Senate of the tales with which he won Desdemona, they are those of survival rather than action: 'the battles, sieges, fortunes that I have pass'd', 'most disastrous chances', 'moving accidents by flood and field', 'hairbreadth scapes i' th' imminent deadly breach' (I.iii.130–6). This is undoubtedly the speech of a man of action, but at no point in it do we hear of him actively *doing* anything, much less killing anybody. What Desdemona loves Othello for is what he has suffered rather than what he has achieved. It is again his capacity for endurance to which other people testify as the mark of his former greatness when, in the later part of the play, he becomes all but unrecognisable. Lodovico, seeing him strike Desdemona, asks incredulously:

> Is this the nature
> Whom passion could not shake, whose solid virtue
> The shot of accident nor dart of chance
> Could neither graze nor pierce?
>
> IV.i.262–5

Shakespeare could characterise the soldier otherwise, from the overachieving, honour-hunting Hotspur through the majestic warrior-king old Hamlet to the awesome battlefield berserkers Macbeth and Coriolanus. It is the more significant that he chose to show in Othello rather the passive strength of standing firm, the specifically Christian heroism which Milton was to call 'the better fortitude'. This is what makes Othello, although a Moor, the appropriate defender of Christendom against the Turks, enforcing a value-system associated with war in the play, a value-system so signally absent in *Troilus and Cressida*.

In *Troilus and Cressida*, Hector is the nearest we are shown to a model warrior. But in the context of the brutal realities of Greek warfare, his ideals of chivalry may be merely misguided, 'fool's play' rather than 'fair play' as Troilus forcefully insists. *Troilus and Cressida* constantly opens up gaps between the vicious and point-less war we watch, and the various specious justifications of it. In *Othello*, by contrast, the text, as one of its starting-points, expects us to share belief in a heroic order of harmony, integrity, stability. 'Farewell the tranquil mind, farewell content', says Othello in his great valedictory. This is not just a sentimental retrospective, idealising what is past because it is unlike the anguished present. Othello's vision of war here as a ceremonialised stasis is entirely consonant with the serene and heroic strength of which he is exemplar.

Given, however, that the war against the Turks dematerialises so early on, that the play seems to abandon concern with a wider world when it moves into the domestic interior of Cinthio's narra-tive in Act II, what significance, if any, do these amplitudes have in the tragedy? The traditional sense of the limited scope of the play, a 'story of intrigue rather than a visionary statement',[9] is supported by its more or less complete concentration on love and jealousy, by the contingency of Iago's deception, by the fact that Othello and Desdemona's fates are not central to their society as Hamlet's is or Lear's. Not only that; the action of *Othello* is socially concretised and particularised more than any other of the tragedies. This specificity of social interaction, and the intimacy it gives us with the characters, may tend to distract attention from the broader orders of meaning they figure.

Such broader orders of meaning are there, nonetheless. The relationship with *Troilus and Cressida* is again one of illuminating contrast. No play, notoriously, is more full of abstractions than *Troilus and Cressida*. But they are curiously uninhabited abstrac-tions, ideas and principles; the characters seem constantly to struggle with them as with a dead language. The characters in *Othello* enact what they mean in a style which leaves no gap between their individual being and what they signify beyond

themselves. Shakespeare did not merely prefix the threatened war
with the Turks to the tale of love and jealousy he found in Cinthio
to provide it with, as it were, a grand overture. He created a
seamless dramatic world in which the military and the domestic,
Othello's soldiership and his love, are integrated within a pattern
of immanent ideas.

We can see this from the beginning in the rapidly sketched-in
professional situation of Iago, Cassio and Othello. Iago in his long
opening speech places himself as a man with a grudge, a man who
has been passed over for an (in his view) deserved promotion.
There might, notionally, be some sympathy for the veteran who
sees his place supplanted by the newly graduated cadet, 'that
never set a squadron in the field, Nor the division of a battle knows
More than a spinster' (I.i.22–4) Arguably, some in Shakespeare's
audience might have been convinced by Iago's grumble about
favouritism:[10]

> Why, there's no remedy; 'tis the curse of service:
> Preferment goes by letter and affection,
> Not by the old gradation, where each second
> Stood heir to the first.
>
> I.i.35–8

Yet the speech that follows broadens out the individual grievance
into an ideology of self-serving which must surely have immediately damned him.

> We cannot all be masters, nor all masters
> Cannot be truly follow'd. You shall mark
> Many a duteous and knee-crooking knave
> That, doting on his own obsequious bondage,
> Wears out his time, much like his master's ass,
> For nought but provender; and when he's old, cashier'd.
> Whip me such honest knaves. Others there are
> Who, trimm'd in forms and visages of duty,
> Keep yet their hearts attending on themselves;
> And, throwing but shows of service on their lords,
> Do well thrive by 'em and, when they have lin'd their coats,
> Do themselves homage – these fellows have some soul;
> And such a one do I profess myself.
>
> I.i.43–55

This is a provocative challenge to orthodox pieties as strong, though less intellectually showy, than Edmund's 'Thou Nature art my goddess'. It inverts and parodies, but thereby reinforces, the ideal of which Adam in *As You Like It* was type:

> O good old man, how well in thee appears
> The constant service of the antique world,
> When service sweat for duty not for meed!
>
> II.iii.56–8

As Iago simultaneously sneers at the stupidity of the loyal servants and doubts their sincerity – 'Whip me such honest knaves' – as he scandalously takes to his doctrine of egotism the honoured terms of feudal duty – 'their hearts *attending* on themselves', 'Do themselves *homage*' – he makes of the speech as manifest a declaration as Richard III's 'I am determined to prove a villain'.

The opening two scenes establish Othello and Iago not only as commanding officer and disgruntled subordinate, but as antithetical principles. This is hinted already in the riddling lines of Iago:

> Were I the Moor, I would not be Iago.
> In following him I follow but myself –
> Heaven is my judge, not I for love and duty,
> But seeming so for my peculiar end.
> . . . I am not what I am.
>
> I.i.58–66

The hypothetical exchange of identity is either a meaningless redundancy – of course if he were the Moor he would not be himself – or it signals its own impossibility – he is inescapably Iago, though he might prefer to be the Moor. There is a piguancy in earnestly taking Heaven to witness the inversion of Heaven's principles, even if we do not see in the last half-line a fully blasphemous parody of the divine fiat, 'I am that I am'.[11] The contrast with Othello when we meet him in the second scene is striking. Iago (naturally) would have him conceal himself from Brabantio's posse; Othello will have none of it:

IAGO: . . . You were best go in.
OTHELLO: Not I; I must be found.

My parts, my title, and my perfect soul
Shall manifest me rightly.

> I.ii.30–2

It is essential to Othello's persona not only that he believes in himself, but believes in a necessary identity of inner self and outer projection. He stands ready to account for the whole of himself, as the soul made perfect by confession must stand prepared before God.

This image of confession Othello uses again in the Senate scene, when he is arraigned on Brabantio's charge of having used 'practices of cunning hell' to win his daughter:

> as faithful as to heaven
> I do confess the vices of my blood,
> So justly to your grave ears I'll present
> How I did thrive in this fair lady's love
>
> I.iii.122–5

Here Othello defends himself as confidently as he defends himself and others in battle. It is an essential part of his peculiar role as the Moor of Venice that in this scene he should be both defendant and defender, summoned to the Senate both as wanted man and needed man – wanted for spiriting away Desdemona, needed to lead the Venetians against the Turks. The two plot strands come together as it were accidentally and, for the Senate, most unfortunately: there is a moment of ironic humour as the Senators realise with dismay who it is that Brabantio is accusing:

BRABANTIO: . . . Here is the man – this Moor whom now, it seems,
Your special mandate for the state affairs
Hath hither brought.
ALL: We are very sorry for't.

> I.iii.71–3

You may be sure they are. It is not, though, mere narrative convenience which links the love between Othello and Desdemona with the war between the Christians and the Turks; and they are positively associated, not at odds.

Desdemona is determined to accompany Othello to the war:

> if I be left behind,
> A moth of peace, and he go to the war,
> The rites for why I love him are bereft me
>   I.iii.255–7

Othello seconds this appeal, with such muting of Desdemona's bold emphasis on physical love as is necessary to convince the Senate that his marriage is a reciprocally loving union not a mere sexual infatuation, and one which will not interfere with his generalship in the Turkish wars. What the two of them share is the willingness to acknowledge their love as a public event, to speak up for it in a context which includes also the 'serious and great business' of the war. Their attitude is strikingly unlike that of Troilus and Cressida.

In *Troilus and Cressida* Shakespeare took on a somewhat battered and grubby version of the courtly love conventions in which passionate love was almost invariably extramarital. Troilus' affair with Cressida is a furtive night-world apart, a distraction from the war. Disillusionment with his love drives Troilus to battle-fury. Love and war in *Troilus and Cressida* are akin in so far as they are both appetitive forces, forces more often than not clashing with one another. With *Othello* it is marriage that is central and, as a sacramental image of unity and harmony, felt to be central to a world far beyond itself. We see this particularly during the storm which separates Othello and Desdemona and then brings them together again in Cyprus, the storm which also destroys the Turkish fleet.

Cassio prays for the safe delivery of the general:

> Great Jove, Othello guard,
> And swell his sail with thine own powerful breath,
> That he may bless this bay with his tall ship,
> Make love's quick pants in Desdemona's arms,
> Give renew'd fire to our extinct'd spirits,
> And bring all Cyprus comfort!
>   II.i.77–82

Othello's longed-for arrival as relieving military commander is here also the anticipation of his marriage night. Cosmic imagery blends with the erotic, from Jove as sky-god filling Othello's sails, through the metaphorically erect tall ship in the bay, to the literal climax of marital consummation. Sexual union is imagined as a joyful delivery from fear, the renewal of life in the world. Similarly Cassio's salute to Desdemona, which follows immediately, is more than mere courtier's hyperbolic language:

> O, behold!
> The riches of the ship is come ashore!
> Ye men of Cyprus, let her have your knees.
> Hail to thee, lady! and the grace of heaven,
> Before, behind thee, and on every hand,
> Enwheel thee round.
>
> II.i.82–7

The icon of Desdemona here is rich in Marian suggestion, in the Ave, in the contiguity of lady and grace, in the hint of the Virgin. Yet the wording is not Catholic – she is surrounded by grace rather than being full of it – and the nimbus of Our Lady is laicised.

The great duet between Othello and Desdemona on reunion has been critically examined by those who believe that telltale signs of strain *must* be apparent in this relationship to make sense of the way in which it so disastrously founders. So, for example, Stephen Greenblatt, glimpses in Othello's ecstatic speech a 'potential disruption' of the control of Christian orthodoxy by passion. He cites the antiphonal close of the exchange –

> DESDEMONA: The heavens forbid
> But that our loves and comforts should increase
> Even as our days do grow!
> OTHELLO: Amen to that, sweet powers!
>
> II.i.191–3

– and comments: 'the plural here eludes, if only slightly, a serene affirmation of orthodoxy: the powers in their heavens do not refer unmistakably to the Christian God, but rather are the nameless transcendent forces that protect and enhance erotic love.'[12] This is subtly seen and said. But this need not be interpreted as a tension between an ascetic Christian order and an alternative erotic (dis)order. Instead the language here, as in Cassio's speeches earlier in the scene, represents a synthesis or fusion of the spiritual and the erotic in a doctrinally non-specific sacred ethos.

It is always difficult to know how much weight to give to oaths and invocations of heaven and hell in a Renaissance poetic drama, how seriously the language of religion is to be read. Helen Gardner, for example, argues that the very proliferation of such language reduces its significance: '"Devil" is a cliché in this play, a tired metaphor for "very bad", as "angel" is for "very good"'.[13] It is true that there is no more than rhetorical gesture, histrionic stock-in-trade, in many of the allusions to the infernal or the divine. Yet at key points Shakespeare makes such gestures significant by the breadth and indefiniteness of their reference. In a pivotal moment, as it turns out to be, Othello watches the departing Desdemona:

> Excellent wretch! Perdition catch my soul
> But I do love thee; and when I love thee not
> Chaos is come again.
>
> III.iii.91–3

This is lightly said, 'Damn me, but I love her' as much as 'May I be damned if I don't'. Still the lines are spoken out of Othello's deepest feeling. They contain not only an allusion to the classical legend of Love as the first of the gods to spring out of original chaos,[14] but a Christian eschatology in 'Perdition catch my soul', which lends Christian as well as pagan colouring to Chaos. Glancingly we are taken from Last Judgement back to Creation; the loss of love is at once the damnation of the soul, the uncreation of the world. This it is which we are to witness in what follows immediately, Othello's failure of faith in Desdemona.

The love between Othello and Desdemona is idealised in the first half of the play not only by metaphorical language which makes it cosmically central, but by the sustaining human realities of character in action. Take, for instance, the contrast between Cassio and Iago. Cassio is a hard character to be sure of, one of those subordinate figures in a dramatic text who seem to be shaped by the contingencies of the play's narrative needs. Shakespeare evidently thought of him first as married, 'A fellow almost damn'd in a fair wife' (I.i.21), and then thought better of it. Although an idealising adorer of Desdemona, he is required by the plot to have a courtesan mistress Bianca and a cynical contempt for her devotion to

him. The young lieutenant of Act I, on (presumably) his first
military campaign is most improbably appointed substitute governor
of Cyprus in Act IV. But one fixed datum appears to be a class
difference between lieutenant and ensign; William Empson, in his
famous analysis of the word 'honest', was surely right to see an
element of patronising condescension in its continued application
to Iago.[15] The same nuance is there when Cassio greets Emilia,
after he has saluted Desdemona:

> Welcome, mistress.
> Let it not gall your patience, good Iago,
> That I extend my manners; 'tis my breeding
> That gives me this bold show of courtesy. [*Kissing her.*]
> II.i.96–9

It was an English social custom much remarked on by visitors that
people of different sexes used full kisses as casual greeting: 'For us
to salute strangers with a kisse, is counted but civilitie, but with
forraine Nations immodestie'.[16] Cassio locates this difference of
social mores as class difference. He realises that Iago, with a more
middle-class idea of marital possessiveness, might misinterpret what
is for him 'but civilitie', and takes pains to forestall that misinterpretation.[17] How different this is in spirit from the scene in *Troilus and
Cressida* where Cressida is 'kissed in general' by all the Greek leaders.
There the superficial show of gallantry scarcely masked the predatory
contempt of the Greeks for Cressida, and her participation in the
kissing-game seemed to validate Ulysses' cynical identification of her
as a 'daughter of the game'. Here a kiss is an innocent courtesy and to
suspect it to be otherwise is socially stigmatised.

This sort of nuance is ignored in Terry Eagleton's analysis:
'Within the double bind of patriarchy, there is no way in which
Desdemona can behave "properly" towards Cassio without being
continually open to the suspicion of behaving "improperly", no
firm borderline between courtesy and lechery. For the woman, to
be free is always to be too free.'[18] Desdemona is established as
behaving properly to Cassio precisely by Iago's perceived misrepresentation of it as impropriety. Iago watches voyeuristically a
tableau of courtship between Desdemona and Cassio:

He takes her by the palm. Ay, well said, whisper. . . . Very
good; well kissed! and excellent courtesy! 'Tis so indeed . Yet

again your fingers to your lips? Would they were clyster-pipes
for your sake!

II.i.166–76

For this to work dramatically it must be apparent that the obscenity
is all in the mind of the envious voyeur. The exact analogy is the
scene of Leontes overlooking the silent exchanges between Hermione and Polixenes, and there too it must be apparent as a
misprojected sexual fantasy or the whole point of the play is lost.

The later casual conversation between Cassio and Iago on the
wedding-night brings out the same contrast:

> IAGO: . . . Our general cast us thus early for the love of his
> Desdemona; who let us therefore not blame. He hath not yet
> made wanton the night with her; and she is sport for Jove.
> CASSIO: She is a most exquisite lady.
> IAGO: And, I'll warrant her, full of game.
> CASSIO: Indeed, she is a most fresh and delicate creature.
> IAGO: What an eye she has! Methinks it sounds a parley to
> provocation.
> CASSIO: An inviting eye; and yet methinks right modest.
> IAGO: And when she speaks, it is not an alarm to love?
> CASSIO: She is indeed perfection.

II.iii.13–25

Iago is of course here trying to manoeuvre Cassio into showing
sexual interest in Desdemona to give some substance to his fiction
of a love affair between them. But Cassio, though he could use a
vivid image of marital consummation in his prayer for Othello's
safety – 'make love's quick pants in Desdemona's arms' – will not
collude with Iago in his fantasies of the couple's wedding night,
his vulgar male reduction of woman to sex object. Without snub-
bing, he re-translates each of Iago's prurient leers into a chivalrous
language of admiration. Here, and throughout the play, social
observation underwrites and illustrates moral principle. We see a
readily recognisable human interchange, the upper-class young
officer politely fending off the would-be collaborative masculine
camaraderie of his somewhat older, lower-class subordinate. At
the same time, what is asserted here, by Cassio's protection of it
and Iago's attempts to deny it, is a high ideal of sexual love.

That ideal actually exists in *Othello*, is realised in the relationship between Othello and Desdemona. To look for flaws in their love from the beginning, to detect hair-line cracks from which the rending fissure will open up, is to misconstrue the play's action. Critical suspicions of the quality of Othello's love and signs of sexual strain have been detected beneath his language even, or especially, in his speech of joyful reunion with Desdemona in Act II.

> If it were now to die,
> 'Twere now to be most happy; for I fear
> My soul hath her content so absolute
> That not another comfort like to this
> Succeeds in unknown fate.
>
> II.i.187–91

To some this has seemed characteristic of Othello's anxiety or his egotism, his lack of Desdemona's proper sense of this moment not as an ultimate climax but the beginning of the rest of their lives together:

> The heavens forbid
> But that our loves and comforts should increase
> Even as our days do grow!
>
> II.i.191–3

A glance back at Troilus' speech as he is about to consummate his love points up, by contrast, how little Othello's lines here are intended to suggest sexual unease. For Troilus is, without question, anxiety-ridden, anxious about his own possible inadequacy, about the failure of event to live up to expectation:

> I am giddy; expectation whirls me round.
> Th' imaginary relish is so sweet
> That it enchants my sense; what will it be
> When that the wat'ry palate tastes indeed
> Love's thrice-repured nectar? Death, I fear me;
> Swooning destruction; or some joy too fine,
> Too subtle-potent, tun'd too sharp in sweetness,
> For the capacity of my ruder powers.
>
> III.ii.17–24

This is indeed a one-sided apprehension of sexual love, desire turning into fear of its own force, the root ambivalence towards sex which linked it to death in the recurrent *double entendre* on 'die'. By comparison with this vivid dramatisation of the instability of sexual feeling, we can appreciate the depth and maturity of Othello's joy in love.

What we see in the first half of *Othello* is the reality of high love which is yet tragically vulnerable to its traducer. We need not see tensions within Othello and Desdemona's moving greeting in Cyprus to apprehend the destructive force of Iago's aside:

> O, you are well tun'd now!
> But I'll set down the pegs that make this music,
> As honest as I am.
>
> II.i.197–9

Nowhere in the play is the charge of envious resentment more fully felt than here. The audible inverted commas round 'honest' bespeak Iago's injured awareness of the condescension involved in the term: he will show these people who pat him on the head, clap him on the shoulder, what 'honest Iago' is capable of doing. Yet what is embodied here is more than one specific instance of human littleness. It suggests the much more radical hatred on which Milton drew for his comparable scene in Book IV of *Paradise Lost* when Satan watches Adam and Eve in Eden. In *Othello*, as in *Paradise Lost*, nothing serves more completely to authenticate the vision of goodness than the envy of evil which it attracts.

The tragedy of *Othello* derives from something as ordinary as human inattention, yet enacts something as fundamental and deep-seated as the Fall. Labelling Iago as 'honest' dispenses those around him from thinking seriously about him. It is often remarked, for example, that nobody at any point considers that Iago might be feeling slighted at losing out to Cassio over the lieutenancy. Cassio seems such a 'natural' choice for lieutenant, the dependable Iago for the lower rank of ensign, that it never occurs to anyone that he might resent this 'natural' order of things. Cassio and Desdemona can enjoy his misogynistic clowning as rough bluntness – 'You may relish him more in the soldier than in the scholar' (II.i.164–5) – without seeing it as seriously threatening. It is this same functional stereotype which gives him so much credit with Othello. Othello has been frequently condemned for his readiness to trust Iago against his own wife, a readiness seen as indicating a lack of true knowledge of Desdemona. But it is Iago not Desdemona that Othello does not really know, and would not have seen the need to get to know intimately or individually. He is trusted as (on all the evidence) a trustworthy subordinate, in a professional relationship precluding speculation on any inner life which might lurk within the mask of honesty.

For modern readers, so to characterise the attitude of Othello and the others towards Iago may be to condemn it, even to give some justification to Iago's actions. In the democratic ethic the failure to credit each human being with a full measure of autonomous individuality is a serious moral offence. Yet within the text the unobservant trustfulness of Cassio, Desdemona, Othello is a mark of innocence, the resentful egotism of an Iago characteristic of evil. Coleridge's brilliant phrase 'the motive-hunting of motiveless malignity' has elicited any number of glosses from those who want to track down a motive for Iago or from those who see him as truly motiveless, malignity incarnate. It might seem as if the alternative twin poles of critical possibility in *Othello* are to allegorise or to psychologise. Either Iago is seen as Vice or Devil,[19] Desdemona as the principle of Christian virtue, Othello Everyman who chooses between; or Iago is Othello's darker other self, speaking his own unspeakable fears about his relationship with Desdemona. But it is implicit in the allegorical representation of the Morality tradition that the Vice figure should be *both* motiveless and motivated.

The design by which the Morality plays worked, and out of which they originated, involved the illustration of an abstract principle by a life-like human situation. The recognisability of the human relations represented drew the listeners/watchers into an understanding of the general truths of which they were examples. This produced a constant two-way process in which individual and universal sustained one another, a process which is still at work in Iago, and is exemplified in the poised balance of Coleridge's formulation. In so far as he is Malignity, he needs no motives: he is malign by definition rather than from some cause. But the way in which Iago behaves, rationalising with a series of mutually inconsistent 'motives' a hatred which is prior to all of them, reminds us forcibly of a certain sort of envious person who is temperamentally disposed to feed his grudge against the world with whatever pabulum he finds. Similarly Desdemona is associated with images of heavenly beauty, is invested with symbolic significance; yet that does not prevent her being an entirely believable young girl, bold in commitment to her love, yet inexperienced enough to make mistakes (as in her pathetic misjudgement of Othello's tone in relation to the handkerchief which she cannot believe he can take so seriously), and shell-shocked under the impact of his anger when it comes. Othello may be identified as the exemplary Christian knight, self-assured in the values he defends, and still show a dreadfully realistic collapse of confidence into the tortured creature of anxiety and inadequacy that Iago makes him.

III.iii has traditionally been identified as the temptation-scene, a term which those who wish to see the play in secular moral terms find inappropriate.[20] But an analogy with the Fall, as the archetype of all temptations in Judaeo-Christian culture, is relevant and illuminating. For the scene presents both the inch-by-inch movement of the tempting strategy, and yet also the instantaneity of yielding with the absoluteness of the change which it brings about. Iago winds into his objective with a sinuous trail of hints and half-hints, false starts designed to lead on. These could be mere tricks, Othello knows, but not coming from someone such as Iago:

> I know thou art full of love and honesty,
> And weigh'st thy words before thou giv'st them breath,
> Therefore these stops of thine affright me the more;
> For such things in a false disloyal knave
> Are tricks of custom; but in a man that's just
> They are close delations, working from the heart
> That passion cannot rule.
>
> III.iii.122–8

Iago here makes crucial use of his reputation for honesty, plays the comedy of the reluctant witness, as we saw him do so successfully when called to testify against Cassio after the drunken brawl in II.iii. He puts Othello in the position of commanding officer urging his diffident subordinate to speak out. There are virtuoso touches too, as when he appropriates Cassio's views on reputation and intones sententiously:

> Good name in man and woman, dear my lord,
> Is the immediate jewel of their souls
> > > III.iii.159–60

It was Cassio who in the earlier scene had exclaimed, 'O, I have lost my reputation! I have lost the immortal part of myself, and what remains is bestial' and it was Iago who made light of his complaint: 'Reputation is an idle and most false imposition' (II.iii.255–9). Within a dramaturgy where a slanderer was by convention credible, Shakespeare took great pains to make of the temptation a plausibly extended development.

Iago works Othello into making a formal disavowal of all capacity for jealousy, a complete statement of his faith in his wife and in his marriage:

> > 'Tis not to make me jealous
> To say my wife is fair, feeds well, loves company,
> Is free of speech, sings, plays, and dances well;
> Where virtue is, these are more virtuous.
> Nor from mine own weak merits will I draw
> The smallest fear or doubt of her revolt;
> For she had eyes and chose me.
> > > III.iii.187–93

It is this almost boastful and unguarded assurance which gives Iago the opening for the darting body-blow which he has been deliberately holding back:

> Look to your wife; observe her well with Cassio;
> Wear your eyes thus, not jealous nor secure.
> > > III.iii.201–2

After all Iago's deferential formulae, his circling recessions before the general's superior rank, suddenly there are three piercing imperatives which reverse the power relations of the two. From here until the first break in the scene with Iago's strategically judged exit, the choreography is altered: it is Iago who is always moving forward in language, Othello who can produce only stunned half-lines – 'Dost thou say so?', 'And so she did' – as he goes back under the onslaught.

It is possible to play Othello as gradually responding to the graduated moves in Iago's gamesmanship, taking the bait bit by bit. There must, though, always be a terrible suddenness in the moment when he becomes convinced:

> She's gone; I am abus'd; and my relief
> Must be to loathe her.
>
> III.iii.271–2

This is an absolute transformation, like the Fall, in the complete gulf which it marks between before and after. Iago's gloating comments stress this radical and irreversible metamorphosis:

> The Moor already changes with my poison. . . .
> Look where he comes! Not poppy, nor mandragora,
> Nor all the drowsy syrups of the world,
> Shall ever medicine thee to that sweet sleep
> Which thou owed'st yesterday.
>
> III.iii.329–37

As with Adam and Eve, the gained knowledge of good and evil becomes a pure evil, transmuting in retrospect what was innocence into ignorance:

> What sense had I in her stol'n hours of lust?
> I saw't not, thought it not, it harm'd not me.
> I slept the next night well, fed well, was free and merry;
> I found not Cassio's kisses on her lips.
>
> III.iii.341–5

The tainted imagination is driven to pollute what were its sacred places of purity:

> I had been happy if the general camp,
> Pioneers and all, had tasted her sweet body,
> So I had nothing known.
>
> III.iii.349–51

The appalling, degrading fantasy of a whole army, down to its lowest ranks, enjoying Desdemona overruns Othello's memory of his own love-making with her.

Othello takes within himself, is invaded by, the Iago view of things. That is not necessarily to say that it was latent within him from the start, or that Iago is a previously suppressed part of his consciousness. Iago makes him see himself as others see him, or as they might see him, turns him into object and thus alienates the confident subjectivity by which he has lived. Here, once again, the emphasis is on the astonishing immediacy of the alteration. Othello's trust in Desdemona was bound up with a trust in himself. He could afford to ignore all the vicious racial prejudices against him, the almost universal sense of his marriage as a terrible and disgraceful misalliance for Desdemona, because of his confidence in his own identity and the free reciprocity of his love and hers – 'for she had eyes and chose me'. Iago makes him doubt all that he had previously held most certain. When Brabantio had fired his parting shot:

> Look to her, Moor, if thou hast eyes to see;
> She has deceiv'd her father, and may thee.
> > I.iii.292–3

Othello could reply without hesitation, 'My life upon her faith'. Now when Iago makes exactly the same point, it strikes home:

> IAGO: She did deceive her father, marrying you;
> And when she seem'd to shake and fear your looks,
> She lov'd them most.
> OTHELLO: And so she did.
> > III.iii.210–12

Othello's previously unself-conscious self-consciousness is turned into a corrosive self-doubt.

> > Haply, for I am black
> And have not those soft parts of conversation
> That chamberers have, or for I am declin'd
> Into the vale of years
> > III.ii.267–70

His race, his soldierly lack of courtliness, even his age, he had before accepted, even proclaimed with a measure of pride; suddenly they are seen as potential weaknesses. Just so, Adam and Eve after the Fall: 'And the eyes of them both were opened, and they knew that they were naked'.

It is possible, of course, to interpret this scene as revealing

insecurities that were there all along, inherent in Othello's situation as the Moor of Venice, the older black man who has married
the young white noblewoman. Othello's supposed unfamiliarity
with the Venetian social world is certainly a key part of Iago's
attack:

> I know our country disposition well:
> In Venice they do let God see the pranks
> They dare not show their husbands
>
> III.iii.205–7

This, however, helps to specify the nature of Othello's vulnerability
rather than to account for it. What is represented here is a much
more general and more tragic openness of goodness to evil. The
idealising innocence of an Othello is apt to trust the posture of
reductive knowingness of an Iago, if only because it is so very
unlike itself. Iago makes a virtue out of his cynical fault-seeking,
which he too truly describes in mock-modest terms:

> I confess, it is my nature's plague
> To spy into abuses, and oft my jealousy
> Shapes faults that are not
>
> III.iii.150–2

Both the tendency and its admission win him further credit for
'honesty'.

> This fellow's of exceeding honesty,
> And knows all qualities, with a learned spirit,
> Of human dealing.
>
> III.iii.262–4

Iago is here granted the expertise in human depravity which he
claims for himself. And so the best defers to the worst, the spirit of
affirmation cedes itself to doubt and denial.

Doubt is an unnatural state for Othello. He craves certainty, even if
it is to destroy what he most believed in. Yet it proves impossible
to achieve that unwavering forward logic with which he had

brushed aside Iago's *agent provocateur* warning of the tortures of
jealousy:

> I'll see before I doubt; when I doubt, prove;
> And, on the proof, there is no more but this –
> Away at once with love or jealousy!
>
> III.iii.194–6

He is to discover that neither love nor jealousy are so easily
disavowed. Under the Iago influence, he tries to imagine Desdemona as an untamable hawk:[21]

>   If I do prove her haggard,
> Though that her jesses were my dear heart-strings,
> I'd whistle her off and let her down the wind
> To prey at fortune.
>
> III.iii.264–7

But even as he thinks of discarding the bird, cutting her loose, the
image bespeaks the self-mutilation that this will involve in cutting
his own heart-strings. When she actually appears, the certainty of
the worst with which he had tried to arm himself dissolves:

>   Look where she comes.
> If she be false, O, then heaven mocks itself!
> I'll not believe it.
>
> III.iii.281–3

For Othello, as for Troilus, the identity of appearance and
reality, of beauty and truth, are crucial to the integrity of a moral
universe. Othello's one line, 'If she be false, O, then heaven mocks
itself' is an elliptical figure for the extended denial by Troilus that
Diomed's Cressida can be his Cressida:

> If beauty have a soul this is not she;
> If souls guide vows, if vows be sanctimonies,
> If sanctimony be the gods' delight,
> If there be rule in unity itself,
> This was not she.
>
> V.ii.135–40

Troilus has here the evidence of his senses which Othello later demands from Iago –

> Villain, be sure thou prove my love a whore –
> Be sure of it; give me the ocular proof
>   III.iii.363–4

– yet he continues to struggle to disbelieve, to 'swagger himself out on's own eyes', as Thersites unkindly puts it. Cressida's infidelity, however, once taken in, begets in him a black disillusionment which is a complete annihilation of his love and the belief that went with it. 'Words, words, mere words, no matter from the heart', he exclaims, as he tears the letter from her which Pandarus brings him and scatters the pieces: 'Go, wind, to wind, there turn and change together' (V.iii.108–10). In just such a way Othello imagines himself disposing of the 'haggard' Desdemona. Othello's love, though, cannot be so shaken off, it continues alive to torture him, and to cause him to torture her. What is more, he continues to believe in the principles which he thinks she has betrayed, and even tries to convince himself that murdering her will vindicate them.

The fundamental difference between *Othello* and *Troilus and Cressida*, of course, is that Desdemona is faithful and Cressida is not. Cressida *is* what Iago only makes Othello imagine Desdemona is. The plays are, as a result, something like antithetical counterparts in their understanding of what love can be. Troilus' love for Cressida is perceived to be an overvaluing illusion, projected out of the self, treated poignantly and sympathetically but ironically understood. In Othello's case it is his disbelief in Desdemona which is chimerical; the play exposes the tragic liability to delusion within a love which is indeed true on both sides. To see misapprehensions and mutual misconstructions as the basis of the initial relationship of Othello and Desdemona is to try to turn them into Troilus and Cressida.

The critical conditions which have made it possible to understand Cressida more sympathetically as the victim of the male constructs laid upon her, have made it more difficult to respond fully to the figure of Desdemona. Modern readers tend to be uneasy particularly with her passivity in the second half of the play, after the boldness with which she appeared to challenge female stereotypes in her affirmation of an independent sexuality earlier in the Senate-scene:

> That I did love the Moor to live with him,
> My downright violence and storm of fortunes
> May trumpet to the world.
>
> I.iii.248–50

There is what seems a disconcerting reversion to type in such lines as her defence of her chastity to Othello:

> If to preserve this vessel for my lord
> From any other foul unlawful touch
> Be not to be a strumpet, I am none.
>
> IV.ii.84–6

Yet such an uncritical acceptance of the patriarchal view of the married woman's body as her husband's sacred preserve is only superficially inconsistent with Desdemona's earlier characterisation; for in the Senate-scene as well she subscribed to the orthodoxies of patriarchy, speaking of her 'divided duty' between her two lords, father and husband, claiming only what her mother had claimed before, a woman's right to choose husband over father.

In such a context, the attitudes of Emilia to sex and marriage can come to seem attractive in comparison. Emilia, who is given little to say in the first half of the play, becomes more forward, indeed from a Renaissance point of view froward, as Desdemona is driven back into the silence of hurt and anguish. There appears to be something like proto-feminist anger in her denunciation of male sexual consumption:

> They are all but stomachs, and we all but food;
> They eat us hungerly, and when they are full,
> They belch us.
>
> III.iv.105–7

Even more engaging, from a modern point of view, is her fierce attack on the double standard:

> Let husbands know
> Their wives have sense like them; they see and smell,
> And have their palates both for sweet and sour
> As husbands have. What is it that they do
> When they change us for others? Is it sport?
> I think it is. And doth affection breed it?
> I think it doth. Is't frailty that thus errs?
> It is so too. And have not we affections,
> Desires for sport, and frailty, as men have?
> Then let them use us well; else let them know
> The ills we do their ills instruct us so.
>
> IV.iii.91–101

This, like Shylock's speech 'Hath not a Jew eyes', on which it is evidently closely modelled, seems to speak out with a righteous indignation for the oppressed, the insulted and injured. And it is Emilia's role finally, most magnificently, to speak out:

> I, peace!
> No, I will speak as liberal as the north.
> Let heaven and men and devils, let them all,
> All, all, cry shame against me, yet I'll speak.
>
> V.ii.222–5

One can understand why, for at least one critic, 'Emilia seems to be nothing less than the most complete person in the play'.[22]

Yet to read *Othello* in this way is surely to read it perversely, against the grain. Emilia is designed as a contrasting and supporting role to Desdemona, not to act as spokesperson for an admirable ethic of independence which her mistress fails to adopt. She is in several ways believably the wife of Iago, struggling to be loyal to a code of wifely obedience, visibly embittered by marriage to what she calls 'my wayward husband'. Her misandry is the equivalent, as it must also be in some sort the reaction to, his misogyny. Her brave testimony at the end is all the more moving because it represents a final breaking-point in her marriage, as she refuses to go home at Iago's command:

> Good gentlemen, let me have leave to speak.
> 'Tis proper I obey him, but not now.
> Perchance, Iago, I will ne'er go home.
>
> V.ii.198–200

But it is worth registering, also, in that final scene, that she shares
Iago's racist view of Othello: Desdemona, she claims, was only too
faithful: 'She was but too fond of her most filthy bargain'. 'O gull!
O dolt!', she shouts at Othello, 'ignorant as dirt' (V.ii.161–7).
Emilia, magnificent as a champion of truth in this last scene, is
nonetheless a character conditioned by circumstance and situation,
designed within the text to illustrate by contrast the deeper principles by which Desdemona lives.

This is true even in the exchange in the willow-scene, where
Emilia's wry worldly wisdom may seem to score over Desdemona's apparent naivety.

> DESDEMONA: . . . Dost thou in conscience think – tell me,
>   Emilia –
> That there be women do abuse their husbands
> In such gross kind?
> EMILIA: There be some such, no question.
> DESDEMONA: Wouldst thou do such a deed for all the world?
> EMILIA: Why, would not you?
> DESDEMONA: No, by this heavenly light!
> EMILIA: Nor I neither by this heavenly light;
> I might do't as well i' th' dark.
> DESDEMONA: Wouldst thou do such a deed for all the world?
> EMILIA: The world's a huge thing.
> It is a great price for a small vice.
>
>   IV.iii.59–68

There is a delicate comic irony in the contrast between Desdemona's
wondering incredulity and Emilia's knowingness. Throughout the
scene, Emilia's dry tone, her raised-eyebrows jokes, her teasing
refusal to accept Desdemona's words on their own metaphoric terms,
are all engaging. Yet the conversation at cross-purposes marks a split
between two orders of value, Emilia's relativism, Desdemona's commitment to absolutes. Behind Desdemona's repeated question,
'Wouldst thou do such a deed for all the world?' lies the thrust of the
Gospels – 'What shall it profit a man, if he shall gain the whole world,
and lose his own soul?' A spiritually sanctioned law of love is here
affirmed, even as Emilia's scepticism serves to underline how exposed it is.

The love between Othello and Desdemona is credibly realised from first to last, both in the mutuality of its beginning and its terrible falling apart. That is what makes it at once so significant and so painful to contemplate. If it were something less than love, imagined at its most reciprocal, then its destruction might be more like an ordinary casualty of human weakness. But Shakespeare, in dramatising an authentic marriage of true minds, authenticated in part by the social impediments which it has had to overcome, in associating it with the very principles of order and harmony in the world, lets us off nothing in watching it violated. If we could think Othello the self-deceiving egotist of the Eliot–Leavis line of interpretation, if we could see signs of incomprehension in the relationship from the start, we might find the play easier to endure. But we are locked in with Othello, as his sense of self is locked in with that of Desdemona, and we must suffer with him the hideous degradation that is sexual jealousy without the comforting distance of diagnosis or disapproval.

Troilus and Cressida, with its constantly shifting angles of vision, its alienating ironies, wilfully frustrates the impulse towards engagement with character and emotion. *Othello* demands involvement to the point of dramatic claustrophobia. This, rather than the requirements of a merely domestic tragedy, is why, after the grander spaces of the first half, the action contracts in to the bed-chamber. Othello has invested all of the meaning previously diffused through a widely ranging life of action into his marriage, something which in itself was imagined as a bounding within doors:[23]

> For know, Iago,
> But that I love the gentle Desdemona,
> I would not my unhoused free condition
> Put into circumscription and confine
> For the seas' worth.
>
> I.ii.24–8

This is why he feels the need to say farewell to all that his previous life has meant – 'the big wars that make ambition virtue' – when he has to turn inward to face denial at what must now constitute the very heart of his being. At the height of his anguish, it is his previous role as stoic enduring outer affliction with which he contrasts the now unendurable inwardness of torment:

> Had it pleas'd heaven
> To try me with affliction; had they rain'd

All kinds of sores and shames on my bare head,
Steep'd me in poverty to the very lips,
Given to captivity me and my utmost hopes,
I should have found in some place of my soul
A drop of patience; but, alas, to make me
The fixed finger for the time of scorn
To point his slow unmoving finger at! – O, O!
Yet could I bear that too; well, very well;
But there, where I have garner'd up my heart,
Where either I must live or bear no life,
The fountain from the which my current runs,
Or else dries up – to be discarded thence!
Or keep it as a cistern for foul toads
To knot and gender in! Turn thy complexion there,
Patience, thou young and rose-lipp'd cherubin –
Ay, here, look grim as hell.

                                        IV.ii.48–65

The story of Othello's life as told to Desdemona had been a story of survival of hardships, including capture by the 'insolent foe'; he here imagines the extremity of such hardships, a ransomless captivity, and can yet credit himself with a self-reliance which might have pulled him through it. Even the public shame of cuckoldry is not at the quick of suffering; that too is something against which he could have braced himself. But Desdemona was the self within the self, and 'to be discarded thence' is total self-alienation which no patience can make tolerable.

The images of fountain and cistern convey the transformation from the constantly renewed flowing of love to the stagnant tank of sexual jealousy in which obsessive thoughts 'knot and gender'. The word 'change' occurs more frequently in *Othello* than in any other play in the canon,[24] and the second half of the tragedy is dominated by the awesome sense of change in Othello and the consequent change which it brings about in Desdemona. It is at its most terrible in the brothel-scene, comparable to, but even more painful than the nunnery-scene in *Hamlet*. Othello there acts out the phantasmagoria of his own alienation with the double charade of pretending to be a stranger who has wandered into the whorehouse which his own home has become:

I cry you mercy, then.
I took you for that cunning whore of Venice

>   That married with Othello.
>   IV.ii.89–91

We are forced to enter into the hatred and self-hatred that engenders this, and at the same time to live through it also with its unwitting victim:

> EMILIA: . . . How do you, madam? How do you, my good lady?
> DESDEMONA: Faith, half asleep.
>   IV.ii.97–8

The shock of totally unprovoked attack from the very source of love and tenderness feels like a state of suffering somnambulism. There is no special explanation needed for the withdrawn passiveness, the retreat towards infantilism of the later Desdemona, other than the terror of what is being done to her and by whom.

Both Desdemona and Othello are what they were, as well as what they become. Though the spirited woman declaring her love before the Senate, the joyously playful wife, may seem to shrink to the helpless and much younger seeming girl of the last two acts, the principles that inform her remain. The commitment to her love was irreversible:

>   My heart's subdu'd
>   Even to the very quality of my lord:
>   I saw Othello's visage in his mind;
>   And to his honours and his valiant parts
>   Did I my soul and fortunes consecrate.
>   I.iii.251–4

It is a devotion which, with the extraordinary reversal of her husband's feeling, can seem almost masochistic:

>   my love doth so approve him
>   That even his stubbornness, his checks, his frowns
>   . . . have grace and favour in them.
>   IV.iii.18–20

Desdemona is no willing martyr: she is ordinarily frightened by
Othello's murderous looks and cannot believe that he is going to
kill her. But the completeness of her altruism, the self-denying
refusal to blame the loved one within love, is represented in her
impulse to exculpate Othello even as she dies. We can be in no
doubt that it is love itself which Desdemona embodies, and it is
love which Othello thus destroys.

To claim a continuity, a wholeness in the Othello of before and
after the temptation-scene, may seem more problematic, if we do
not accept that the confident soldier–lover is to be seen as in-
cipiently the insecure imaginary cuckold. The collapse of Othello is
so complete, so literally dramatised in the scene where he falls
down in a trance, that it appears to figure some sort of ultimate
disintegration, a man in breakdown, a man possessed. He *is*
possessed by the Iago vision of things and, as has so often been
remarked, his language becomes contaminated with Iago's language. But this is not the same as saying that he becomes Iago, or
even that some latent Iago side to his personality has become
dominant. The image of poison – 'The Moor already changes with
my poison' – rather suggests a violent struggle between the
healthy organism and the venom which transmutes it. Where Iago
uses his language of reductive animality with precise and pointed
control, in Othello it thrashes and plunges like an alien thing.
Nothing better illustrates the difference between Othello and his
tormentor than his anguished cry at the thought of Desdemona's
infidelity, and the merciless way it is received:

OTHELLO: . . . But yet the pity of it, Iago! O, Iago, the pity of it,
Iago!
IAGO: If you be so fond over her iniquity, give her patent to
offend; for, if it touch not you, it comes near nobody.

IV.i.191–5

Iago here keeps Othello up to the mark of hate-filled violence he
has induced within him. For Othello, by himself, is incapable of
sustaining the one-way tide of vengeance he had earlier vowed:

my bloody thoughts, with violent pace,
Shall ne'er look back, ne'er ebb to humble love,
Till that a capable and wide revenge

Swallow them up.

III.iii.461–4

Every sight, every thought of Desdemona, moves him to 'ebb to humble love' and it is the conflict between that impulse and his deluded imagination of her betrayal which tears him apart.

In Act V we see Othello try to put himself back together again, to recreate his controlled and deliberate earlier self. The soliloquy, 'It is the cause, it is the cause, my soul' represents a painful effort of the will to this end. The justice which he supposes himself to be administering on Desdemona is the summary justice of the court-martial. He tries to summon up the tone, regretful but firm, which he used when dismissing Cassio:

> Cassio, I love thee;
> But never more be officer of mine.

II.iii.240–1

This, however, is no disagreeable duty of a commanding officer, reluctantly executed. Othello casts himself in no less a role than the agent of divine retribution. He associates himself with the icon of justice holding her sword, a sternly benevolent deity that shows its benevolence in chastisement:

> This sorrow's heavenly;
> It strikes where it doth love.

V.ii.21–2

The 'cause' which he refuses to name is impersonalised: 'Yet she must die, else she'll betray more men' (V.ii.6). This line moves out from the original offence towards the general moral and meta-physical principle at issue. At a literal level, Desdemona could not betray any other man as she has Othello; only the husband can be cuckolded, and Othello is certainly not hypothesising the betrayal of future lovers. Once again it is the identity of the good and the beautiful which is at stake. In not being what she appears to be, Desdemona betrays men by destroying moral coherence in the world. That is why in dying she could be restored to the exemplary status of a funeral effigy – 'as smooth as monumental alabaster'.

At the same time, another train of Othello's thought in this

soliloquy resists the idealisation of the murder as an impersonalised ritual which could enact justice and restore integrity. For the
dead monument of Desdemona will not be Desdemona:

> once put out thy light,
> Thou cunning'st pattern of excelling nature,
> I know not where is that Promethean heat
> That can thy light relume.
>
> V.ii.10–13

In death she cannot be the exemplum of renewed purity Othello
would like to think because it is in her living being that she is truly
exemplary, as the 'cunning'st pattern of excelling nature'. With the
Promethean imagery we are close to the sense of Othello's lines,
from what seem a life-time away, 'when I love thee not, Chaos is
come again'. Even as he tries to imagine what he is doing as loving
retributive sacrifice renewing order, he acknowledges that it is an
act of destruction which sends the world back into darkness.

In the last act of *Othello* the language of salvation and damnation is
unusually prominent; the final spiritual destiny of the central
characters is more explicitly alluded to than in any of the other
tragedies. Where Hamlet casually sends Rosencrantz and Guildenstern to their deaths – 'not shriving time allowed' – Othello is
punctilious in urging Desdemona to confess 'any crime unrecon-
cil'd as yet to heaven and grace', 'I would not kill thy unprepared
spirit' (V.ii.27–8, 31). It is true that he cannot sustain this role of
executioner/father-confessor, and is driven to rage by Desdemona's refusal to collaborate with it. The naturalness of Desdemona's
reaction tellingly shows up the illogic of Othello's resolution to
murder: 'That death's unnatural that kills for loving' (V.ii.45).
When he does finally kill her, it is in an uncontrollable spasm of
jealousy which refuses to allow her even time to 'say one prayer'.
Yet for the remainder of the play the murder becomes the focus for
an insistently eschatological imagination.

The desolation of realising what he has done – 'My wife! My
wife! what wife? I have no wife' (V.ii.100) – brings a return of the
sense of chaos which is now a vision of apocalypse:

> Methinks it should be now a huge eclipse
> Of sun and moon, and that th' affrighted globe
> Did yawn at alteration.
>
> V.ii.101–3

Yet to Emilia he repudiates Desdemona's self-sacrificial declaration
that she had killed herself with a vehement assertion of her
damnation:

> She's like a liar gone to burning hell:
> 'Twas I that kill'd her.
>
> V.ii.132–3

Othello must believe that his wife was false or accept Emilia's
charge that it is he that is the devil, Desdemona the angel:

> O, I were damn'd beneath all depths in hell
> But that I did proceed upon just grounds
> To this extremity.
>
> V.ii.140–2

One or other must be true, either she is damned or he is. So, when
he is forced to accept that his whole illusion of her infidelity was a
fabrication, he must accept what that means:

> O ill-starr'd wench!
> Pale as thy smock! When we shall meet at compt,
> This look of thine will hurl my soul from heaven,
> And fiends will snatch at it.
>
> V.ii.275–8

Othello, the Christian convert, takes his Christianity more in
earnest than any other of Shakespeare's Christian tragic heroes.

How seriously do we take Othello's damnation? For those suspicious of an element of excess in Othello's language, there is a
locus for such suspicion in his masochistic verbal self-punishment:

> Whip me, ye devils,
> From the possession of this heavenly sight.
> Blow me about in winds, roast me in sulphur,

> Wash me in steep-down gulfs of liquid fire.
>   V.ii.280–4

In the view of others, Othello believes whole-heartedly in his damnation, and confirms that belief in committing the ultimate sin of suicide.[25] This may be overliteral: the theatrical convention of heroic last-act suicides probably precluded Shakespeare's intending, or the audience apprehending, precise theological implications. Yet we are dealing here, as throughout the play, with a rhetoric which reaches out towards a world of universals, and that rhetoric is surely not there merely to illustrate the characters' hyperbolic delusions of grandeur.

We may wonder how literally to interpret Othello's damnation. Othello himself puzzles over the question of how literally Iago is a devil.

> I look down towards his feet – but that's a fable.
> If that thou be'st a devil, I cannot kill thee.
>   V.ii.289–90

The lunge at Iago is an attempt to test one other fable, the indestructibility of a demonic spirit, and in fact Othello only succeeds in wounding, not in killing him. The bewildered questioning of Iago and his final retreat into silence are fitting emblems for the enigma of evil:

> OTHELLO: . . . Will you, I pray, demand that demi-devil
> Why he hath thus ensnar'd my soul and body?
> IAGO: Demand me nothing. What you know, you know.
> From this time forth I never will speak word.
>   V.ii.304–7

'Demi-devil' pinpoints the hybrid nature of Iago, something between evil incarnate and humanly comprehensible psychopath. The withdrawal from language of the infinitely agile wordsmith figures a final blankness behind the mask of the devilish intriguer. It draws from Othello a curious approval: 'Well, thou dost best'. Because nothing Iago could say could extenuate what he has done? Or because his refusal to open his mouth even to ask for mercy – 'What, not to pray?' exclaims Lodovico – is right for someone quite beyond grace?

Mark Rose has argued that '*Othello* . . . is one of the most secular of Shakespeare's tragedies. . . . What Shakespeare is doing in this play is appropriating spiritual conceptions, turning them into metaphors for secular experiences'. But he goes on:

> metaphors work two ways. If *Othello* incorporates a process of demystification, the assimilation of the supernatural to the natural world, it also incorporates the antithetical movement. The story may not literally be the temptation and fall of man from faith, but the play is not purely domestic tragedy either. An interpretation may legitimately stress either the process of naturalization or the way the domestic drama suggests events of cosmic significance.[26]

Of the two alternatives presented, this chapter has been concerned with the latter, with the resonances of the play beyond its individual world of lived reality. In such a perspective, *Othello* can not accurately be described as a secular tragedy. Although as Rose says, it 'may not *literally* be the temptation and fall of man from faith', it adumbrates a movement in human experience as absolute and as precipitous as the Fall itself. The play draws heavily upon images and situations associated with the Christian tradition:[27] Iago as tempter/devil/Vice, Desdemona as the incarnation of love/virtue/chastity, Othello the superficially black man as the true Christian knight. But these are not only naturalised, in Rose's terms, into humanly real figures of the domestic drama. The process of naturalisation, of eroding their iconographic or allegorical specificity, can release them into a realm of cosmic significance which is not limited to the Christian frame of reference. The famous 'Othello music' shadows undefined powers that orchestrate the universe, just as the wilfully discordant Iago suggests an antithetical 'divinity of hell'. The meeting of the lovers in Cyprus, the calm moment after the tempest of thwarting forces prayed for by Cassio as salvation, represents the possibility of perfect erotic union untroubled by Christian asceticism, which is nonetheless tragically momentary, terribly at risk.

Troilus and Cressida is a true tragedy of human mutability, of the proneness of people to imagine ideals grander than they can enact, of a bias within action itself towards disillusionment. There has been a tendency in modern criticism to read *Othello* as if it were *Troilus and Cressida*, to be distrustful of its high language, as the text itself teaches us to distrust the language of the Greeks and Trojans. Part of the difficulty has been that, as Robert Hapgood so shrewdly remarks, 'critics, in their detached and sceptical rationality, are by profession all too Iago-like'.[28] *Othello* is a play that invites us to give ourselves up to the ideal values it posits rather than to stand ironically aloof from them, Iago-like. It makes such a yielding easier by domesticating its human figures, implicating us in their privacies. So involved, we have to face the terror of the destruction both of the ideals and the human beings that have lived by them.

Among the many frustrations which *Troilus and Cressida* inflicts upon its audience is the withholding of death. Neither hero nor heroine are granted, at the end, the end which we might expect for them. Cressida disappears, Troilus looks in vain for the battlefield death he so desires. Though with Hector dead the final cataclysm of the fall of Troy impends, it impends beyond the context of this play which concludes, whether with Pandarus' scurrilous epilogue or not, in a declaration of its own broken incoherence. By contrast, in few plays are deaths so final, or the ending so closed, as in *Othello*. Its very finality, indeed, and lack of apparent consequences, have made it appear less of a universal tragedy than the wrecked kingdoms which surround the deaths of Hamlet, Lear, Macbeth. But it is literal-minded and superficial to feel that because no imaginary society depends on the fate of Othello and Desdemona, it is less significant as a result. Nor should we let a modern taste for open-endedness, a suspicion of the staginess of the strong curtain associated with a nineteenth-century theatrical tradition, make us read ironies between the lines of Othello's last speech. It is surely intended as the fitting climax of his tragedy, recalling though not restoring the heroic persona of the Moor of Venice, living through with the clarity of alienated understanding what he had done in killing Desdemona, and completing that alienation in the act of self-destruction.[29] In *Troilus and Cressida* nothing that purports to be a transcendent ideal goes unchallenged: the characters must go on living in a world unillumined by significance. In *Othello* there are absolutes, destroyed but not denied by the play's action. Desdemona, Othello, even Emilia, are granted the grace of death in which they stand for principles of love, truth and loyalty, even as they enact their tragic annihilation by a power of evil that survives in silence.

6
Timon of Athens

Timon of Athens could not be more unlike *Othello*.[1] Where *Othello*
gave its audience an all but contemporary Mediterranean world,
oriented initially at least around the grand conflict of Christian and
Turk, the Athens of *Timon* is an indeterminate place with the
vaguest of classical associations. The characters, situation and
atmosphere of *Othello* were rendered with an almost unnecessary
specificity: the age of Iago, Cassio's Florentine origin, the
strawberry-spotted handkerchief and its history, Desdemona's
maid Barbary, all filled the play with the thickening detail of
human identities. In *Timon* there is no such individuation. We start
with a conversation between the Poet and the Painter (only so
named), as it might be an exposition between First and Second
Gentleman, and then discover disconcertingly that the play is
made up of nothing but (more or less nameless) first and second
gentlemen. We do not so much as know whether Timon is old or
young, much less whether he has brothers or sisters, living
parents, a wife or lover.[2] What plot details we are given are
evidently exemplary, the imprisonment for debt from which Timon
rescues one friend, the advantageous marriage which he enables
one of his servants to make. Everything in the play seems subordinated to the abstractness of its parable-like design.

'I have in this rough work shap'd out a man' (I.i.46), says the
Poet in the play's opening scene, of the composition he is about to
offer Timon. The Poet's 'rough work' is an allegory and a satire: an
allegory of Fortune's hill up which a man 'of Lord Timon's frame'
is beckoned, a satire on those who follow him slavishly while he is
Fortune's favourite, desert him when she 'spurns down her late
beloved'. The poem described is *Timon* itself in little, though
ironically the Poet will be foremost among those fair-weather
friends his poem satirises. The play, allegoric/satiric like the poem,
remains puzzling as it leaves us uncertain as to what the allegory
signifies or what is the point of the satire. What scheme of things is
represented in Timon's dramatic fall from good fortune into bad
fortune or what does it illustrate? By what standard of judgement

are the satirised characters found wanting? The difficulty in answering these questions is bound up with the indeterminacy of the play's setting.

Timon is unlike the Roman plays in which Shakespeare dramatised more or less well-known episodes of Roman history. It is equally unlike *Troilus and Cressida* where the familiarity of Homer's epic action in its various recensions was a *donné* from which the play could start. Some features of the story of Timon would probably have been known to a Renaissance audience: his almost proverbial reputation as a misanthrope and a recluse, the incident with the fig-tree on which he invited the Athenians to hang themselves, his burial by the sea.[3] He was very frequently identified as Athenian; the title Shakespeare gave to his play seems to have stuck with him, almost by way of traditional formula, as in Painter's gloss on his story in *The Palace of Pleasure*: 'Of the straunge and beastlie nature of Timon of Athens, enemie to mankinde, with his death, buriall, and Epitaphe' (Bullough, VI, 293). There is an emphatic focus on the Athenian setting in *Timon*, but an emphasis curiously dislocated from what one might expect to be its associations. A well-established historical figure such as Alcibiades, for example, whose life Shakespeare knew from Plutarch, is disconcertingly blankly drawn, deprived of many of the defining details of his character and situation. Though Corinth, Lacedaemon and Byzantium are alluded to, no other place in Greece besides Athens ever really figures in the play. Athens stands as the type of a city, any city of any time, surrounded by a featureless wilderness of wood and sea, hardly more specified here than in the comic nowhere-land of *A Midsummer Night's Dream*.

Athens in the play seems a test-case for what it is to live in human community. For Timon, in his positive phase of the first two acts, being Athenian is a metaphor for belonging to one another. In Act II when the first of many creditors puts in his claim, Timon asks for the password:

CAPHIS: My lord, here is a note of certain dues.
TIMON: Dues! Whence are you?
CAPHIS: Of Athens here, my lord.
TIMON: Go to my steward.

                                                  II.ii.18–21

This might be an exclusive local chauvinism, implying that if Caphis were from somewhere else he would not get paid. But there is nowhere else in the play for him to be from, and the spirit of Timon's question is rather one of astonishment: can someone from Athens really be doing something so un-Athenian as to dun me? Timon's ideologically charged citizenship even embraces the anti-citizen Apemantus. Though Apemantus is a 'churl', with 'a humour [that] does not become a man', he too is comprehended in Timon's bounty, for the sake of his city: 'Th'art an Athenian, therefore welcome' (I.ii.34–5).

To be Athenian is to be part of the fellowship of the human race for Timon; it is equally the special focus of Apemantus' virulent cynicism. Timon's friends are all by definition knaves:

> TIMON: Why dost thou call them knaves?
> Thou know'st them not.
> APEMANTUS: Are they not Athenians?
> TIMON: Yes.
> APEMANTUS: Then I repent not.
>
> I.i.184–7

His aggressive hatred compounds insult within insult:

> TIMON: Whither art going?
> APEMANTUS: To knock out an honest Athenian's brains.
> TIMON: That's a deed thou'lt die for.
> APEMANTUS: Right, if doing nothing be death by th' law.
>
> I.i.192–6

If there were such a thing as an honest Athenian, Apemantus would knock his brains out, if he had any. Apemantus here anticipates Timon's own later violent detestation of the city he has idealised, and as with Apemantus, Athenophobia is identical with misanthropy. When Timon, in the first of his great speeches of Act IV, takes a last look back and curses Athens, it is the whole of humanity he is cursing:

>   O thou wall
> That girdles in those wolves, dive in the earth
> And fence not Athens!
>
> IV.i.1–3

The walled Athenian city is the symbol of pretended human society, its only alternative the wild woods and the beasts. The city should be levelled and the people behave openly like the beasts they actually are. Coriolanus' banishment and exile bring a switch of allegiance: 'My birthplace hate I, and my love's upon this enemy town' (IV.iv.23–4), he says wonderingly, looking round the Antium he had done so much to depopulate. The disillusioned Timon, by contrast, is like Lear on the heath in his lack of any alternative place, any alternative set of values, to turn to in his disillusionment.

From the beginning, through the sparring of Timon and Apemantus, an abstract debate is initiated on the nature of human nature, and Athens is no more than its emblematic locus. Art serves as one point of entry into the debate. Timon graciously accepts the Painter's picture:

> Painting is welcome.
> The painting is almost the natural man;
> For since dishonour traffics with man's nature,
> He is but outside; these pencill'd figures are
> Even such as they give out.
>
> I.i.159–63

Timon speaks more truly than he knows: those people who surround him are indeed 'but outside'. 'Traffic' is to be a key-word in the play, like 'commodity' in *King John*, in defining the marketplace mentality which governs human relations. Timon's intended meaning here, however, is the conventional neo-classical claim for art, most eloquently expressed by Sidney in the *Apology for Poetry*, that it represents man as he should and might be. For Timon, significantly, that idealising form is the natural man, not an artificial unreality. Painting gives us what man is essentially, dishonourable false-seeming being only an imitation of that essence. Apemantus supplies something like the complementary opposite of this point of view when he is asked his opinion:

TIMON: How liks't thou this picture, Apemantus?
APEMANTUS: The best, for the innocence.
TIMON: Wrought he not well that painted it?
APEMANTUS: He wrought better that made the painter; and yet he's but a filthy piece of work.

> I.i.197–201

The standard gloss for Apemantus' response 'The best, for the innocence' is 'Perfectly well, because, being a mere picture, it can do no harm', carrying the implication that the picture can do no good either. Apemantus' punch-line is the counter-argument to Timon's vision of man and art: painting is no more than botching by a creature botched-up himself.

If the classical setting of _Timon_ is little more than nominal, it makes for uncertainty as to what values are being invoked to enable us to judge in the Timon/Apemantus debate. There are occasional Christian references in the text, though almost without exception they appear in sections of the play ascribed to Middleton by those who argue for his co-authorship.[4] In the Shakespearean sections, the language is nearly as consistently pagan as in _King Lear_. The collaborative authorship may help to account for the difficulty of understanding how the Christian allusions in _Timon_ bear upon the world presented. Take Apemantus' commentary on Timon's feast:

> O you gods, what a number of men eats Timon, and he sees 'em not! It grieves me to see so many dip their meat in one man's blood; and all the madness is, he cheers them up too . . . the fellow that sits next him now, parts bread with him, pledges the breath of him in a divided draught, is the readiest man to kill him.
>
> I.ii.38–47

This allusion to the Last Supper and the betrayal of Judas is re-echoed later in the comment of one of the Strangers, 'Who can call him his friend that dips in the same dish?' (III.ii.64–5). If there is a hint here of Timon as Christ-figure it is seen askew and little else in the portrayal of Timon supports it. As Emrys Jones puts it, 'the comparison is oddly unilluminating. A relation is made between the story of Timon and the story of Christ – but one of contrast as much as similarity.'[5]

The image of Timon eaten up by his flatterers, so relentlessly repeated through so much of the first half of the play, enforces a satiric vision of man's predatoriness. It suggests cannibalism rather than the mystery of the Redemption offered through the body and blood of Christ. Timon never sees himself as self-sacrificial; he is rather the type of the sociable man who believes in a principle of mutuality:

> O you gods, think I, what need we have any friends if we should ne'er have need of 'em? They were the most needless creatures living, should we ne'er have use for 'em. . . . We are born to do benefits.
>
> I.ii.86–95

What is expressed here is a social–ethical rather than a Christian-spiritual ideal. Later in the play, an invocation of Christian doc-trine appears strikingly absent where it might be expected. Alcibiades' plea to the Senate for his unnamed soldier friend, who is under sentence of death, has obvious parallels with scenes in *The Merchant of Venice* and *Measure for Measure*. But where Portia and Isabella invoke as their absolute sanction the divine principle of mercy itself, Alcibiades argues only in terms of honour, desert, extenuating circumstances. The steward Flavius, moralising on Timon's fate after his fall from fortune, glancingly alludes to the teaching of the Sermon on the Mount.

> How rarely does it meet with this time's guise,
> When man was wish'd to love his enemies!
> Grant I may ever love, and rather woo
> Those that would mischief me than those that do!
>
> IV.iii.465–8

The Christian injunction to love our enemies is turned into a sardonic comment: we had better love those who are our declared enemies than those who are our professed friends, the latter are much the more dangerous. Flavius, who is the nearest thing to a redeeming figure in the play, whose loyalty to Timon in his fallen fortunes might be seen as Christian exemplar, invokes the Chris-tian ethic only to make a satiric point.

The awkwardness of the disjunction between 'this time's guise' and the implied time 'when man was wish'd to love his enemies' is significant. In the satiric mode of city comedy, to which *Timon* is clearly in some ways related (and which has helped to make Middleton seem so plausible a collaborator), there is a stance of deploring the degeneracy of present times by the acknowledged moral standards of the audience. It was not necessary for the plays to be set in contemporary London for this to be true. Jonson, Marston or Chapman could base their actions in Augustan Rome, in Italy, or in Ephesus, and still depend on a shared frame of reference in the audience's present. But *Timon* is a generic hybrid, the milieu and mode of which leaves no secure vantage-point from which to view it. Hence the notoriously polarised interpretations of the play: Timon as the satirised gull or as the much-wronged idealist, a figure of prodigality or of generosity. No interrogation of signals in the text enables us to decide on one evaluation or another. The story of Timon has been cast adrift from any sure shorelines of judgement. This is not a satire of a degenerate 'nowadays' because there is nothing to connect it with any given 'now'; it is not a timeless allegory either, for its setting in classical Athens suggests a semi-historical standing.

Willard Farnham has noted how Timon's misanthropy, in earlier sixteenth-century versions, was identified with the medieval tradition of the contempt of the world, and used in counterpoint to the antithetical Renaissance humanist celebration of man.[6] Shakespeare, in the initial opposition of Timon and Apemantus, seems constantly to be suggesting such a dialectic, only to frustrate any attempt to see it in those terms. Apemantus' comments on Timon's masque of Amazons appears to be in a traditional homiletic vein:

> Hoy-day, what a sweep of vanity comes this way!
> They dance? They are mad women.
> Like madness is the glory of this life,
> As this pomp shows to a little oil and root.
> We make ourselves fools to disport ourselves
>
> I.ii.126–30

This is comparable to Vindice's great meditation in *The Revenger's Tragedy* – 'Surely we are all mad people and they, Whom we think are, are not'[7] – and is all the more effective as a reflection on the masque, that great Jacobean symbol of power and glory. The conspicuous consumption of Timon's feasting might seem an excellent target for moralising homily, the dance of the Amazons to be read as a dance of death, the masque an antic-masque. However the testimony of Apemantus dog-cynic is tainted. It is not only that as cankered satirist his motives are suspect, even if he speaks the truth. In his 'grace', he proclaims a self-sufficiency which is an assault on the central Christian ethic of human altruism:

> Immortal gods, I crave no pelf;
> I pray for no man but myself.
> Grant I may never prove so fond
> To trust man on his oath or bond,
> Or a harlot for her weeping,
> Or a dog that seems a-sleeping,
> Or a keeper with my freedom,
> Or my friends, if I should need 'em.
> Amen. So fall to't.
> Rich men sin, and I eat root.
>   I.ii.60–9

Apemantus here stands alienated in a total moral isolationism.

Timon's opposed vision of man as social animal can be viewed equally critically. Of the passage in which he proclaims his faith in friendship – 'We are born to do benefits' – L.C. Knights comments: 'it is not moral truth that we recognize but self-indulgence in easy emotion'.[8] Knights sees the play as a thorough-going exposure of the facile self-satisfaction of Timon's initial generosity, and of the self-hatred which is the driving-force of his later misanthropy. Yet this is surely to override the signs of respect for Timon's character which condition our response to him. The passing Strangers of III.ii, who are introduced purely to offer choric commentary on the denial of Timon by his friends, are outraged by it:

> FIRST STRANGER: For mine own part,
> I never tasted Timon in my life,
> Nor came any of his bounties over me
> To mark me for his friend; yet I protest,
> For his right noble mind, illustrious virtue,
> And honourable carriage,
> Had his necessity made use of me,
> I would have put my wealth into donation,
> And the best half should have return'd to him,
> So much I love his heart.
>   III.ii.75–84

The satiric sequence of scenes in which this appears is so devastating in its revelation of the gap between profession and practice,
that we may be tempted to see irony here too.[9] All Timon's former
friends say what the First Stranger says, and wouldn't he also find
excuses like Lucullus, Lucius and Sempronius, if he had actually
been put on the spot? However, in a play of heavily emphasised
ironies, it is unlikely that such an ironic construction, if intended,
would have been left merely implied. The First Stranger's assertion, rather, seems to stand as a quite disinterested statement
underwriting Flavius' later loyalty to the dispossessed Timon:

> That which I show, heaven knows, is merely love,
> Duty, and zeal, to your unmatched mind
>
> IV.iii.515–16

There is that within Timon, his 'heart', his 'unmatched mind',
which attracts love and admiration, even though the impulses of
that heart and the assumptions of the mind prove spectacularly
misguided.

The play thus sets up within its first half a tension between an
idealism which is somehow admirable, even though it is seen to be
deluded, and its distorting mirror image in an annihilating cynicism. The result is a debate-like mode, somewhat akin to the
relativism of *Troilus and Cressida*, in which anything proclaiming
itself as truth is answered by a counter-truth. The issue of the
debate is nothing less than the life of man, its value and significance. Yet the metaphysical dimensions of such a debate are
seemingly closed off to restrict it to a moral and ethical field. The
spiritual criteria represented by a Christian scheme of things are
not absolutely excluded, in spite of the play's non-Christian setting, but they appear only intermittently and ambiguously in their
application to the action. We cannot confidently align Apemantus'
cynical preaching with the tradition of Christian ascetic pessimism
any more than we can identify Timon as a Morality lesson in
Prodigality or a type of Renaissance Magnificence. We are distanced from the action by the low relief representation of its
satiric–allegoric mode and by the sense of a deliberately limited
imagination of a world of human society reaching out to no
transcendent order.

For all the roughness of its execution, *Timon* is a play of extraordinarily symmetrical design; many critics have remarked on how deliberately the second half reproduces the first in altered mood.[10] Placed right in the middle of Act III, the mock banquet acts as pivot and theatrical centrepiece. It reassembles the festive crowd of Act I, only to have the feast turned into a premeditated travesty of itself. The quite perfunctory embarrassment of the feasters, who have so recently denied Timon money, makes its own sharp satiric point. The salivation is almost audible as the banquet is brought in:

> LUCIUS: All covered dishes!
> LUCULLUS: Royal cheer, I warrant you.
>
> III.vi.49–50

But the covered dishes, misread as signs of the lavishness of the hospitality, conceal Timon's true message. The theatrical principle is like that in the bloody banquet of *Titus Andronicus* where the show of social harmony is vehicle for the ferocious wit of revenge. In Timon, it is show only. The idea for the scene (possibly derived from the academic comedy of Timon where the mock feast had stones painted like artichokes) is purely emblematic.

Timon's ironic benediction acts as recapitulation of Apemantus' grace, but also as the inversion of his own celebration of friendship in I.ii. From the veiled paradox of enjoining the gods to give sparingly 'lest your deities be despised', which the inattentive guests might well hear as conventional blessing, he warms into denunciation of men, women and Athenians – 'Senators' and 'the common lag of people' – ending with present company:

> For these my present friends, as they are to me nothing, so in nothing bless them, and to nothing are they welcome.
>
> III.vi.82–4

With the uncovering of the empty dishes, nothing is revealed, here as in *King Lear*, the cipher for all that might be thought to bond man to man. Uncovered now, too, is the full and direct force of Timon's anger as he denounces his whited sepulchres of friends for what they are:

> Live loath'd and long,
> Most smiling, smooth, detested parasites,

> Courteous destroyers, affable wolves, meek bears,
> You fools of fortune, trencher friends, time's flies,
> Cap and knee slaves, vapours, and minute-jacks!
> Of man and beast the infinite malady
> Crust you quite o'er!
>
> III.vi.93–9

Timon's imagination here searches restlessly through the human and animal world to find fit terms of execration, whether as beasts of prey taking to themselves the nominally antithetical qualities proper to men, courtesy, affability, meekness, or as the kitchen parasites that buzz about the domestic preparation of food. The denunciation ends with a formal curse, which is also a vow by which Timon creates himself the implacable misanthrope with which his name was so firmly identified:

> Burn house! Sink Athens! Henceforth hated be
> Of Timon man and all humanity!
>
> III.vi.104–5

The symmetry of structure in some sort prepares us for what we find in Acts IV–V of *Timon*: the gregariousness of the first half is met by the isolation of the second, the absoluteness of Timon's idealism is matched by the absoluteness of his misanthropy. In all of this there is an inevitability of narrative design. Yet with that predestined form, comes a sense also of disproportion, of the play moving into unexpected and disconcerting modes. There is, for example, the sudden surfacing of sexuality as a dominant subject of Timon's hate-filled vision. In the first half of the play Timon has lived in what is apparently an exclusively masculine world, the masque of the Amazons apart. There is, therefore, little cue for the frequency with which he harps on sexual corruption as a main instance of human depravity. Explanations in terms of the individual character seem unsatisfactory: 'Timon's horror is of anarchic impulses that he knows within himself when the picture of noble Timon is destroyed'.[11] We are not shown enough that might suggest Timon's inner life to verify this hypothesis, certainly no sign that his self-image involves a repression of potentially anarchic sexuality. As with the similarly unprepared eruption of sexual imagery in the tirades of Lear, a broader vision of chaos is involved.

Deviation from the norms of socially sanctioned behaviour in sex is only one, if one of the most strident, in the examples of moral breakdown which Timon wishes on Athens, in his first major apostrophe of Act IV:

> Matrons, turn incontinent.
> Obedience, fail in children! Slaves and fools,
> Pluck the grave wrinkled Senate from the bench
> And minister in their stead. To general filths
> Convert, o' th' instant, green virginity.
> Do't in your parents' eyes.
>
> IV.i.3–8

The most scandalous, the most outrageous instances of traditional orders of hierarchy and decorum inverted, are here invoked, both as punishment on the city and as a true representation of its essence. Sexuality may be unexpectedly prominent only because, as the strongest of man's animal drives, it most obviously and urgently threatened the apparatus of social structure. Timon catalogues, in order to excoriate, the aggregate of abstractions that went to make up the Renaissance idea of a human commonwealth:

> Piety and fear,
> Religion to the gods, peace, justice, truth,
> Domestic awe, night-rest, and neighbourhood,
> Instruction, manners, mysteries and trades,
> Degrees, observances, customs and laws,
> Decline to your confounding contraries
> And let confusion live.
>
> IV.i.15–21

This is like Ulysses' order speech in *Troilus and Cressida*, though more movingly intimate in the values it adumbrates – 'night-rest, and neighbourhood'. But in the case of Ulysses, the speech is seen to be a set-piece with a monitory end in view, the chastening of the insubordinate Greeks. What is disturbing with Timon, and what prompts the feeling of disproportion, is an uncertainty as to where the energies which drive the speech forward come from, or where they are going to.

Timon's hatred spirals outward from the cursed Athens, in its ingratitude the parody of what a city should be, to a longed-for cosmic disorder. The expected paradigm would be a contrast between the corruptions of the city/court and the austere purities of the natural. There is an analogy with the pastoral mode of *As You Like It* in the movement of the play, as the city empties and the forest fills. Apemantus echoes Duke Senior's 'Sweet are the uses of adversity' in a harsh and penitential spirit:

> What, think'st
> That the bleak air, thy boisterous chamberlain,
> Will put thy shirt on warm? Will these moist trees,
> That have outliv'd the eagle, page thy heels
> And skip when thou point'st out? Will the cold brook,
> Candied with ice, caudle thy morning taste
> To cure thy o'ernight's surfeit?
>
> IV.iii.220-6

At times it would seem as though Timon had learnt the lesson of this form of ascetic naturalism. 'Why should you want', he asks the Banditti:

> Behold, the earth hath roots;
> Within this mile break forth a hundred springs;
> The oaks bear mast, the briars scarlet hips;
> The bounteous housewife Nature on each bush
> Lays her full mess before you.
>
> IV.iii.415-19

Yet there is relatively little such idealisation of Nature, and Timon's flight is more away from the human than towards the natural. He tears his clothes off because they are Athenian, not because they are in themselves 'lendings'. Timon is not alienated from the world of man to find himself at home in the world of nature, and the play allows us no such straightforward version of pastoral.

Nature, as in *King Lear*, is invoked to forward the protagonist's desire for vengeance on the wrongs of humanity.

> O blessed breeding sun, draw from the earth
> Rotten humidity; below thy sister's orb
> Infect the air!
>
> IV.iii.1-3

But Nature is not set over against a man-polluted culture as a neutral or benevolent transcendent force. Instead it seems implicated in, even the agent of corruption; the 'blessed breeding sun' becomes like Hamlet's 'good kissing carrion', its fecundity proximate to rottenness. There is an apparent perversity in the earth's yielding gold rather than the roots Timon wants. In Lucian, with whom this incident originates, there is an elaborate narrative explanation: the impoverished Timon digs for treasure at the insistence of Hermes who has been sent down by Zeus to restore Timon to his former fortunes. With the removal of the Lucianic spoof of a supernatural superstructure, the cruelty of giving Timon the worthless precious metal in place of food seems nature's own. Though Timon initially rejects the gold, as he did in Lucian, as an unwanted divine gift – 'No, gods, I am no idle votarist' (IV.iii.26–7) – by association of ideas it becomes earth's 'most operant poison'. The element itself is alive with the evil it spreads among mankind:

> Come damn'd earth,
> Thou common whore of mankind, that puts odds
> Among the rout of nations, I will make thee
> Do thy right nature.
>
> IV.iii.41–4

Gold is an anti-elixir, bringing death and disease instead of eternal youth, transmuting what it touches to dross. In Timon's comprehensive abreaction from the human, the natural world is suffused with the deformations of culture.

The ultimate expression of this vision comes in Timon's exhortation of the Banditti to ply their trade, for which the universe itself gives precedent:

> The sun's a thief, and with his great attraction
> Robs the vast sea; the moon's an arrant thief,
> And her pale fire she snatches from the sun;
> The sea's a thief, whose liquid surge resolves
> The moon into salt tears; the earth's a thief,
> That feeds and breeds by a composture stol'n
> From gen'ral excrement – each thing's a thief.
>
> IV.iii.434–40

This, the wildest of all Timon's flights of disillusion, provokes one of the play's few moments of comedy in its effect on the Banditti:

> THIRD BANDIT: Has almost charm'd me from my profession by
> persuading me to it.
> FIRST BANDIT: 'Tis in the malice of mankind that he thus advises
> us; not to have us thrive in our mystery.
> SECOND BANDIT: I'll believe him as an enemy, and give over my
> trade.
>
> IV.iii.449–54

The solemn seriousness about their 'mystery' of thieving, like
Abhorson's 'mystery' of hanging in *Measure for Measure*, their
literal-minded bewilderment at Timon's mad eloquence, allow the
respite of laughter. But the intended effect of Timon's speech
remains very difficult to construe.[12] It resembles the shock-tactic
administered by Marlowe in *Tamburlaine* with the great paean to
power, 'Nature that fram'd us of foure Elements, Warring within
our breasts for regiment, Doth teach us all to have aspiring
minds'.[13] As in Marlowe the vision of a world of God-given order
and harmony which underwrote a hierarchical social cosmos is
reversed to license unlimited aggression, so here a corrupt society
of predation and desire is sanctioned by an imagined universe of
lawless force. The status and intention of Timon's magnificent
poetry of derangement are still problematic. It provokes in the
most acute form the question raised by the whole second half of
the play: how are we supposed to react to the extremities of
Timon's misanthropy?

Timon's traditional reputation, in so far as it may be judged by
earlier versions of his story or references to him in the Renaissance,
would have conditioned an audience to disapprove. Painter's
description, quoted earlier, of the 'straunge and beastlie nature of
Timon of Athens' is typical in advertising Timon as monstrous
freak in his antipathy to his own kind. Yet it is essential to the
dramatic effect that Timon should pursue his misanthropy to its
limits; we would be almost disappointed by any failure of his to
stick to his misanthropic principles. There is a certain suspense
when we see Timon apparently taken in by the blandishments of
the Poet and Painter in Act V, even though, having seen him

overhear them earlier, we know that his anger is simply preparing
for them a satiric ambuscade. His mock relenting with the Senators
similarly causes momentary anxiety:

> But yet I love my country, and am not
> One that rejoices in the' common wreck,
> As common bruit doth put it.
>
> V.i.189–91

There is a certain sigh of satisfaction when this proves only the
beguiling build-up for the gullible Senators to the invitation to the
Athenians to come and hang themselves on Timon's fig-tree.

In incidents such as this, we will Timon on to maintain the
integrity of his hatred because he is the instrument of satire, and
we would not have the flatterers and hypocrites let off with less
than their due discomfort. But how is Timon to be judged in other
contexts such as his 'flyting' with Apemantus? This scene puts up
to us the question as to which is the more authentic and more
justified misanthrope, the professional cynic Apemantus who
hates mankind on a priori principles, or Timon whose bitterness
has origins in experience. In the argument each of the debating
antagonists hits home with valid points. Timon's is merely contingent disillusionment, Apemantus says:

> This is in thee a nature but infected,
> A poor unmanly melancholy sprung
> From change of fortune.
>
> IV.iii.201–3

His has been a reactive change from one absolute to another; as
Apemantus puts it, in a judgement often quoted as the moral of
the play: 'The middle of humanity thou never knewest, but the
extremity of both ends' (IV.iii.299–300). Yet Timon fights back
effectively with the traditional accusation against the envious
railer, common in satiric plays of the period, that he is only
righteous by default.

> If thou hadst not been born the worst of men,
> Thou hadst been a knave and flatterer.
>
> IV.iii.274–5

The effect of the quarrel, which ends with an almost farcical exchange of insults, is to engage the mind with well-weighed contrary viewpoints without allowing moral or emotional commitment to one or the other. It is like the formal debates of *Troilus and Cressida*, moved into a fiercer key.

Willard Farnham suggested that Shakespeare may have found a hint for the contrast between Apemantus and Timon in Montaigne.[14] Montaigne remarks, in his essay 'Of Democritus and Heraclitus', that 'we can never bee sufficiently despised, according to our merit. . . . We are not so full of evill, as of voydnesse and inanitie.' This leads him to prefer Diogenes the cynic as

> a more sharp, a more bitter, and a more stinging judge, and by consequence, more just and fitting my humour, than *Timon*, surnamed the hater of all mankinde. For looke what a man hateth, the same thing he takes to hart. *Timon* wisht all evill might light on us: He was passionate in desiring our ruine.
>
> (Bullough, VI, 241)

It is just this passion, however, which gives Timon the emotional edge in the scene with Apemantus, and makes its current flow against the superior pessimism advocated by Montaigne. The very intensity of Timon's anger, the way he takes his injuries to heart, make his the more human misanthropy. There is a grandeur in Timon's headlong sense of hurt which involves us with him, however marginally. In *King Lear* Shakespeare took this disproportionate but humanly implicating anger as one of the central driving forces and key themes of the play. In *Timon* it is one more disconcerting source of dislocation, unbalancing the otherwise controlled structure of the parable mode.

The second half of *Timon* does offer a number of opportunities for him to relent, affords openings for alternative perspectives on his absolute relentlessness. The most significant such scene is the encounter with Flavius.[15] The Steward is the one just man of the play, the only visitor to Timon in his wretchedness who visits out of loyalty, compassion, love. At first he too is comprehended in the simple syllogism of Timon's general misanthropy:

FLAVIUS: Have you forgot me, sir?
TIMON: Why dost thou ask that? I have forgot all men;
Then, if thou grant'st th'art a man, I have forgot thee.
                                                        IV.iii.472–4

Yet the evident sincerity of Flavius' feeling moves Timon to something like a change of heart.

> What, dost thou weep? Come nearer. Then I love thee
> Because thou art a woman and disclaim'st
> Flinty mankind, whose eyes do never give
> But thorough lust and laughter. Pity's sleeping.
> Strange times, that weep with laughter, not with weeping!
>   IV.iii.482–6

This is an extraordinary passage, not only because of the softening
in Timon but because of the terms in which that softening is
expressed. 'Man', up to this point, has always been generic in
Timon's execrations of him. Women are as prominent examples of
human depravity as men, their whorish venality the counterpart of
male lust and greed. Yet here Timon seems to glimpse the possibility of some principle of feminine tenderness antithetical not to
the masculine but to 'flinty mankind'. This womanliness is not
seen as the normal attribute of women; there is a trace still of
Timon's usual fierce irony in his proclamation of love for a man
'because thou art a woman', behaving in such a womanish way as
to weep. There is ambiguity also in Timon's later wondering
contemplation of Flavius:

> Let me behold thy face. Surely, this man
> Was born of woman.
>   IV.iii.493–4

To be 'born of woman' may mean merely to be mortal – Timon is
showing astonishment that his Steward so little resembles his
fellow humans; or he could be exclaiming at having found at last a
man truly akin to the mother in him.

'Pity's sleeping. Strange times, that weep with laughing, not
with weeping.' Timon here implies that there might be a time with
pity awake, unlike the perverse present of senseless laughter, but
he is incapable of imagining what or when it might be, just as the
feminine compassion of Flavius bears no relation to anything known
in the actual world of men and women. So the example of the loyal
Steward points nowhere, leads to no conversion. 'It *almost* turns my
dangerous nature mild.' In the event, what opens like a confession
of error, a formal conversion testimony, turns into just one more of
Timon's rhetorical ploys to give force to his refusal to relent.

> Forgive my general and exceptless rashness,
> You perpetual-sober gods! I do proclaim
> One honest man – mistake me not, but one;
> No more, I pray – and he's a steward.
> How fain would I have hated all mankind!
> And thou redeem'st thyself. But all, save thee,
> I fell with curses.
>
>   IV.iii.495–501

The Christian principle by which the one can redeem all the others is suggested only to be rejected; Flavius redeems himself only, the rest of humanity remains reprobate. Flavius is rewarded with gold for his loyalty, but only on condition that he be a true disciple of Timon's terrible gospel of anti-humanity:

>   Go, live rich and happy,
> But thus condition'd: thou shalt build from men;
> Hate all, curse all, show charity to none,
> But let the famish'd flesh slide from the bone
> Ere thou relieve the beggar.
>
>   IV.iii.525–9

Timon carries on his nihilistic crusade, undeflected by the one instance of altruism he meets and acknowledges.

In the formal design of the play, Alcibiades is evidently intended to pair Timon as a secondary victim of Athenian ingratitude to serve for foil, comparison or contrast. The difficulty in construing the meaning of Alcibiades' role is often put down to the ill-finished or collaborative nature of the text. Certainly the lack of preparation or explanation for Alcibiades' appearance in III.v, pleading for his soldier friend whose very name or identity we never learn, seems a striking case of narrative hiatus. (It is just possible that the letters brought in by the Page to Timon and Alcibiades in that other loosest of loose ends in the play, the scene with the Fool in II.ii, were intended to carry the news of the duel, putting the audience into the picture.) But there are signs, too, that the coherence of Alcibiades as a character may have been sacrificed to the play's narrative needs, rather like Cassio in *Othello*, only more so.

The association of Alcibiades with Timon originates in Plutarch, where it is a manifestation of Timon's anti-Athenian prejudice: he cultivates Alcibiades out of spite 'bicause I know that one day he

shall do great mischiefe unto the Athenians' (Bullough, VI, 251). In
Act IV of Shakespeare's play, he is thus used as an engine of
Timon's hatred against Athens. But elsewhere discrete elements of
Alcibiades' reputation are developed as they are needed. He is
established as 'Captain Alcibiades' at his first appearance, a soldier
of rather alarming bloodthirstiness:

> TIMON: You had rather be at a breakfast of enemies than a
> dinner of friends.
> ALCIBIADES: So they were bleeding new, my lord, there's no
> meat like 'em; I could wish my best friend at such a feast.
>
> I.ii.73–7

Though jokingly spoken, this accords all too well with the pervasive imagery of cannibal banqueting. When he pleads before the
Senate, however, his soldier's ethic of honour seems solidly re-
spectable, his case for his friend intended to attract sympathy
against the harsh inflexibility of the judges. Alcibiades' well-
known dissoluteness is nowhere in evidence in the first half of the
play, though it may have provided warrant for his two accompanying whores when he meets Timon in Act IV. Yet there is the
sense of Timandra and Phryna as rather *ad hoc* creations. The name
Timandra comes from Plutarch, where she was the loyal concubine
who contrived to give Alcibiades honourable burial after he had
been murdered. Phryna, one suspects, was a name coined out of
the associations of the sentence in Plutarch which supplied
Timandra – 'Now was Alcibiades in a certen village of Phrygia,
with a concubine of his called Timandra' (Bullough, VI, 262) –
Phrygia yielded Phryna. This deliberate doubling of Alcibiades'
women appears to be undertaken less to blacken his character as a
whoremaster, than to supply Timon with whores (plural) as
targets for railing and recipients for his ill-intentioned gold-giving.

It is this opportunistic characterisation of Alcibiades which
leaves us so uncertain what to make of his part in the play's
ending. He seems unlike the other evidently corrupt visitors of
Timon in that he meets the recluse by chance, and appears genuinely to wish him well. He is aligned with Timon in having some
justifiable grievance against Athens, however little Timon will
accept this as grounds for friendship with him. But there is too
little definition to the figure of Alcibiades to make of his action in
sparing Athens at the end a positive moral example in contrast

with the unforgiving hatred of Timon. He is used rather, adventitiously, as the necessary stage manager and choric commentator who is needed to give the play its formal close. In so far as Alcibiades does supply a contrasting alternative to the extremity of Timon, it is with the blankness and normative neutrality which serves to make manifest the distinctiveness of the tragic protagonist's fate.

For the last surprise of this strange play is the sense of tragic destiny surrounding Timon's end. Timon's burial by the sea, his abusive epitaph, were integral parts of his story from Plutarch on. In Plutarch the appropriateness of his tomb's isolation is accidental – 'buried upon the sea side . . . it chaunced so, that the sea getting in, it compassed his tombe rounde about, that no man coulde come to it' (Bullough, VI, 252). But later commentators developed this into a deliberate design on Timon's part, representative of a masochistic self-hatred persisting beyond death: as Painter put it, 'by his last will, he ordeined himselfe to be interred upon the sea shore, that the waves and surges might beate and vexe his dead carcas' (Bullough, VI, 294). Although Shakespeare stays close to this, the effect is very different, repeated as it is twice, in Act IV and Act V:

> Then, Timon, presently prepare thy grave;
> Lie where the light foam of the sea may beat
> Thy gravestone daily
>
> IV.iii.375–7

There is a lyric tenderness in the lines here which quite alters the idea of the sea-washed body. The later passage has more sense of disturbance:

> Come not to me again; but say to Athens
> Timon hath made his everlasting mansion
> Upon the beached verge of the salt flood,
> Who once a day with his embossed flood,
> The turbulent surge shall cover.
>
> V.i.212–16

Here too, though, the image is composed into a stately and sonorous icon.

The tomb as 'everlasting mansion' moves us out towards ideas
of eternity and the afterlife naturally suggested by the sea. Again
unexpectedly, some of Timon's language as he approaches death
takes on a distinctly Christian colouring.

> My long sickness
> Of health and living now begins to mend,
> And nothing brings me all things.
>   V.i.184–6

What is exploited here is the paradox, so endemic in Christian
literature, of dying into life. There is nothing for Timon to look
forward to in death except release, and yet that nothing brings him
'all things', as it does the Christian believer for whom the annihilation of death through the Resurrection of the body promises life
everlasting. Awe surrounds the death of Timon with a sense of the
sacred, almost as it does the end of Oedipus in *Oedipus at Colonus*.
The unregenerate anger overtaken by the intuition of coming
death, the mysterious apartness of the death itself, reinforce the
analogy. But in Sophocles, the sacredness of the death-place, the
shrine at Colonus, is the given from which the play starts, and
the fatedness of Oedipus' end is bound up with the terrible tragic
pattern of his life.[16] In *Timon*, the haunting sea-music which intermittently plays around the death of the hero seems to come from
nowhere and connect with nothing else in the action. For the
world of *Timon*, with its ethical morality structure and its sharply
satiric stance, appears everywhere else to shut out a transcendent
order of the imagination.

Timon may have been a dramatic experiment, an experiment that
did not altogether work. For whatever reasons Shakespeare chose
to collaborate with Middleton (if that is what he did) to produce a
form of tragedy in the satiric/allegorical key of Jonsonian comedy,
it looks as though the play was left aside unfinished and possibly
unproduced. It may be that he went on to write *King Lear* instead.
Even if it seems unfair to *Timon* to call it the 'still-born twin of
Lear',[17] suggesting that it is nothing else but a *King Lear* that did not
happen, the relationship between the two plays is certainly a
striking one. They share not only the central theme of ingratitude,
but a basic movement as well: from the city/court through the

barren wilderness towards the sea is the rhythm of *Timon* as of *King Lear*. Much of *Timon's* peculiarity, many of the features even which seem least satisfactory about it, reappear in *King Lear*. There is, for example, the central structural reduplication. Parallel plotting is everywhere in Shakespeare, but in no other plays in the tragic mode is the action centred around two precisely comparable figures in analogous situations as it is with Timon and Alcibiades, Lear and Gloucester. Both plays risk monotony to achieve an almost obsessive thematic concentration and repetitive use of related figures. The alternate versions of the misanthrope, represented by Timon and Apemantus, are comparable to the several voices of madness of Lear, Poor Tom and the Fool. In *Timon*, as in *King Lear*, the designed effect is a dramatic intensification by monochrome variations on a single theme.

The milieu in which the story of Timon was embedded, however, the formal mode in which it was conceived, denied the possibility of what was realised in *King Lear*. Timon might be of an Athens emptied of all historical Athenian content, an Athens turned into an emblematic city-space merely, yet its classical origins were bound to define its nature, more or less. It was a world in which the spiritual had no roots, however often it was looted by Renaissance writers for moral and ethical exemplars. Timon, inherited from Plutarch and Lucian, belonged in this tradition of exemplification. Whether as an allegorical or a satiric illustration of man's ingratitude to man, a meditation on ill-requited generosity or its resultant misanthropy, Timon was a figure within a field of secular moral abstraction. Shakespeare had to go further back imaginatively to a world consciously archaic and primitive in order to explore the violent anger of disillusionment which forces a tormented rediscovery of man in the universe, to release the visionary or mythic power only sensed fitfully in *Timon*.

7
King Lear

'Some Stonehenge of the mind' G.K. Hunter says is the impression
made by *King Lear*;[1] the image is a suggestive one because it reflects
a common modern sense of the play's primitivism. But it is difficult
to define how much of this notion of the primitive or prehistorical,
the legendary or mythic, would have attached to the story of Lear
in Shakespeare's time. Lear, apparently an invention of Geoffrey
of Monmouth as one of the successors to Brutus, Britain's Trojan-
descended first founder,[2] by the time he reached Holinshed in the
sixteenth century had been historicised into the chronicle: 'Leir the
sonne of Baldud was admitted ruler over the Britaines, in the yeare
of the world 3105, at what time Joas reigned in Juda' (Bullough,
VII, 316). Yet there was some shakiness in the historical status of
this sort of record, and the antiquarian Camden was sceptical of
Lear as the eponymous founder of Leicester (*Leir-cestre*): 'that it
was built by the fabulous King Leir, let who will believe for me'.[3]
Its origins in folk-tale, its adoption into chronicle, its associations
with myths of origin, gave to the storystuff of *King Lear* its complex
quality. As a result, the play is both more and less historical than
Timon. The figure of Timon, notionally attached to the datable
Athens of Alcibiades, vouched for by Plutarch, yet belonged essentially in a timeless and placeless space of moral exemplum. Lear's
never-never source in folklore was overlaid by the historicising
chronicles; as a monarch of ancient Britain he could be located in
some mythic and primal past.

What sort of world do we enter in the first scenes of *King Lear*?
How is an audience situated in relation to them? The first thing to
notice, perhaps, is how little Shakespeare is concerned to turn the
story of Lear to homiletic purpose, as had been done with *Gorboduc*. Sackville and Norton had used Gorboduc's division of the
kingdom between his sons Ferrex and Porrex, also taken from
early British pseudohistory, as a monitory text to enforce the
political doctrine of centralised, unified monarchy. By contrast, the
opening exchange between Kent and Gloucester is quite neutrally
expository:

149

KENT: I thought the King had more affected the Duke of Albany than Cornwall.

GLOUCESTER: It did always seem so to us; but now, in the division of the kingdom [kingdoms, Q], it appears not which of the Dukes he values most; for equalities [qualities, F] are so weigh'd that curiosity in neither can make choice of either's moiety.

I.i.1–6[4]

For the very observant among the audience, there may be a hint here of the moral differentiation of Albany and Cornwall which is to emerge in the action. But there is no choric disapproval, no sucked-in breath or head-wagging, at the proposed division of the kingdom in itself, only court curiosity about its details.[5] This is the more striking in view of Kent's later vehement opposition to the division when Cordelia is excluded from it. At this stage, in fact, three daughters are not even mentioned and the alignment of the two plots is set up initially in a misleadingly binary form, the two sons-in-law of Lear matched with the two sons of Gloucester. Shakespeare seems to have wanted his audience to accept the division of the kingdom as a plot given, but to witness the love-test as a completely unforeseen drama.

From the moment that three daughters appear and the love-test is announced, it is written into the script that the first two will flatter and be rewarded, the third and best will refuse to flatter and be unjustly punished. How, though, are we intended to construe this folk-tale situation as Shakespeare dramatises it? There was precedent for a threefold division of the kingdom within legendary British history in Brutus' allocation of land to his three sons, Albanact, Camber and Locrine, providing an originary myth for the three nations of Scotland, Wales and England. Similarly in *King Lear*, with the Dukes of Albany and Cornwall associated with the north and west, it is tempting to see the 'third more opulent' designed for Cordelia as England. Certainly Shakespeare took the trouble to make such a geographical distribution plausible in that he reassigned Goneril to Albany, Regan to Cornwall, as in Geoffrey of Monmouth, where in his immediate source, the old play of *King Leir*, Gonorill had been married to the King of Cornwall and Ragan to the King of Cambria.[6] It has been argued that Lear's initial plan in the division of the kingdom was a shrewd political scheme for attaining a balance of power in a situation where there was no male heir, an alliance planned between a Home Counties Cordelia and Burgundy, with the strategically important Kent giving support, against the potentially dangerous ambitions of Albany and Cornwall.[7]

Such a thesis may seem oversubtle, but there is nothing to suggest in the opening scene that Lear's desire to divide the kingdom 'that future strife may be prevented now' (I.i.43–4) was to be seen as a foolish one. The foolishness begins when the love-test miscarries and Cordelia is banished. The real difficulty with a territorial–political reading of the first scene is its lack of specificity. What Lear hands over to Goneril and Albany does not sound particularly like Scotland:

> all these bounds, even from this line to this,
> With shadowy forests and with champains rich'd,
> With plenteous rivers and wide-skirted meads
> I.i.62–4

Contrast Brutus' legacy to Albanact in the anonymous *Locrine*:

> Take thou the North for thy dominion,
> A country full of hills and ragged rockes,
> Replenished with fearce untamed beasts[8]

The emphasis in *King Lear* is rather on the goodness of the goods the father is dispensing, than on any actual territory. This is what makes it so different from that other mapped division of Britain in Shakespeare, the rebels' premature share-out in *1 Henry IV*, III.i. What is striking there is the irresponsibility of Hotspur's proposal to re-route the Trent to increase his share. This helps to emphasise the literal carve-up of what ought to be the kingdom of Britain, the treatment of a whole country as robbers' booty. In *King Lear* there is no such image of national dismemberment because there is so little real sense of a nation to be dismembered.

Lear's abdication is not so much a political ceremony as a public family ritual. Shakespeare heightened the ritual by removing the scaffolding of motivation and intrigue which supported it in the older play of *King Leir*, where it is the death of the King's wife which prompts his desire to abdicate, he plans the love-test to manoeuvre Cordella into marrying as he wishes, the other two sisters have prior warning of the plan from the evil counsellor, and so on. In Shakespeare, no contingencies of plot weaken the dramatic sovereignty of the scene or impede the inexorability with which it runs its course. It seems inappropriate to interrogate Lear's motives at the level of individual character, either to detect a hidden political design, or psychological weaknesses – a reprehensible craving for flattery, the desire to control even in appearing to relinquish control, a covert incestuous feeling for Cordelia. The scene enacts a basic paradigm of power and family relationship which precludes this sort of political or psychological analysis.

One of the puzzles of the love-test has always been its exact function: if the division of the kingdom is pre-drawn, what is there to compete for? If the shares of Goneril and Regan are so even (Q's reading, 'equalities are so weigh'd'), and a 'third more opulent' reserved for Cordelia, isn't the contest palpably rigged? It would be, if it were a real contest with rewards for success. But this is a children's party with prizes for everyone; all that is required is that they should join in the game which is, of course, what Cordelia refuses to do. The solemn charade of the love-test figures the paradoxical nature of the parent–child relationship, at once personal and impersonal, voluntary and compelled. The father's power is his to give, but he is bound to give it to his children and in fair proportion; the children must love the father for himself, and not for the gifts with which they are rewarded for their love. It is this uncontractual contract between parental generosity and filial love which is to be celebrated in the public drama of Lear's love-auction.

Yet as drama it may be merely acted and as public drama it can become empty show, a travesty of what it is supposed to signify. It is in this spirit that Goneril and Regan make their professions, and make it impossible for Cordelia to play her part. Goneril mouths what Cordelia means:

> Sir, I love you more than word can wield the matter;
> Dearer than eyesight, space, and liberty;
> Beyond what can be valued, rich or rare;
> No less than life, with grace, health, beauty, honour;
> As much as child e'er lov'd, or father found;

A love that makes breath poor and speech unable:
Beyond all manner of so much I love you.

                                                          I.i.54–60

We will see in the course of the play how true this is – of Cordelia,
Cordelia who will show that she loves Lear 'as much as child e'er
lov'd, or father found'. Here Goneril, in lyingly acting out such an
attitude, has corrupted the language in which love might be
spoken, pre-empting and reducing to rhetorical hyperbole even
the gesture of the inadequacy of language: 'I love you more than
word can wield the matter'. There are no words left: 'What shall
Cordelia speak? Love, and be silent' (I.i.61). It is not only that
Goneril and Regan profess what they do not mean and thus
destroy the possibility of meaningful speech; they make their
public declarations of love seem an obscenity. Such love, even if
felt, could scarcely be spoken aloud, much less declaimed in a
court ceremony.
    Cordelia's response, however much it is foreseen, comes as a
shock in the theatre:

> LEAR: . . . what can you say to draw
> A third more opulent than your sisters? Speak.
> CORDELIA: Nothing, my lord.
>
>   I.i.84–6

The effect is of a wilful disruption of the spectacle, of the actress
throwing up her part and forcing the play to break down. What
follows is a tense attempt to find some way of communicating in
the ruins of Lear's public ritual, fraught lines and half-lines replac-
ing the stately verse periods exchanged with Goneril and Regan.

> CORDELIA: Nothing, my lord.
> LEAR: Nothing!
> CORDELIA: Nothing.
> LEAR: Nothing will come of nothing. Speak again.
> CORDELIA: Unhappy that I am, I cannot heave
> My heart into my mouth. I love your Majesty
> According to my bond; no more nor less.
>
>   I.i.86–92

Cordelia and Lear, under the pressure of the public scene in which they are now embedded, fail to reach one another, a failure culminating in the mirrored misunderstanding of the last exchange:

> So young and so untender?
> So young, my lord, and true.
> I.i.105–6

'I love your Majesty according to my bond' is Cordelia's riddle, equivalent to the folk-tale's 'loving like salt'. It is the cipher for infinity which so closely resembles the zero for which Lear takes it. An element of perversity has been detected in Cordelia's response. Coleridge saw in her 'Nothing', 'something of disgust at the ruthless hypocrisy of her sisters, some little faulty admixture of pride and sullenness'.[9] Cordelia is indeed protesting, indignantly, satirically, against her sisters – 'Sure I shall never marry like my sisters To love my father all' (I.i.102–3) – but it is part of a more fundamental protestantism in her attitude. Where Lear trusts in ritual to embody meaning, Cordelia insists that only in the innerness of the individual spirit can true truth live. The irony is that the bond according to which Cordelia loves her father is that same bond which he sought to have enacted in the love-test. It is from this radical split between two means of expressing an ideal of mutuality that the tragedy opens out.

'We are born to do benefits', Timon asserted as the key doctrine in his creed of philanthropy. In *King Lear* our membership of one another is equally at issue. By focusing on the family, though, Shakespeare rooted the question in a deeper and more fundamental matrix of experience. The image of the father distributing lands to his children is nearer to an archetype of human relatedness, at least in patriarchal culture, than the generous host feasting his friends. The generalised and abstract concept of ingratitude which obsesses Timon becomes the filial ingratitude which in its inwardness drives Lear mad. Some of the sense of the mythic in *King Lear* which is absent in *Timon* may be attributed to the primacy of the image of family on which the play is structured. But the pre-Christian, prehistorical milieu of *King Lear* is also of key importance in creating the mythic field of imagination of the tragedy.

Shakespeare removed the many explicitly Christian references found in his source-play and created in *King Lear* a remarkably consistent pagan world.[10] This did not involve any general squeamishness about the use of anachronism, however; as in his other plays, he felt free to draw on the immediate experience of his audience. When Gloucester talked of 'these late eclipses of the sun and moon' they may have very recent indeed for the original audiences if, as scholars have argued, they allude to eclipses in autumn 1605.[11] The devils which possess poor Tom had previously possessed followers of the Catholic exorcist Edmunds in 1580s Buckinghamshire, as reported by Samuel Harsnett in his 1603 pamphlet *A Declaration of Egregious Popish Impostures*.[12] In dress, in speech, in topical reference, the characters of *King Lear* could be occasionally, and without apparent anomaly, the contemporaries of its audience. It was only in systems of belief that the illusion of their otherness was sustained. Thus in *King Lear* there are few, if any, unmistakably Christian references; with the one arguable exception of Lear's phrase, 'as if we were God's [Gods, QF] spies' (V.iii.17), consistently plural deities preserve the convention of polytheism.

This imagination of a pagan world gives to nature an animistic force, as we see first in Lear's disowning of Cordelia:

> by the sacred radiance of the sun,
> The mysteries of Hecat and the night;
> By all the operation of the orbs
> From whom we do exist and cease to be;
> Here I disclaim all my paternal care,
> Propinquity and property of blood,
> And as a stranger to my heart and me
> Hold thee from this for ever.
>
> I.i.108–15

The principles which Lear takes as witness to his oath are the natural forces on which man depends for life, and they are, by implication, the principles Lear imagines Cordelia to have flouted. As mankind takes his being from the universe, so the child derives from the parent, and to deny that dependency in either case is blasphemy. Though analogous to the Christian patriarchal system in which the authority of the human father is reinforced by an Almighty one and *vice versa*, this is different in so far as it is nature itself which is deified. The idea of the natural in human relations is extended out into the universe; hence the thoroughgoing exploration of the nature of nature which is integral to *King Lear*. Where in *Timon* there was a somewhat ill-defined opposition between culture and nature, represented by the city and the wilderness, in *King Lear* a metaphysic of nature is central from the start, and human nature central to it.

King Lear is concerned with the family and has, as a result, a basic human accessibility, even intimacy. It would be possible to argue that *King Lear*, and not *Othello*, is Shakespeare's one domestic tragedy with its vivid representation of sibling rivalry, the frictions of the generation gap, the loves and hatreds that parents and children together generate. Yet the legendary status of the story, Lear's position as monarch of ancient Britain, invest this family with vast and reverberating significance for the kingdom, for the world even. The combinations of king/father, kingdom/family mean that the elaborately ritualised public style of the opening scene can nonetheless plunge unexpectedly into the most direct and urgent language of confrontation. We see this happen first when Lear and Cordelia face each other over the cryptic 'nothing'. The abrupt descent from formal and declarative utterance to a charged immediacy is repeated with the intervention of Kent. He begins in a style appropriate to addressing a king, though significantly making of his servantship something as personal as sonship:

> Royal Lear,
> Whom I have ever honour'd as my king,
> Lov'd as my father, as my master follow'd,
> As my great patron thought on in my prayers –

when he is interrupted with Lear's terse warning:

> The bow is bent and drawn; make from the shaft.
> I.i.138–42

This elicits an outburst of shocking energy in its assault on decorum:

> Be Kent unmannerly
> When Lear is mad. What wouldst thou do, old man?
> I.i.144–5

It is the loyal Kent who first sounds that word 'mad' which is so to resound through the play; it is Kent who first strips the King of all his titles but bare 'old man'.

In the English history plays, Shakespeare's kings are treated with more or less the ceremonious respect paid to Renaissance monarchs, with the dubiously legitimate King John a partial exception. Lear can be addressed by Kent with a bluntness which would have been unthinkable in a counsellor of Elizabeth or James, because his kingship is conceived of as something remote from a complex hierarchy of state. The folk-tale shape of Lear's story simplifies his role; his kingship is an awesome magnification of his power as father and head of family. We are thus able to see him in this first scene both as dread king on whose decrees a country depends, and as father whose will may be challenged by the independent-mindedness of a daughter like Cordelia or a substitute son like Kent. The effect is of primitiveness in so far as it seems to take us back to the origins of monarchy in an ur-family ruled over by an ur-father.

No other opening scene of a Shakespeare tragedy puts before us so swiftly, so inevitably, so irreversibly its tragic node. What begins as an orderly set-piece ceremony is aborted into the successive disasters of Cordelia disinherited, Kent banished, the kingdom split two ways, and Lear left an anomalous king and no king. The brief prose dialogue between Goneril and Regan at the end of the scene offers us a breathing-space to judge all that has happened and, in their comments, a potential judgement on it and Lear:

GONERIL: You see how full of changes his age is; the observation we have made of it hath not been little. He always lov'd our sister most; and with what poor judgment he hath now cast her off appears too grossly.
REGAN: 'Tis the infirmity of his age; yet he hath ever but slenderly known himself.

I.i.287–93

A surprising number of critics quote with apparent approval Regan's last line as a key to the understanding not only of this first scene but of the play. Lear's royal egotism, his susceptibility to flattery, his angry aggressiveness when his will is thwarted, are all symptoms of a lack of self-knowledge which only the fearful events which follow will make him discover. Yet surely the very

fact that this view of Lear's character is expressed by Goneril and
Regan should give us pause. They, who have most benefited from
their father's ill-judgement, can with least grace complain of it.
There is a chilling contrast, not only in sentiment but in style,
between their orotund verse declarations of love and this scalpel-
like prose. We can already sense in them the steady predatoriness
of those for whom what they have been given merely confirms the
need to take more. They discredit the attitude of analysis they
adopt, not just as cold-hearted and self-interested, but as shallow
and inadequate. The scene we have just witnessed can not be
reduced to the erratic behaviour of an almost senile old man who
'hath ever but slenderly known himself', as Goneril and Regan
would have it. Nor can we revert to a comfortable schema of moral
judgement on Lear's actions. The failure of the love-test, the
disastrous division of the kingdom, belong within some fated tragic
scheme of things beyond complacent psychological diagnosis.

Goneril and Regan, as the two elder sisters, are by the prescriptive
conventions of the Cinderella tale-type bound to be the bad elder
sisters. Their badness, however, though implied and assumed
from the start, does not initially take any very explicit or dramatic
form. It is for Edmund to supply them with an avowed ideology in
the second scene which begins the sub-plot. In *Timon* the second
mirroring plot of Alcibiades was a late introduction in the play,
hardly more than embryonically there at all. In *King Lear* the two
plots are intricately intertwined to create a complex system of
correspondence and difference. Although there is the effect of
reduplication in matching Gloucester with Lear as rash misguided
fathers, Edgar with Cordelia as the loving children misjudged, the
variations between the plots are as important as the identifications.
If, for example, the king's three daughters fall into a traditional
pattern of youngest-best, in the Gloucester family the wicked
Edmund is not only the bastard but the younger son. He invokes
the goddess Nature to sanction his assault on primogeniture as
much as legitimacy:

> Wherefore should I
> Stand in the plague of custom, and permit
> The curiosity of nations to deprive me,
> For that I am some twelve or fourteen moonshines

Lag of a brother? Why bastard? Wherefore base?
I.ii.2–6

This double challenge to the traditional twin principles of inheritance must have made Edmund especially scandalous to the original audience. It also makes it possible for him, in his forged letter,
to have Edgar the older son appear to express what are precisely
Goneril and Regan's sentiments: 'I begin to find an idle and fond
bondage in the oppression of aged tyranny, who sways, not as it
hath power, but as it is suffer'd' (I.ii.46–7). This corresponds to
Goneril's restiveness with what remains of Lear's power at the end
of the previous scene: 'Pray you, let us hit together; if our father
carry authority with such disposition as he bears, this last surren-
der of his will but offend us' (I.i.303–4).

Ann Thompson has pointed out how, when characters within
the play comment on analogies between the two plots, their
perception is skewed by misinterpreting their own part.[13] Gloucester's comment in I.ii is the first example of such partial vision. As
part of the train of disasters presaged by 'these late eclipses', he
sees 'the bond crack'd 'twixt son and father'.

This villain of mine comes under the prediction: there's son
against father. The King falls from bias of nature: there's father
against child.
I.ii.105–8 (F only)

Lear thought it was Cordelia who had fallen from 'bias of nature':
Gloucester has identified the wrong one of his sons as the villain
who has turned against him. This pattern, however, does not
merely illustrate a general human inability to take the mote out of
one's own eye. The principle of crossed comparisons and imper-
fect analogies sets up resistance to oversimplifying interpretation.

Edmund, for instance, in what amounts to a eugenics of illegit-
imacy, justifies his driving hunger for power by reference to the
circumstances of his birth. Bastards, he claims,

in the lusty stealth of nature, take
More composition and fierce quality
Than doth, within a dull, stale, tired bed,
Go to th' creating a whole tribe of fops
Got 'tween asleep and wake?
I.ii.11–15

(Coleridge marvellously deflates this with an allusion to Mr Shandy.[14]) Where then, do Goneril and Regan, perfectly legitimately got, come by their acquisitiveness, already in this scene established as cognate to Edmund's? The legitimate may be no more naturally kind than the unnatural 'natural' son. And the son may be just as monstrous in his unkindness as the daughters. Feminists complain, with good reason, of the play's bias against women. 'The misogyny of King Lear,' concludes Kathleen McCluskie, 'both the play and its hero, is constructed out of an ascetic tradition which presents women as the source of the primal sin of lust, combining with concerns about the threat to the family posed by female insubordination.'[15] Maybe, but it is Gloucester's male lust and its legacy in Edmund which is most prominent early in the play, and it is Edmund's male aggressiveness, unrestrained by law or feeling, which represents initially the most fully drama-tised threat to the family.

The action is organised around key thematic concepts, such as nature and the natural, explored at an abstract or metaphysical level; yet there is always a complicating dramatic concreteness which makes interpretation problematic. What status, for instance, has Gloucester's astrological belief or the scathing mockery of it by Edmund? W.R. Elton has identified Gloucester's attitude as that of a certain sort of pagan superstitiousness which would have been recognised and stigmatised as such by a Renaissance audience.[16] Certainly in modern productions it is hard to play Gloucester's lines about the 'late eclipses' as other than foolish old maunder-ings. The self-respect of a sophisticated twentieth-century audi-ence will tend to demand an alignment with Edmund's scoffing scepticism. Yet it will not do to set Gloucester's speech entirely aside as credulous doom-mongering, if only because it fits too well with the sense of oncoming disaster within the play. 'Though the wisdom of nature can reason it thus and thus, yet nature finds itself scourged by the sequent effects' (I.ii.98–9). This has a certain force in context, however little we may be disposed to accept it as a justification of astrology against the claims of natural science. It is akin to Lafeu's comment on miracles in *All's Well*:

They say miracles are past; and we have our philosophical persons to make modern and familiar things supernatural and causeless. Hence it is that we make trifles of terrors, ensconcing ourselves into seeming knowledge when we should submit ourselves to an unknown fear.

Edmund's snorting iconoclasm may be identified as such 'seeming knowledge', and Gloucester's submission 'to an unknown fear' to be preferred to it.

Edmund does a brilliant demolition job on his father's superstition:

> This is the excellent foppery of the world, that, when we are sick in fortune, often the surfeits of our own behaviour, we make guilty of our disasters the sun, the moon, and stars; as if we were villains on necessity; fools by heavenly compulsion; knaves, thieves, and treachers, by spherical predominance, drunkards, liars, and adulterers, by an enforc'd obedience of planetary influence; and all that we are evil in, by a divine thrusting on
>
> I.ii.115–22

Yet the denunciation, so compelling and so apparently comprehensive, twists away from its detached rationalism to reveal the animus of the speaker. It is no accident that the list of crimes excused by astrological influence ends with adultery, or that the sexual so dominates the speech in what follows:

> – an admirable evasion of whoremaster man, to lay his goatish disposition on the charge of a star! My father compounded with my mother under the Dragon's tail, and my nativity was under Ursa Major, so that it follows I am rough and lecherous. Fut, I should have been that I am, had the maidenliest star in the firmament twinkled on my bastardizing.
>
> I.ii.122–7

Even as Edmund exposes the absurdity of horoscope determinism, the conjunction of planets at his birth shaping his being, he betrays his belief in another sort of determinism. He *is* rough and lecherous, and could be no other way because of the physical rather than supernatural circumstances of his birth, circumstances on which he dwells obsessively. In his own view, he is lustful because a product of his father's lust, and must justify his own nature by seeing all humanity as 'whoremaster man'. Any attempt to disguise this naked truth is mere foppery – the same word he used to dismiss legitimate heirs, 'a whole tribe of fops'. Thus, Edmund's posture of unillusioned existential autonomy is undermined from within; he is the creature as much as the exponent of the naturalism he preaches.

King Lear arouses from the beginning a sense of awe; it is this which an audience shares with Gloucester, for all his vulnerability to Edmund's sardonic ridicule. It may be a mistake to blame it on the stars, but something terrible is happening in the world of *King Lear*, and its causes are obscure. An irresistible movement is on towards the expulsion of the good, a movement so apparently arbitrary and convulsive as to suggest something beyond the · observable concatenation of human characters and event. Banishment and self-exile are features which *King Lear* has in common with *Timon*. Lear's banishment of Kent, with its threat of direr punishment if it is not acted on within a strictly limited term, reads like a rhetorical development of the Senate's blank sentence on Alcibiades:

> If after two days' shine Athens contain thee,
> Attend our weightier judgment.
>
> III.v.101–2

But the banishment of Alcibiades comes, unexpectedly, halfway through the play as part of what seems a contrived design to parallel the (nearly simultaneous) indignant withdrawal from Athens of Timon. Kent's exile, which is bound up with that of Cordelia, takes place at the very start of the action, as part of a momentum which will drive out in turn Edgar, the Fool, the enraged Lear and the blinded Gloucester. It is a pattern which we experience as mysterious and inscrutable, though much of the play is devoted to anguished efforts to understand it.

'The best lack all conviction, while the worst Are full of passionate intensity': such was Yeats's imagination of coming apocalypse. Disconcertingly, almost the opposite appears to be true in *King Lear*. In Edgar and in Albany, we see something of the paralysis of goodness confronted by the implacable certainty of evil conjured up by Yeats's lines. But for the most part through the first two acts of the play, a passionate intensity of anger is the distinguishing characteristic of the best characters, while the worst appear con-

tained and undemonstrative. The rash and misguided anger of the
two fathers, Lear and Gloucester, is structural to the plot, making
possible an interpretation of the whole play as 'a tragedy of wrath
in old age'.[17] But Kent too has a hairtrigger temper, Kent who has
'years on [his] back forty-eight' and is thus young enough to know
better. A smouldering anger against her sisters animates Cordelia's
response in the love-contest.

> Why have my sisters husbands, if they say
> They love you all?
>
> I.i.98–9

We are told (with no further explanation) of 'France in choler
parted' (I.ii.23), as though to thicken further the atmosphere of
violent indignation which swirls through the opening scenes.

When Timon marvelled at Apemantus' ill-humour, it was to
place it as pathological: 'They say, my lords, Ira furor brevis est;
but yond man is ever angry' (I.ii.28–9). Apemantus' aggressiveness in the first half of *Timon* is eccentric, and though it anticipates,
it hardly prepares us for Timon's own later rage which seems
disproportionate, in excess. That sense of angry excess, however,
is an informing mood of *King Lear* from the beginning. It is particularly striking in the case of Kent, because his original in *King Leir*
was the meek old man Perillus whose role was to suffer with,
never to oppose, his king. He does not intervene on behalf of
Cordella but merely comments chorically after Leir has made his
exit. 'Reason to rage should not have given place' (Bullough, VII,
345), he remarks sententiously, an observation apt enough to the
conduct of his counterpart Kent. Kent rebukes his master's 'hideous rashness', yet his own speech is hardly more temperate,
certainly not well calculated to allay Lear's anger. We see the same
characteristic of vehement belligerence in his attacks on Oswald. In
disguise as Caius, his first service to the King is to trip the 'base
football player'; his later assault on the luckless servant of Goneril
in II.ii may seem almost as unprovoked to an audience as it does to
Oswald himself, who asks in bewilderment, 'Why dost thou use
me thus? I know thee not' (II.ii.9–10). Though there are reasons for
Kent's anger revealed in II.iv – Oswald, as messenger of Goneril,
has soured Kent's welcome as the King's emissary with Cornwall
and Regan – significantly he does not bother to explain them either
to Oswald, or subsequently when questioned by Cornwall. It is

enough that Oswald's 'countenance likes me not'. When this is followed up by an ironic riposte from Cornwall, 'No more, perchance, does mine, nor his [Edmund's], nor hers [Regan's]', Kent does not flinch from the implications:

> Sir, 'tis my occupation to be plain;
> I have seen better faces in my time
> Than stands on any shoulder that I see
> Before me at this instant.
>
> II.ii.85–90

It is understandable that Cornwall should conclude:

> This is some fellow
> Who, having been prais'd for bluntness, doth affect
> A saucy roughness, and constrains the garb
> Quite from his nature.
>
> II.ii.90–3

There is, as it were, a race-hatred between good and evil in *King Lear*. Kent needs no immediate cause to attack Oswald, or Edmund, for that matter, whom he launches at in the brawl – 'With you, goodman boy, an you please' (II.ii.41); he does not attempt to justify himself to Cornwall but instead extends his aggression to him and his Duchess. Oswald is the initial focus of his attack because Oswald is his antithesis, the type of the bad servant as he is the type of the good. 'Why art thou angry?' asks Cornwall. Kent replies:

> That such a slave as this should wear a sword,
> Who wears no honesty. Such smiling rogues as these,
> Like rats, oft bite the holy cords a-twain
> Which are too intrinse t' unloose; smooth every passion
> That in the natures of their lords rebel;
> Bring oil to fire, snow to their colder moods;
> Renege, affirm, and turn their halcyon beaks
> With every gale and vary of their masters,
> Knowing nought, like dogs, but following.
>
> II.ii.66–75

Apart from caste disdain for Oswald, who has proved that he is a

slave and not a gentleman entitled to wear a sword by putting up
with being tripped and assaulted without retaliating, there is here
also an indictment of false service. For Kent, service means 'absolute loyalty to his master and absolute loyalty to the truth',[18] never
one at the expense of the other. To serve truly may thus mean, on
occasion, to stand out against one's master on behalf of truth. This
is a paradox expressed again by Cornwall's nameless servant when
he opposes the blinding of Gloucester:

> Hold your hand, my lord.
> I have serv'd you ever since I was a child;
> But better service have I never done you,
> Than now to bid you hold.
>
> III.vii.71–3

Oswald, by contrast with this true service of truth, stands for all
those bad servants who, in humouring their master's moods however ill-disposed, destroy the very principles on which service rests.

Chaucer's Parson distinguished a good from a bad anger: 'The
goode Ire is by jalousie of goodnesse, thurgh which a man is
wrooth with wikkednesse, and agayns wikkednesse'.[19] It is this
'jalousie of goodnesse', this 'noble anger', as Lear calls it, which
possesses Kent and which moves most of the good characters in
the first two acts of the play. Cordelia protests against the travesty
of love in the professions of Goneril and Regan, as Kent attacks the
deformation of service in Oswald. Both Lear and Gloucester rage
against the imagined unnaturalness of their children's behaviour.
The effect produced is of a strange emotional imbalance, with the
immoderate overreactions of the virtuous constantly playing into
the hands of their adversaries. Evil has little to do but sit tight and
watch as goodness undoes itself by its strenuous militancy. A dry
diagnosis – 'He hath ever but slenderly known himself' – or a cool
contempt – 'A credulous father and a noble brother' – express the
detached ascendancy of an observing pragmatism over the vulnerable zeal of the idealists.

It is, of course, in Lear himself that the fierceness of indignation
seems most disproportionate and most disastrous. In his confrontation with Goneril in I.iv her speeches are so low-key in comparison to the King's Titanic abuse that some critics and theatre
producers have accorded a measure of justification to the 'detested
kite'.[20] Though this may be a reading against the grain of the text, it

is hard not to be horrified by Lear's curse, hard to imagine that anything Goneril can be seen to have done so far quite justifies something so horrific. Once again, as with Cordelia, Lear's anger is fired by the failure of 'natural' feeling in his daughter, and Nature is prayed to take revenge by denying to Goneril a 'babe to honour her', or to give her only such a 'thwart disnatur'd torment' of a child as she has proved to Lear. It is in a sort of retrospective justice to Cordelia's 'most small fault', that Lear feels bound to outgo in denouncing Goneril his former denunciation of his youngest daughter. In the violence of Lear's reaction can be sensed both its impotence and the desperate urgency of his need to affirm a threatened order of belief.

Goneril, so far from taking Lear's curse to heart, shrugs it off to the bewildered Albany who asks 'whereof comes this?'

> Never afflict yourself to know more of it;
> But let his disposition have that scope
> As dotage gives it.
>
> I.iv.290–3

To Goneril, Lear's antics are no more than the tantrums of a senile second childhood and have to be treated with sharp parental discipline.

> Old fools are babes again, and must be us'd
> With checks as flatteries, when they are seen abus'd.
>
> I.iii.20–1 [Q only]

In a play centrally concerned with the relations of parents and grown-up children, this is part of a pervasive pattern of childishness in the parent, parental roles taken on by the child. For Lear's behaviour can indeed be seen as childish, in the unreasonableness of his anger, the violence of his resentment of imagined slights, most of all in his threats of an unimaginable revenge, when both his older daughters have turned against him:

> I will have such revenges on you both
> That all the world shall – I will do such things –
> What they are yet I know not; but they shall be
> The terrors of the earth.
>
> II.iv.278–81

Here speaks the child in his frustration at not being able even to conceive of punishment adequate to his sense of hurt. Goneril and Regan, allowing him to fling out into the storm, are pseudoparents disclaiming responsibility to enforce on the child a salutary lesson.

> 'Tis his own blame; hath put himself from rest,
> And must needs taste his folly.
>
> II.iv.289–90

Shakespeare's great daring in the play is to ground the opposition of good and evil in such inverted parent–child relations, the child-ish irrationalism of the father against the hard reasonableness of the daughters.

The inversion of the roles of parent and child is only one sign of that deep disorder in the kingdom in which authority is usurped, goodness expelled or driven to defend itself in passionate un-reason. The sinister adulthood of Goneril and Regan disciplining their father/child will eventually be answered by their good counter-parts, Cordelia and Edgar, who take on the loving protective-ness of true parents/children. In this pattern the Fool has a special role. He is wise child to Lear, the child who knows better than his father and with child-like tactlessness will not forbear from telling him so again and again. He is merciless in teaching Lear the simple lesson of his folly with the homeliest of images: 'thou mad'st thy daughters thy mothers . . . thou gav'st them the rod, and put'st down thine own breeches' (I.iv.171–2). Yet the truth Lear rejected in Cordelia, banished in Kent, he tolerates from the Fool, even if it is often hard to tell how much he is really listening. The Fool's special status of privileged child allows him to talk to his 'nuncle' the King with a combination of unceremonious directness and a waywardness which dances in and out of sense. For Goneril his unbiddable antics are associated with the unruliness of Lear which must be brought under control. Significantly, the Fool, and Lear's defence of him, are among her causes of grievance: 'Did my father strike my gentleman for chiding of his fool?' (I.iii.1–2). The Fool arouses Goneril's antagonism by his truth-telling and his licensed fooling, but also by the sense of his bond with Lear.

It is an odd alliance between them, difficult to describe without misrepresentation or sentimentality. As a personal relationship it is fitful and intermittent, buried within the structural roles of king and jester. The Fool's theatrical function makes him a commentator at large on the scene, answerable to nothing and nobody, the obliqueness and unpredictability of his voice essential to his part. Yet in masked and dislocated form, he shares Kent's dual loyalty to Lear and truth, and acknowledges the affinity to Kent with the ironic accolade of the offer of his coxcomb. When in the third act the Fool follows Lear out of the court confines on to the heath, we see glimpses of a tenderness and solicitude on both sides. The Fool 'labours to out-jest' Lear's 'heart-struck injuries' (III.i.16–17), by re-playing his set-piece paradoxes in this newly desperate scene to coax the King back towards sense and shelter:

> O nuncle, court holy-water in a dry house is better than this rain-water out o' door. Good nuncle, in; ask thy daughters' blessing. Here's a night pities neither wise men nor fools.
>
> III.ii.10–13

Though Lear is too absorbed in his apostrophes to the elements to respond to this, yet its concern is matched at the end of the scene by the King's paternal compassion for his companion:

> Come on, my boy. How dost, my boy? Art cold?
> I am cold myself. . . .
> Poor fool and knave, I have one part in my heart
> That's sorry yet for thee.
>
> III.ii.68–73

The Fool is not by this reduced to mere object of pathos: he retains his downstage knowingness, standing outside the dramatic situation, with a wittily apt reprise (for the original audience) of what he, the actor Robert Armin playing Feste, had sung at the end of *Twelfth Night* – '. . . the rain it raineth every day'. Yet there are strains within the relationship of Lear and the Fool of that mutuality of feeling as between parent and child which the play's situation has so disrupted and distorted.

The movement of the first half of the play is to drive goodness and truth of whatever sort out of control and authority into silence, disguise or disfigurement. 'Truth's a dog must to kennel; he must be whipp'd out' (I.iv.110–11), says the Fool, who yet contrives to tell his truths through riddles, songs and jests. Kent's 'likeness' is 'raz'd', though as the good servant Caius he is identifiably himself. Edgar's assumption of the role of Poor Tom involves a deeper sinking of the personality: 'Edgar I nothing am' (II.iii.21). From this moment he vanishes from the play, until he erupts from the hovel like the spirit the Fool takes him for, exorcised by Kent's command, 'Come forth' (III.iv.44). Truth, like the sun and moon of Gloucester's omens, is under eclipse; it is exiled into the language of the mentally retarded, the mad, the possessed. 'Lurk, lurk', Edgar's watchword to himself as poor Tom at the end of III.vi (Q only), is all that he and his fellow outcasts can do, hovering on the outside in darkness. This vision of a whole world of dispossession and derangement informs the central dramatic focus on Lear's breakdown into madness.

The play takes an audience with Lear stage by stage through into madness, giving to his alienation from the world which has betrayed him a different status from the comparable movement in *Timon*. We are never able to judge just how pathological Timon's virulent disillusionment is, whether it is to be seen as a massively amplified paranoia or a dystopian cosmic vision designed to contrast with his initial idealism. The movement of Lear through his successive encounters with his three daughters in Acts I and II is a believable progress from anger to anger. His first outburst of rage against Cordelia requires the even more savage curse on Goneril. But this climbing graph of aggression cannot be sustained, and by II.iv when he meets with Regan, the monolith of his anger is beginning to break up. He by now desperately needs to find in his last remaining daughter the 'tender-hefted nature' which he failed to recognise in Cordelia and which Goneril so manifestly lacked. Though incensed by the stocking of Kent and Cornwall's refusal to see him, for the first time he backs away from his anger. Gloucester, in the thankless part of diplomatic go-between, has tried to explain Cornwall's resolution not to come, in a way which all too obviously and unfortunately exposes the changed power relations between the Duke and King:

> My dear lord,
> You know the fiery quality of the Duke;

> How unremovable and fix'd he is
> In his own course.
>
> II.iv.89–92

Lear is apoplectic at the idea that anyone in the kingdom should dare to be fierier than himself, that any 'quality' should stand above his own as monarch. Still, he bites back the riposte that is about to break from him:

> Fiery? the fiery Duke? Tell the hot Duke that [Lear, Q] –
> No, but not yet. May be he is not well.
>
> II.iv.102–3

The threat of madness forces him to rein in that anger which unrestrained in earlier scenes expressed his absolute sovereignty.

In this scene Lear makes recurrent efforts to control his gusts of rage, to find an attitude of dignified patience as alternative to the inchoate emotions which drive him beside himself. He does not immediately react against Regan's tone of patronising firmness with him, concentrating his venom on the absent Goneril. When Goneril appears, and he must face the harsh truth of their alliance against him – 'O Regan, will you take her by the hand?' (II.iv.193) – he can at least momentarily find words of real pathos to express his estrangement from his eldest daughter:

> I prithee, daughter, do not make me mad.
> I will not trouble thee, my child; farewell.
> We'll no more meet, no more see one another.
>
> II.iv.217–19

Immediately, however, the effort rebounds on itself:

> But yet thou art my flesh, my blood, my daughter;
> Or rather a disease that's in my flesh,
> Which I must needs call mine; thou art a boil,
> A plague-sore, or embossed carbuncle
> In my corrupted blood.
>
> II.iv.220–4

Such is the intestine nature of filial ingratitude which means that Lear's hatred cannot be projected out on to an external adversary, but must be taken into a self which fragments under its force.

But just because of the greater naturalisation of Lear, it is possible to misrepresent by a psychological or moralistic interpretation
the complexity of what happens in the play. Madness can too
readily be seen as a way forward to new levels of understanding,
the lack of self-knowledge in the sane Lear, remarked on by Regan,
leading on to an eventual true self-discovery. There is no doubt
that what Maynard Mack calls the 'archetypal theme . . . of the
Abasement of the Proud King' is there in *King Lear*.[21] The proud
and egotistical king of the first scene, who cannot tell the difference between love and flattery, comes through alienation to understand the selfless feeling he has banished in Cordelia, learns to go
out to the experience of others in compassion and humility. The
great address to the 'poor naked wretches' suffering in the storm is
a key moment in this development; the denunciation of authority
in the mad scenes in Act IV is another. Yet overall to read the play
thus, as a series of staged lessons in a moral or political learning
process, is to read it selectively: to pick and choose from among
Lear's mad speeches, to deny or downplay the apocalyptic force of
the central storm scenes and their metaphysical urgency.

Paul Jorgensen, in his book *Lear's Self-Discovery*, comments that Lear's
apostrophes to the heavens in III.ii remain on the whole 'an enlarge-
ment from microcosm to macrocosm of his private tantrums'.[22] Those
speeches certainly resemble Lear's earlier childishness in their vola-
tility, their egotism, their self-pity, and they could be construed as
one gigantic act of attention-seeking exhibitionism. The scene,
though, hardly allows an audience the mental space to make such
a judgement. Lear's rhetoric assaults us with too fierce an energy
to enable us to sidestep it as 'rhetoric'. The desire for the destruction of the world in revenge for Lear's wrongs may indeed be
paranoia on the grand scale, like Timon's curse on Athens, but it
draws upon a daunting imagination of apocalypse. Visitation by
fire and flood, the Deluge, Sodom and Gomorrah devastated, are
only types of the comprehensive annihilation that Lear wishes on
the world:

> Crack nature's moulds, all germens spill at once,
> That makes ungrateful man.
>
> III.ii.8–9

Though Lear varies between commanding and accusing the elements, treating them now as vengeful ministers of justice, now as unfair allies of his unkind daughters, there is more here than a 'private tantrum' projected out on to the heavens.

'I am a man more sinn'd against than sinning' (III.ii.59–60) – the 'I' is stressed in self-righteous contrast to those sinners who *should* tremble before the storm. Lear's attitude here is comparable to that of Cassius in *Julius Caesar*, who remarks complacently of the night of terrible disturbances before the Ides of March that it is 'A very pleasing night to honest men'. As the proof that he belongs in such a category, Cassius tells Casca,

> I have walk'd about the streets,
> Submitting me unto the perilous night,
> And, thus unbraced, Casca, as you see,
> Have bar'd my bosom to the thunderstone
>   I.iii.46–9

The comparison brings out the entirely different effect of the two plays. In *Julius Caesar*, the storms and omens are liable to various interpretations as Cicero notes:

> men may construe things after their fashion,
> Clean from the purpose of the things themselves.
>   I.iii.34–5

It is with some such measured scepticism that an audience views the credulous fear of Casca, the bravado attitudes of Cassius. The storm in *King Lear* is far more awesome and directly threatening. The idea of a real if inscrutable connection between the world of nature and the actions of man is imaginatively immediate throughout, whether in the images of a universal destruction brought about by human wickedness or of a last judgement with individual sinners called to account:

> Close pent-up guilts,
> Rive your concealing continents, and cry
> These dreadful summoners grace.
>   III.ii.57–9

Under the impact of this accusatory force, it is hard to resist the metaphoric claims of the elements as the great gods' arresting officers.

Shakespeare strikingly naturalised what the thunder said in his source. In the *King Leir* play, a peal arrives exactly on cue to prevent Gonorill's messenger from carrying out her command to murder Leir and his faithful servant Perillus: 'It thunders. He quakes, and lets fall the Dagger' (Bullough, VII, 379). In *King Lear* the thunder is never the token of this sort of naive providentialism. For all Lear's denunciations, its/his enemies are safe within doors, and the storm hurts no-one but himself and those loyal to him. It is a natural not a supernatural phenomenon, wetting and chilling with real wind and rain, forcing those exposed to it to seek shelter. In spite of this actuality of the elements, Lear's address to the storm is not mere posturing absurdity. For Lear, as Maynard Mack points out, the thunder has transcendent meaning: 'his (and our) consuming questions are what it means – and if it means – and whose side it is on'.[23] Those questions are intensified rather than removed by the naturalisation of the storm, by taking away the clear symbolic significance which it had in *King Leir* as the theatrical guarantor of a God-directed scheme of things. It is divested of a ready-made metaphoric association only to push back to the origins of metaphoric power in the actual.

It is natural to be scared of thunderstorms; they are, after all, dangerous. Terror before the force of nature as manifested in a storm, the feeling of human helplessness against it, are as near universal as any emotions are likely to be. Myths of apocalypse, of almighty powers above, angry with sublunary humanity, draw inevitably on this basic experience of the terrible in nature. A part of the primitivism of *King Lear* is the way in which it returns us to an originating awe and uses it to charge again the transcendental images which it generates. As the play reaches back to a primary identity of the kingdom with the family, so it takes us to an imaginative starting-point where 'heavens' are simultaneously literal and metaphoric. This is again made possible by the paganism of the setting. Because Lear's belief in sacred order is invested in the natural universe, its disruption involves an anguished interrogation of nature. 'What is the cause of thunder?', he asks his 'philosopher' Poor Tom (III.iv.151). The question expresses a metaphysical demand for first causes, prompted and blown wide open by the raging storm that accompanies it.

The action of the play drives towards extremities which are also basics, origins; the metaphoric must re-find itself in the literal. This movement is precipitated by the literalism of the evil characters. The first shaping of Lear's impulse out into the storm comes as a rhetorical gesture, when it is proposed that he go back to Goneril:

> Return to her, and fifty men dismiss'd?
> No, rather I abjure all roofs, and choose
> To wage against the enmity o' th' air,
> To be a comrade of the wolf and owl –
> Necessity's sharp pinch!
> II.iv.206–10

Goneril, in reply, calls the rhetoric's bluff by obtusely misreading its intention: 'At your choice, sir', she shrugs. This same reductive transformation of metaphor into reality is shown at its most terrible in the blinding of Gloucester. 'Tied to the stake' and forced to 'stand the course' of Cornwall and Regan's terse and relentless questioning as to his part in sending off the King to Dover, Gloucester at last abandons his timid defence of equivocation. When for the third time he is asked by Regan, 'Wherefore to Dover?', he bursts out in indignation:

> Because I would not see thy cruel nails
> Pluck out his poor old eyes
> III.vii.55–6

This is a figure of speech, a hyperbolic image of Regan's cruelty to her father, and Gloucester's final prophecy of revenge is similarly figurative:

> I shall see
> The winged vengeance overtake such children.
> III.vii.64–5

There is a sickening inevitability in Cornwall's grimly literal reply, 'See't shalt thou never'. In the most horrifying moment of the play we have to watch hyperbole enacted, the metaphorically imagined embodied in the pain of the flesh.

The extremities of the third act, and of this scene of the blinding of Gloucester in particular, develop both good and evil out of

latency. Goodness in the earlier acts had been registered largely by
impotent indignation, evil by its lack of feeling one way or the
other. Evil is still characterised as lack, lack of imagination as much
as feeling, but that now emerges as a steady will to power undeflected by moral considerations. Edmund comments on his betrayal of his own father as though it were a law of physics: 'The
younger rises, when the old doth fall' (III.iii.25), an amoralism
which makes all the more obscene his impersonation of an unctu-
ous moral queasiness to Cornwall:

How, my lord, I may be censured, that nature thus gives way to
loyalty, something fears me to think of.
                                                        III.v.2–3

Like Iago's mimicry of the language of 'honesty', Edmund here
depletes loyalty of meaning. Edmund, though, does not have
Iago's whiff of the Satanic; he is the purer psychopath, in no way
abnormal except for the absence of the normalities of love and
guilt. The later stages of the play force us, and the good characters,
to confront evil in this blankly psychopathic form.

It is as though, after the fatal failure of goodness to recognise its
own, represented by Lear and Gloucester's misjudgement of
Cordelia and Edgar, the nature of good and evil must be pain-
fully re-discovered as something other than received metaphysical
categories. In an inverted world of values, evil has appropriated
not only power but the appearance of legitimacy and its sanctioning vocabulary. Thus Edmund is a model of 'loyalty', his father is
'the traitor Gloucester' to be arrested and interrogated. Though
colour is given to such accusations by the Earl's confederacy with
the French invasion, Cornwall himself betrays what a kangaroo-
court it is to which he summons Gloucester:

Though well we may not pass upon his life
Without the form of justice, yet our power
Shall do a court'sy to our wrath, which men
May blame, but not control.
                                                        III.vii.23–6

Due process of law is here reduced to mere 'form of justice'. The
idea of the blinding as a 'court'sy to our wrath' has a special horror,
in the grotesqueness of the image's perversion of the meanings of

the word 'courtesy'. It brings out also the contrast between the anger of goodness, of which we have seen so much in the play, and this evil anger which now for the first time appears as such. The anger of Lear, Kent, Gloucester was headlong, unguarded, lashing out in indignation at real or imagined denials of the principles they uphold. The animus of Cornwall knows itself better as the exercise of power, knows just how far it can indulge itself.

This emergent evil demands a response, forces goodness out of quiescence. We see this first in Gloucester himself who has been so convincingly uneasy in his relations with the Goneril/Regan party, caught between a temporising deference before their power and a growing anxiety about their treatment of Lear. The final outburst against Regan, therefore, represents a compelled need to testify on behalf of truth. It is echoed by the challenge of Cornwall's servant, an astonishing movement of rebellion against tyranny, coming from nowhere theatrically. The unexpectedness is repeated in Act IV with the transformation of Albany, Goneril's 'mild husband' of Act II, into a figure of fierce reprobation (however much fiercer in Q than F):

> O Goneril!
> You are not worth the dust which the rude wind
> Blows in your face.
> IV.ii.29–31

Yet the opposition to evil can as yet achieve nothing but the declaration of its own militancy. Gloucester is blinded, Cornwall's servant dies for his act of insubordination, and Albany's full misogynistic denunciation of Goneril (not in F) receives only the derisive retort 'Marry, your manhood – mew!' (IV.ii.68).

With evil so in the ascendant, with goodness reduced to powerless or persecuted witness, the search for meaning is pursued by the outcast, the mad and the blind. There is a long and deep-rooted tradition of attributing to madness and blindness understanding and knowledge denied to the normally sane or sighted. Cassandra and Tiresias stand as archetypes of this association of the special gifts of prophecy with the doom of physical or mental defect. The paradox of the madman who understands more than the wise, the blind man who sees more than the seeing, is exploited in any number of forms and at a variety of levels. The very figure of the fool, both in its social institution and its theatrical counterpart, depends on this interpretation of nonsense as privileged truth. But madness and blindness in *King Lear* are literally themselves, not just figurative constructs for the voicing of knowledge beyond the reach of normal understanding. Gloucester's often-quoted 'I stumbled when I saw' is a confession of the error of his seeing self; yet that does not mean that blinding gives him access to some special new wisdom. Similarly, we need to resist the tendency to read all that Lear says in madness as a higher, if disjointed, form of sanity.

Lear fears madness as a horror and that is what it is when it comes, an uncontrollable turbulence of the mind. The contrast with the Fool brings this out. His professional folly seems a tame, domesticated thing, its free play of language and image hardly free, so trained as it is towards sense. With Lear, the single monomaniacal obsession with his daughters' ingratitude fractures the mind that tries to contain it. As with Timon's misanthropy, Lear's madness spirals outward. In Act III, it is never far from its source in fixation on filial cruelty, projected on to Edgar at the moment of entry into madness, 'Didst thou give all to thy daughters?' (III.iv.49), reflected in the phantasmagoria of the (Q only) mock-trial, picked out in a grotesque detail such as the hiring of Poor Tom as 'one of my hundred' (III.vi.78). Daughters are to Lear what Athenians are to Timon. When we see Lear again, after the relatively long break from the stage, he is much madder, 'mad as the vex'd sea' as the distressed Cordelia puts it (IV.iv.2). In IV.vi, where the mad king meets the blind Gloucester, the whole world is comprehended in his deranged denunciation. However, unlike Timon who holds on tight to the source of his hatred, growing ever angrier in his progress towards the ultimate isolationism of his death, Lear's vision is more fitful and fragmented, full of the shifts and starts of a convincingly alienated mind.

Timon's passionate misanthropy is counterpointed with its variant voice in Apemantus; Lear's madness is flanked not only by the folly of the Fool but by the feigned possession of Edgar/Poor Tom in the triptych of unreason at the structural centre of the play. The function and significance of the part of Poor Tom is the hardest to read of the three crazed figures. It was one of the play's original theatrical draws, to judge at least by the title-page of the Quarto which advertised as a starred feature Edgar's 'sullen and assumed

humour of Tom of Bedlam'.[24] The role of Tom of Bedlam was a
generic one, impersonated briefly by Edmund – 'My cue is villain-
ous melancholy, with a sigh like Tom o' Bedlam [Q them of
Bedlam] (I.ii.129–30) – before being taken on in earnest by Edgar.
As such it might have been placed by the Jacobean audience as a
conventional part, a 'humour', distanced by its very generic status.
As an assumed part, also, it is the donned disguise of an Edgar
recognisably sane underneath. To that extent, at least, it is akin to
the part of the Fool, a manipulated version of non-rational
language. There is some measure of relief in the ventriloquism of
the Edgar/Poor Tom figure. It is certainly less menacing than 'the
thing itself', real madness, in Lear, and by its relative actedness
further enforces the unacted and uncontrollable dementia of the
King. Still, performed as it is, and generic as it may have been,
there is a rawness of theatrical impact in the Bedlam beggar. When
Edgar elects to

> take the basest and most poorest shape
> That ever penury in contempt of man
> Brought near to beast
>
> II.iii.7–9

he does indeed become that shape and stands in for all those who
must permanently inhabit it. It certainly does not diminish the
force of Lear's contemplation of him as 'unaccommodated man'
that we know him to be the disguised and banished heir to the Earl
of Gloucester.

The idea of possession is similarly live though simulated.
Stephen Greenblatt has argued that in Shakespeare, as in Harsnett's pamphlet on which he was dependent for the names of Poor
Tom's devils, this language is 'emptied out' of significance, and
that this is typical of the way *'King Lear* is haunted by a sense of
rituals and beliefs that are no longer efficacious'.[25] Poor Tom's
speeches might have been originally perceived as an alms-giving
rigmarole, further discredited perhaps by its association with the
Popish practices Harsnett denounced. But in the dramatic context
the images of possession take on new and vivid imaginative
power. Though we may not believe literally in the devils with the
outlandish names that possess him, Flibbertigibbet, Smulkin,
Modo and Mahu, Poor Tom's rhapsodies bring an intimacy with
them and with the natural world through which he is driven:

Poor Tom; that eats the swimming frog, the toad, the tadpole,
the wall-newt, and the water; that in the fury of his heart, when
the foul fiend rages, eats cow-dung for sallets, swallows the old
rat and the ditch-dog, drinks the green mantle of the standing
pool; who is whipp'd from tithing to tithing, and stock-
punish'd, and imprison'd
III.iv.126–32

The deprivation and social persecution that Tom and his like suffer
are here tellingly registered. At the same time Poor Tom is imagined as a religious maniac who regards his own madness as
possession, who turns himself into an exemplum of damnation.
He is visited by devils in punishment for his past life, in which he
was a compendium of all the sins:

Wine lov'd I deeply, dice dearly; and in woman out-paramour'd
the Turk. False of heart, light of ear, bloody of hand; hog in
sloth, fox in stealth, wolf in greediness, dog in madness, lion in
prey.
III.iv.88–92

Human nature, monstrous in its combination of the worst of all
animals, must look for something above or below the natural to
account for its own monstrosity.
'Let them anatomize Regan', commands Lear, 'see what breeds
about her heart. Is there any cause in nature that make these hard
hearts?' (III.vi.75–7). The question rings out at the very centre of
the play and pairs with Lear's other enquiry of Poor Tom, 'What is
the cause of thunder?' Both questions are unanswered: the pathol-
ogy of evil remains as impenetrable as the cosmology which is
invoked to punish it. What is figured in the mad scenes is the
primary need to seek out meanings and causes, remaining even
when all capacity for offering rationally conceived answers has
broken down. In this the grotesque demonism of Poor Tom can be
seen as a folkloric version of Lear's grander rage for order. It is a
rage exposing, in the disorder of madness, the uncontrollable
forces it vainly strives to understand. A misogynistic horror of
sexuality and its power comes into the play with Poor Tom's
homilies: 'Let not the creaking of shoes nor the rustling of silks
betray thy poor heart to woman. Keep thy foot out of brothels, thy
hand out of plackets, thy pen from lenders' books, and defy the

foul fiend' (III.iv.92–6). It swells into the appalling speech of Lear later:

> Down from the waist they are centaurs,
> Though woman all above;
> But to the girdle do the gods inherit,
> Beneath is all the fiends'
>
> IV.vi.124–7

Lear himself is appalled by this vision: 'Give me an ounce of civet, good apothecary, to sweeten my imagination' (IV.vi.129–31). Explanations of this eruption of the sexual hardly seem satisfactory, either in terms of the psychopathology of the individual characters, or in the revelation of a root misogyny underlying the play's patriarchal ideology. Sexuality and aggression seem to surface, rather, as the twin animalities of human nature which it can only superficially discipline and control and which madness uncovers with horror in itself.

The simultaneous urge towards explanation and interpretation in madness, with the inchoate display of the naked drives it seeks to interpret and explain, makes construing the play's mad-scenes extremely difficult. In Lear's great speeches in IV.vi there are moments of poetic vision which seem to be the truths the progress into madness was designed to come at: the anarchist repudiation of punitive authority – 'None does offend, none – I say none', or the tragic exposition of the birth-cry to Gloucester:

> Thou must be patient; we came crying hither.
> Thou know'st the first time that we smell the air
> We wawl and cry. . . .
> When we are born, we cry that we are come
> To this great stage of fools.
>
> IV.vi.179–84

But Lear's speech is always, as Edgar describes it, 'matter and impertinency mix'd'; it never steadies into a stable wisdom in madness, a humbled self-knowledge, a radical anti-authoritarianism, or a Christian acknowledgement of common sinfulness, as interpreters of the play might variously wish to see it. For all his denunciation of the false hierarchy of justice, Lear can still claim to be the very origin of authority – 'they cannot touch me for coining; I am the King himself' (IV.vi.83–4). And, instants after he has been preaching patience to Gloucester, there comes the six-times re-peated 'kill', the fierce war-cry of no quarter for his sons-in-law. Shakespeare lets us off none of the nightmarish suffering of the mad consciousness completely at the mercy of its own vagaries. The drive towards a deep or transcendental understanding which is still there in madness can reach no single goal of meaning.

The parallelism of the play's double plot design emerges strikingly again in the fourth act where the banished children, Edgar and Cordelia, are seen supporting and caring for their suffering outcast fathers. In that pattern, the blindness of Gloucester is evidently intended as a counterpart to Lear's madness. For those who like their tragedy moralistic, there is an appropriateness in the form of suffering which each undergoes: Gloucester's is physical in that he first sinned through lust in begetting Edmund, Lear's mental in that it was the sins of pride, anger and intemperance which he displayed in the opening scene.[26] Yet it is doubtful how far an audience watching the agonies of Lear and Gloucester is so edified by the fittingness of punishment to crime, or indeed aware of issues of crime and punishment as such. The complementarity of blindness and madness seems related rather to a dialectic running through the play between acceptance and resistance, patience and protest. At one level, *King Lear* represents a massive dramatisation of Hamlet's question, 'whether 'tis nobler in the mind to suffer . . . or to take arms against a sea of troubles'.

Lear tries to summon patience as a wall against the mounting tide of madness – 'You heavens, give me that patience, patience I need' (II.iv.270). But his efforts to be 'the pattern of all patience' (III.ii.37), never more than intermittent, are borne away in the mind's tempest that sweeps him beyond his sane self. The spirit of indignant protest, the impulse to 'punish home', an aggressive denunciation of the world's inequities, are all strong currents through Lear's mad language. By contrast, the blinding of Gloucester leaves him helpless victim, tortured by and vulnerable to forces infinitely above his control.

> As flies to wanton boys are we to th' gods –
> They kill us for their sport.
>
> IV.i.37–8

Where madness adds energy to Lear's spirit of remonstrance, Gloucester in blindness heads down towards the yielding of despair. It is Edgar's self-appointed mission to transform this defeatism into a stoically positive patience.

Edgar, who has the second longest role in the play in terms of speaking lines, is one of its most problematic figures. In his first appearances barely sketched in as the good legitimate brother to the vividly evil Edmund, his identity all but lost in the discontinuous assumed parts of Poor Tom and other disguises, it seems useless to look for a coherently characterised 'character' of Edgar.[27] Yet there do appear to be some shaping features in his will to endure – 'Whiles I may scape I will preserve myself' (II.iii.5–6) – and a moralising bent towards self-consolation. In a soliloquy of formal couplets (found only in Q), closing III.vi, he distances himself from the haunting trio of mad voices in which he has just joined:

> When we our betters see bearing our woes,
> We scarcely think our miseries our foes. . . .
> How light and portable my pain seems now,
> When that which makes me bend makes the King bow
>
> III.vi.102–9

There is a similar move towards meliorist recuperation in his opening speech of Act IV:

> Yet better thus and known to be contemn'd,
> Than still contemn'd and flatter'd.
>
> IV.i.1–2

These two speeches, however, stand either side of the fearsome scene of Gloucester's blinding, and no sooner has Edgar assured himself that 'The lamentable change is from the best; The worst returns to laughter' (IV.i.5–6), than his maimed father is led in, and he is forced to eat his words in a stunned aside:

> O gods! Who is't can say 'I am at the worst'?
> I am worse than e'er I was.
>
> IV.i.26–7

This moment which so cruelly ambushes Edgar's attitude of stoic resolution seems part of a recurrent quarrel with quietism in the latter part of the play, undermining, among other things, Edgar's efforts to make of Gloucester's disability a spiritual re-education. Under the impact of intense feeling, Edgar feels unable to go on with his pretence, 'I cannot daub it further'. This is humanly so sympathetic that it seems difficult to comprehend the necessity that works against it: 'And yet I must' (IV.i.55). Edgar offers a formal motivation for his action when he has led his father to the imaginary Dover cliff.

> Why I do trifle thus with his despair
> Is done to cure it.
>
>   IV.vi.33–4

There is, if taken literally, an intolerable moral pedagoguery in this, and in the patronising sententiousness with which the moral of the fake fall is enforced: 'Bear free and patient thoughts' (IV.vi.80). The difficulty of accepting Edgar's schooling of his father into stoic acceptance is increased by the dignity, the very orthodox piety of Gloucester's would-be suicide speech. He kneels to pray:

> O you mighty gods!
> This world I do renounce, and in your sights
> Shake patiently my great affliction off.
> If I could bear it longer, and not fall
> To quarrel with your great opposeless wills,
> My snuff and loathed part of nature should
> Burn itself out.
>
>   IV.vii.34–40

This is no reprehensible act of despair, but a reasoned choice of death as the lesser evil, with due deference to the 'mighty gods' that are invoked to witness it, an acknowledgement of the futility of mutiny against their 'great opposeless wills'. As such it surely commands far more respect than the therapeutic strategies of Edgar.

The function of the scene on 'Dover cliff' is not so much to fulfil or discredit Edgar's moral rehabilitation of his father, as to render it irrelevant. Edgar's role as Gloucester's multiply-disguised guardian and tutelary spirit can not be accounted for in terms of his educative intentions. The elaboration of the word-drawn cliff view, the answering perspective upward with the bogey-man fiend imagined at the cliff top, are spectacularly superfluous to Edgar's stated objective. In the strangeness of the dramatic sequence, there is hardly opportunity for attention to motive. What we live through in the scene is a purgatorial phantasmagoria of the blind, equivalent to Lear's mad delusions. In the one as in the other, Edgar may be as much theatrical instrument as agent. Gloucester no more than Lear reaches a secure haven of true doctrine through suffering. Rather, the experience of blindness becomes a dramatised metaphor for the terror and opacity of the world in which man must, against his will, go on living and groping for meaning.

The end of the fourth act brings at last the reunion and reconciliation of parent and wronged child which so much of the act has worked to withhold, with Edgar, for whatever reasons, denying his father the recognition he so craves, Cordelia close to Lear yet apart from him. The father–daughter meeting, when it comes, serves to fulfil expectations postponed, building on and blending with the Edgar–Gloucester misrecognition scenes. Lear, when he returns to consciousness, like Gloucester after his 'suicide', believes he has died and awakes to the afterlife:

> You do me wrong to take me out o' th' grave.
> Thou art a soul in bliss; but I am bound
> Upon a wheel of fire, that mine own tears
> Do scald like molten lead.
>
> IV.vii.45–8

The gap of separation, at the very moment it is to be closed, yawns as the gulf sundering damned from saved. The vision of a loving Cordelia is to the remorse-stricken Lear like the knowledge of lost heaven which is the worst torture of damned souls. As he moves towards coherence, the sense of the anguish of madness and the part of self-reproach within it, is brought home retrospectively. The depths of darkness through which he has suffered are registered in the frail lucidity into which he emerges.

Nothing could be simpler or more natural than the reconciliation of father and daughter, the step-by-step tentativeness with which Lear finds himself again in a real world and gingerly moves

towards recognition, the eloquent compassion poured out by
Cordelia over him asleep, contrasted with the tear-choked half-
sentences with which she greets him awake. Allegorical or symbolic readings seem inappropriate, unnecessary. Cordelia's
humanity is too purely itself to need to be read as the representation of a Christ-like forgiveness. Her response to Lear's self-
accusations completes the design which her answer in the
love-contest set up:

LEAR: . . . I know you do not love me; for your sisters
Have, as I do remember, done me wrong:
You have some cause, they have not.
CORDELIA: No cause, no cause.
                                        IV.vii.73–5

'No cause, no cause', rhymes across the span of the play with the
earlier repeated 'nothing'. The one expounds the meaning within
the other which Lear so failed to understand, the inherent dispro-
portionality, gratuitousness, in the nature of love. Such an idea is
integral to Christian doctrine in the concept of the supererogatory
sacrifice of Christ. Cordelia does have Christian associations, including one of the most evident scriptural echoes in the play. 'O
dear father!', she exclaims in defence of her invasion of Britain, 'it
is thy business that I go about', recalling the twelve-year-old Jesus
in the Temple, 'knewe ye not that I must go about my fathers
busines'.[28] Such a reference does not strike us as puzzling or out of
place in King Lear, in spite of its pre-Christian setting, as the images
associated with the Last Supper do in Timon. This is not because
Cordelia is allegorised as Christ-figure or morality personification
of Charity. It is rather that, as C.L. Barber and Richard Wheeler
say, 'the sort of love Cordelia expresses is the very ground from
which love of God, transcending or fulfilling the love of parents,
would develop in a fully Christian situation'.[29] Here as so often, the
play returns to fundamentals of human experience, to rediscover the
devotion of which the Redemption stands as supreme type.

Through the fourth act signs of self-destruction seem at last to be
appearing among the evil characters, with an equivalent re-grouping
of the banished and scattered representatives of goodness. In the first

half of the play, the evil party is marked by a striking solidarity of
shared self-interest. Goneril and Regan 'hit together' in a sure
partnership of power against their father. Edmund is 'seized on' by
Cornwall as a natural recruit for his service: 'natures of such deep
trust we shall much need' (II.i.115). Though the approaching civil
war between Cornwall and Albany, which is earlier hinted at,
never materialises in that form, dissension does come at last, when
Cornwall is already dead, in the deadly sexual rivalry of the sisters.
The death of Cornwall, and then Oswald, the predatory sexuality
of Goneril and Regan which emerges as though to validate Lear's
horrific misogynist vision, all seem to point towards the defeat of
evil by a combination of its own self-destructiveness and the
rehabilitated forces of goodness.

The fifth act collects as though to such an ending; even though
the King's party is defeated, the virtuous and newly strong Albany
takes reassuring charge. Edmund, whose irresistible rise seems to
be carrying him towards the crown itself, is firmly put back in place
by the Duke with royal status:

> Sir, by your patience,
> I hold you but as a subject of this war,
> Not as a brother.
>
> V.iii.60–2

Within minutes, Edmund's real brother is to appear in his last
disguise, and in ritual single combat prove his title true and
Edmund's false. The scene re-installs not only authority and legitimacy but patriarchy, as the hitherto dominant Goneril is exposed
by Albany with the incriminating evidence of her adulterous letter
to Edmund:

> Shut your mouth, dame,
> Or with this paper shall I stopple it. . . .
> Thou worse than any name, read thine own evil.
> No tearing, lady; I perceive you know it.
>
> V.iii.154–7

Goneril's response is a last desperate attempt to claim independent
sovereignty, 'the laws are mine, not thine', which Albany dismisses as 'most monstrous'. What would have been for the original
audience a proper order and control, absent since the opening

scene, here return to the play. It is this sense of returning order which the last entrance of Lear so stunningly shatters.

Dr Johnson, in his famous protest against the catastrophe of *King Lear*, complained that 'Shakespeare has suffered the virtue of Cordelia to perish in a just cause, contrary to the natural ideas of justice, to the hope of the reader, and, what is yet more strange, to the faith of the chronicles'.[30] Following Johnson, it is almost always argued that the ending, representing an alteration of the narrative shape of the original sources 'the faith of the chronicles', must be seen as a very deliberate decision of Shakespeare's to deny the audience the satisfying conclusion they might have expected. For those who interpret *King Lear* as challenging an orthodox Providentialist Christianity, this deliberateness is tendentious, even polemic. However, because so much turns on it, it is worth questioning whether the ending really does represent an iconoclastic reversal of the narrative direction of the sources.

It is true that in all previous versions of the story, Cordelia was victorious against her wicked sisters and restored her father to his kingdom, thus completing the design of the original love-contest in demonstrating the superiority of the last/best daughter. But most earlier recensions, with the significant exception of the play *King Leir*, closely linked the reign of Lear with its unhappy sequel when Cordelia, succeeding to the throne after her father's death, was defeated by her warring nephews, sons of Goneril and Regan, and committed suicide in prison. Thus, for instance, Spenser in *The Faerie Queene* moves on in one swift stanza from Cordelia's restoration of her father, through her reign, to the tragic concluding alexandrine:

> And overcommen kept in prison long,
> Till wearie of that wretched life, her selfe she hong.
> (Bullough, VII, 334)

In the *Mirror for Magistrates*, Cordelia tells the whole tale of Lear and the love-contest as a monitory recollection from beyond the grave, illustrating the perils of despair which led her to suicide. It may well be that it was the author of *King Leir* who, in providing a happy ending to his play, elected to stop the narrative short of its traditional conclusion, and Shakespeare who reverted to the more usual tragic outcome.[31]

This would make a different sort of sense of the choices involved in having *King Lear* end as it does. Shakespeare might then be seen as telescoping and compressing, for the sake of drama, a double rhythm implicit in the received story: the false security of the king restored by his good daughter, bound to the tragic downturn of her unmerited defeat and death. Restoration is figured not only in the gathering towards a triumph of the good in the final act, but in Lear's 'Come let's away to prison', a triumphalist declaration of victory in defeat. The king may not be restored to his throne, but in his reunion with his daughter achieves a reversal of values like that in a Donne love poem, with the walled prison, like the bed-chamber, becoming the centre of a stable power and meaning, the outer world of politics a shifting environment of ephemeral 'gilded butterflies'. Yet the sight of a Cordelia led off to prison must have been inherently ominous to those with any previous knowledge of the story. Already Edmund's design had been revealed to prevent the mercy which Albany 'intends to Lear and to Cordelia' (V.i.66). In suborning the Captain to kill her, Edmund plans to fake exactly the ending the traditional narrative had in store:

> To hang Cordelia in the prison, and
> To lay the blame upon her own despair,
> That she fordid herself.
>
> V.iii.253–5

The hanging derives from Spenser who needed a rhyme-word, 'long', 'hong'; the despairing suicide was prominent in the *Mirror for Magistrates*. The ending of *King Lear* may thus be read not as a radical upsetting by Shakespeare of expectations aroused by a traditional story, but as a re-shaping of images and ideas inhering in that tradition.

What then was the aim or effect of this re-shaping? The death of Cordelia may not have been a Shakespearean shock-tactic de-signed deliberately to frustrate audience hopes, and thus to de-stroy belief in a 'teleological link between the play's world and a beneficent divine order'.[32] But so much significance is vested in the life of Cordelia that we, like the characters in the play, are bound to struggle to construe the meaning of its violent ending. Looking on the pathetic spectacle of the King's madness in Act IV, the Gentle-man commented:

> Thou hast one daughter
> Who redeems nature from the general curse

Which twain have brought her to.

IV.vi.207–9

Again in the final scene, when Lear fleetingly hopes that Cordelia may still be alive, he exclaims:

> If it be so,
> It is a chance which does redeem all sorrows
> That ever I have felt.

V.iii.265–7

Whether or not we read full Christian resonance into the word 'redeem', both passages underline the crucial value of Cordelia's goodness and love to the moral universe of the play, a value called in question by the brutal extinguishing of her life.

The horror of the scene, and the need to make sense of it, are voiced in the chorus of three half-lines from the three characters by now in charge:

> KENT: Is this the promis'd end?
> EDGAR: Or image of that horror.
> ALBANY: Fall and cease!

V.iii.263–4

The imagination of apocalypse which so haunts the play, has here become a positive desire for apocalypse: it is a 'promis'd end' to be looked forward to, the heavens Albany has so often invoked as guardians of righteousness he now implores to fall and crush the world. But the full expressiveness of the lines is their harmonised inarticulateness, their bewildered and halting improvisation. In this they represent the culmination of a pattern in the last act, the resistance of the action to the efforts of the characters (and the audience) to organise it into meaning.[33] Albany, Edgar and Kent have all, severally and together, tried to shape the play into a significant denouement. Albany has stage-managed the trial by combat planned by Edgar against his brother. Edgar vanquishes Edmund, and reveals himself, making it the occasion for a horrifyingly final and punitive moral:

> My name is Edgar, and thy father's son.
> The gods are just, and of our pleasant vices
> Make instruments to plague us:

The dark and vicious place where thee he got
Cost him his eyes.

                                                              V.iii.169–73

Kent keeps on his disguise deliberately only, we must imagine, to
make possible a more satisfying *anagnorisis* at the very end. But
none of these attempted denouements come off as the triumphs
they are intended to be. Edgar and Albany's wrapping-up
speeches keep getting interrupted by other distractions, including
the deaths of Goneril and Regan. When Lear at last manages dimly
to recognise Kent – 'You are welcome hither' – Kent can only reply
bleakly 'Nor no man else. All's cheerless, dark, and deadly'
(V.iii.289–90).

Such is the confusion of mismanaged denouements and botched
recognition scenes that Lear and Cordelia are, notoriously, lost
from view. 'Great thing of us forgot!', gasps Albany. Cordelia's
death is all the harder to accept because of its apparently random
contingency. The vital but unexplained delay between Edmund's
relenting at the story of his father's death – 'This speech of yours
hath mov'd me, And shall perchance do good' (V.iii.199–200) – and
his acting on it – 'Some good I mean to do, Despite of mine own
nature' (V.iii.243–4) – is filled up with routine narrative unravell-
ing. It is just possible that there are unintentional incoherences
here, brought about by the profusion of plot material which had to
be dealt with. Variations between Q and F suggest a degree of
theatrical uncertainty as to how best to bring together all the
multiple strands of the double plot.[34] But it is hard to resist the
impression that the death of Cordelia is unnecessary, superfluous,
a haphazard accident rather than a tragic inevitability.

Is the aim of this contingent causality, of the action of the whole
play in so far as the death of Cordelia is its culminating catastrophe, to deny any organising principle in the world itself? Many
modern critics have said yes, most notably and unequivocally Jan
Kott: '*King Lear* makes a tragic mockery of all eschatologies: of the
heaven promised on earth, and the heaven promised after death;
in fact – of both Christian and secular theodicies; of cosmogony
and of the rational view of history; of the gods and natural goodness, of man made in the "image and likeness".'[35] Few interpreters
have so thoroughly Beckettified *King Lear* as Kott, but others have
stressed the play's lack of any visible signs of a transcendental.
'The characters appeal again and again to the pagan gods, but the

gods remain utterly silent. Nothing answers to human questions but human voices; nothing breeds about the heart but human desires; nothing inspires awe or terror but human suffering and human depravity.'[36] Yet Stephen Greenblatt, quoted here, goes on to recognise that the 'forlorn hope of an impossible redemption persists . . . ineradicable',[37] and though the play may empty out ritual of its traditional significance it creates in the rites of theatre its own sort of secular sacredness. Kott's militantly absurdist reading of King Lear is inadequate because it fails to represent either the need for meaning shared by characters and audience, or the sense of mystery which the play leaves behind. What we experience at the end of a performance of King Lear is not an assured conviction of the empty absurdity of the world, but a deeply troubled awareness of its inscrutability; not that there is, conclusively, no meaning, but that meaning, intuited as there, is so tragically hard to grasp.

The primitive, pagan setting in King Lear is a reaching back to origins in order to find images for the ultimate: last things, the promised end. The final lines, whether spoken by Albany (Q) or Edgar (F), are suggestive here:

> The weight of this sad time we must obey;
> Speak what we feel, not what we ought to say.
> The oldest hath borne most; we that are young
> Shall never see so much nor live so long.
>   V.iii.323–6

These are delphic couplets and it is hard to be sure how much significance to attribute to them. They are effective partly for their declaration of their own feebleness, the incapacity under the weight of what has happened to do more than 'speak what we feel', inadequate as it may be. But they testify also to what we have witnessed as some primordial rite of suffering which the survivors, and we in the audience, experience in a state of belatedness. To be young is not to look forward to a new beginning, the minimal upturn registered at the close of so many tragedies. Instead, in the limited remaining life of the young who will 'never live so long', we may sense the proximity of the final ending to which the whole action has brought us so close. King Lear thus dramatises at once basics, essentials, origins of meaning, and the ultimates involved in facing death and apocalypse, a doubleness made possible by the imagination of a primitive, pagan milieu, directed towards a latter-day audience.

This primitiveness, and what it made creatively possible, constitute the difference between *King Lear* and *Timon*, to return to the comparison with which this chapter started. *King Lear* resists interpretation because there is too much of it; *Timon* because there is too little. If *Timon* was somehow too abstract a schema, too inherently skeletonic, to put on the full flesh of drama, then *King Lear*, though no less abstract in design, has the effect of being imaginatively overloaded, all but impossible to comprehend in its manifold entirety. The semi-classical setting and parable-like form of *Timon* made for a degree of creative constriction, limiting the play's range and resonance to satiric and moral exemplary modes. By contrast, the legendary pre-history of *King Lear* allowed for an extraordinary imaginative liberation. The divided families at the centre of a divided kingdom, set back at the beginnings of Britain, took on the force of an originary myth. In the natural religion of the pagan characters, a fundamental antithesis between good and evil in the world could be explored without the benefit of the under-writing certainties of a Christian cosmology. Yet the resources of Christian imagery remained available in the play's dramatic iconography. Where the tragedies with a classical pagan setting induce a detached awareness of alternative systems of belief, *King Lear* drives its audience with the central characters through the most intense suffering, beyond reason and rational understanding, towards the essential emotions that animate belief itself.

8
Macbeth *1st scene*

The storm of thunder and lightning which attends the three Witches on their entrance into the first scene of *Macbeth* is not a natural phenomenon. When Lear asks his 'philosopher' Edgar 'what is the cause of thunder', it is an open question. The storm in *King Lear* is at once literal and metaphorical, wet rain that wets, thunder that will not 'peace' at the King's bidding, as well as the manifestation of those 'heavens' to which the characters look up so often and struggle to understand. In *Macbeth* there is no such duality. The Witches belong with the thunder and lightning, and the thunder and lightning with them, in unbreakable association as the theatrical signs of a non-natural supernature. The tiny twelve-line first scene of the play establishes the supernatural as a ground of reality prior to the human action. In *King Lear* the characters reach out from within a natural world to identify transcendent principles of good and evil to shape their experience – 'is there any cause in nature that make these hard hearts?' In *Macbeth*, evil is manifestly there theatrically, other than, external to, the human beings to which it will appear in such equivocal and equivocating form. Which is not to say that such an extrinsic supernatural is absolutely to govern the drama that follows. It is rather that the mini-overture of the Witches signals the supernatural as one of the determining givens of the tragedy. *Quote*

The Witches are certainly there and certainly evil at the start of *Macbeth*. In that knowledge we are given a position of privilege unlike the opening of *Hamlet* where, with the watchers on the battlements, we must await the appearance of the Ghost, and bewilderedly conjecture what the walking 'thing' in armour may be. Yet just *what* the ominous figures are omens of, *how* they are to relate to the actions we see initially, is made no clearer in *Macbeth* than in *Hamlet*. In the Witches' opening incantation there is a confused sense of conflict, 'hurly-burly' and 'battle', swirling around the single distinguishable name of Macbeth. Sure enough, I.ii begins with a 'bleeding captain' reporting from the battlefield, a figure of violence apparently to be linked to the Witches' apparition, just as the Ghost in *Hamlet* is associated by the watchers with the military preparations for coming war with Norway. But the Captain/ Sergeant's reports turn out to be of victory on all fronts in which Macbeth is the illustrious hero. The Witches do not prefigure war, any more than the Ghost did. Our attention instead is projected, beyond the account of how 'the battle's lost and won', towards the meeting with Macbeth which will come after; as in *Hamlet*, the prefigured evil is diverted from the outer conflicts of war to the more inward violences of apparent peace.

Scotland, it would seem from I.ii, is in a bloody mess, a mess which Macbeth, more or less single-handedly, has been cleaning up.[1] Shakespeare compressed into one brief scene three quite distinct campaigns as chronicled in Holinshed: the revolt of Mac- duald, Shakespeare's 'merciless Macdonwald', separate invasions from Norway by King Sueno and from England by his brother the Danish Canute.[2] The resulting atmosphere of confused crisis, resolved as though miraculously by the omnipresent heroism of Macbeth, helps to distract an audience from the otherwise relevant question of what is wrong with Duncan's Scotland. In the English history plays, war and rebellion are always the symptoms of government by a weak, inadequate or illegitimate king. In Ho- linshed Duncan's reign is given similar analysis. It is specifically because the king was so 'negligent . . . in punishing offendors, [that] manie misruled persons tooke occasion thereof to trouble the peace and quiet state of the common-wealth' (Bullough, VII, 488). But in *Macbeth*, remarkably, there is no indication that Duncan's weakness has precipitated the state of disorder in Scotland, nor yet the accompanying view (also to be found in Holinshed) of the stronger Macbeth as better suited in character to the monarchy. Such was the situation in *Richard II*, which the rightful but incom- petent king challenged by his abler rebellious first cousin. With this sort of political analysis *Macbeth* is not concerned.

Instead, in I.ii a visionary relation between action and authority is laid down informing the whole play. The 'bloody man' arriving from the battlefield is identified by Malcolm:

> This is the sergeant
> Who like a good and hardy soldier fought
> 'Gainst my captivity.

> I.ii.3–5

This is to be the function of the man of action, to fight energetically in defence of a royalty apparently incapable of defending itself. Duncan is imagined as a very old man, Malcolm a very young one, so they both have plausible excuses for not distinguishing themselves in battle. Yet together they represent an image of authority as a passive centre whose vulnerability must be protected by a violently championing force, the force most vividly displayed in Macbeth's rough justice visited on the rebel Macdonwald:

> brave Macbeth – well he deserves that name –
> Disdaining Fortune, with his brandish'd steel
> Which smok'd with bloody execution,
> Like valour's minion, carv'd out his passage
> Till he fac'd the slave;
> Which ne'er shook hands, nor bade farewell to him,
> Till he unseam'd him from the nave to th' chaps,
> And fix'd his head upon our battlements.
>
> I.ii.16–23

In Holinshed the incident on which this is based is given as an instance of Macbeth's 'cruell nature' (Bullough, VII, 490–1); here the allegorising epic style ritualises his battle-fury. Macdonwald 'worthy to be a rebel', as his adversary deserves the name of 'brave Macbeth', is given a traitor's death, though the haste of the battlefield makes impossible the formal farewells of the scaffold. There is no irony in the gentle Duncan's salute: 'O valiant cousin! worthy gentleman!'. It is the fitting tribute of validating authority to the energies of action undertaken in its behalf.

Charles I in his execution speech was to declare sovereign and subject 'clear different things'. So it is in *Macbeth*. In the tragedy's distinctive imaginative conception of king and hero, they have separate natures and functions. Duncan is, unlike any other king in Shakespeare, an icon of kingliness rather than an executive head of state. In place of the raw force of a King Lear, with power and authority combined in the figure of the king/father, Duncan is the sacred embodiment of his country's life needing a reverent and tender protectiveness. The emphasis throughout the play is on his innocence, his holiness, his sanctity. His lack of suspiciousness of the traitor Cawdor, for example, might have appeared a culpable lack of a worldly wisdom essential to a monarch –

> There's no art
> To find the mind's construction in the face.
> He was a gentleman on whom I built
> An absolute trust.
>
> I.iv.11–14

– especially when it is followed by an equally trusting greeting to the (equally to be distrusted) next Thane of Cawdor who immediately enters: 'O worthiest cousin!' But the irony here does not cut against the king. Rather, 'Duncan is trust incarnate; and his trust is neither something arbitrarily "given", nor an insensitivity to human deviousness, but a necessary expression of royalty'.[3] Again and again in the play, the tributes to Duncan are to his holy virtues – 'so clear in his great office' (Macbeth), 'a most sainted king' (Macduff). For such a king, the ethic of devoted service enunciated by Macbeth (however little his heart may go with it) is fitting homage. When Duncan declares his incapacity to reward him, Macbeth replies:

> The service and the loyalty I owe,
> In doing it, pays itself. Your Highness' part
> Is to receive our duties; and our duties
> Are to your throne and state children and servants,
> Which do but what they should by doing everything
> Safe toward your love and honour.
>
> I.iv.22–7

The most strenuous endeavour of the subject is no more than the due of a paternalist king, source of all love and honour.

It is against the background of such an absolute separation of power and authority, sovereign and subject, that the Witches introduce the temptation of the kingship to Macbeth. The ascending graph of their triple all-hails implies, as it were, a natural progression from Glamis to Cawdor to King. Macbeth's initial reaction is that 'to be King Stands not within the prospect of belief' (I.iii.73–4). We may well be doubtful of the sincerity of this, like those apparently unequivocal declarations of non-candidacy by possible candidates for the American presidency. Macbeth may need to deny his own dreams of sovereignty when, to his horror, he hears them voiced aloud. But the horror at least is real enough, and in the shocked recoil from the prophetic salutations there is a dislocation of identity involved in the idea of becoming king.

Macbeth may have had designs on the throne before he meets the Witches; their function may be merely to activate his latent ambition. The one line he is given before the encounter with the Witches, with its echo of their words in the first scene, has commonly been taken to indicate a prescient affinity with them: 'So foul and fair a day I have not seen' (I.iii.38). Equally well it could be read as an innocent response to the sudden clouding of the bright day brought about by the proximity of the Witches and the foul weather they conjure up – the one line of innocence Macbeth is to be allowed in the play. We have seen the coven assemble, as arranged, to 'meet with Macbeth', an appointment known to us but not to him; he walks unawares into the encounter. What is crucial here is the coming together of outer evil with inner being. That conjunction makes of Macbeth's desire for the crown something quite other than the ordinary ambition of a power-hungry nobleman.

In terms of the source story, there was nothing inherently implausible about the prophecy that Macbeth should become king. In Holinshed he is given at least some pretext for his open usurpation of the throne in that Duncan, by naming Malcolm prince of Cumberland and thus heir apparent, 'did what in him lay to defraud [Macbeth] of all maner of title and claime, which he might in time to come, pretend unto the crowne' (Bullough, VII, 496). But in the play there is no hint of anything illegitimate in Duncan's announcement:

> Sons, kinsmen, thanes,
> And you whose places are the nearest, know
> We will establish our estate upon
> Our eldest, Malcolm, whom we name hereafter
> The Prince of Cumberland; which honour must
> Not unaccompanied invest him only,
> But signs of nobleness, like stars, shall shine
> On all deservers.
>
> I.iv.35–42

The effect is of a ceremony of succession within a settled hierarchy,

an occasion of celebration in which the whole court may be expected to participate. The imagery with which Macbeth voices his
dismayed reaction in an aside suggests how perverse and guilty it is.

> The Prince of Cumberland! That is a step,
> On which I must fall down, or else o'er-leap,
> For in my way it lies. Stars, hide your fires;
> Let not light see my black and deep desires.
>
>   I.iv.48–51

Although Macbeth may briefly entertain the notion that he might
come by the throne rightfully –

> If chance will have me King, why, chance may crown me,
>   Without my stir.
>
>   I.iii.143–4

– aspiration to the kingship is overwhelmingly an imagination of
transgression.

From his first meeting with the Witches, Macbeth is as though
possessed by the idea that he will be 'King hereafter'. It generates
in him a state of trance, of that raptness from surrounding reality
which is one of the play's dominant images. 'Look how our
partner's rapt', comments Banquo, after Macbeth's long aside/
soliloquy (I.iii.142). That is what it looks like from outside. Macbeth's speech makes us privy, also, to the inner alienation, to what
feels like a physical invasion of the personality, disrupting from
without.

> why do I yield to that suggestion
> Whose horrid image doth unfix my hair
> And make my seated heart knock at my ribs
> Against the use of nature?
>
>   I.iii.134–7

The rendering here of the paralysing surge of adrenalin as a new
idea, at once frightening and exciting, enters the mind, is psycho-
logically completely credible. Yet the idiom of the play makes of
this concept of possession something more than a metaphor for
mental experience. The virtuous Banquo prays to be delivered
from it:

> Merciful powers
> Restrain in me the cursed thoughts that nature
> Gives way to in repose!
>
> II.i.7–9

The play is so peopled with the embodied instruments of darkness, that evil cannot be simply located within the mind of man.

Instead there is an interpenetration of inner and outer which
produces radically ambiguous forms of representation. The
Witches are both actively evil, the malevolent allies of the Devil of
Jacobean imagination, and, as the voices of prophecy, neutral
agents of temptation to Macbeth. It is impossible to tell whether
the image of murder which so instantly arises in Macbeth's mind is
implanted by them, or merely catalysed. Similarly, it is hard to
know how to understand Lady Macbeth's invocation:

> Come, you spirits
> That tend on mortal thoughts . . .
> Come to my woman's breasts,
> And take my milk for gall, you murd'ring ministers,
> Wherever in your sightless substances
> You wait on nature's mischief.
>
> I.v.37–47

This is not literally the conjuring of a would-be witch: it was not at
her ordinary woman's breasts that the witch suckled her familiar,
but at the special teat sought out as the incriminating 'mark' in
witchcraft trials.[4] Lady Macbeth is rhetorically working up the
psychological state necessary for her 'fell purpose'. Yet the rhetoric
with its images of possession, of a witch-like nurturing of the
demonic, of spirits that 'wait on nature's mischief', blends frighteningly with the world of animated evil we have already seen.

There is a resemblance, commented on in an earlier chapter,
between the mental state of Macbeth as the idea of murdering
Duncan first occurs to him and Brutus contemplating the assassination of Caesar:

> Between the acting of a dreadful thing
> And the first motion, all the interim is
> Like a phantasma or a hideous dream.
> The Genius and the mortal instruments

> Are then in council; and the state of man,
> Like to a little kingdom, suffers then
> The nature of an insurrection.
>
> > II.i.63–9

Brutus, though, knew the deed he was contemplating could mark off as interim the gap between conception and execution. Macbeth's more convulsive phantasmagoria abolishes any such fixities:

> My thought, whose murder yet is but fantastical,
> Shakes so my single state of man
> That function is smother'd in surmise,
> And nothing is but what is not.
>
> > I.iii.139–41

By a Roman effort of will, Brutus puts down the insurrection within; for Macbeth there can never again be a 'single state of man'.

Twice Banquo remarks on Macbeth's raptness and both times he refers to him as his partner. 'My noble partner', he says to the Witches

> You greet with present grace and great prediction
> Of noble having and of royal hope,
> That he seems rapt withal.
>
> > I.iii.54–7

Banquo is Macbeth's partner as joint commander of the Scottish forces. The greeting by the Witches makes them also sharers of prophetic knowledge denied to others, hence the whispered asides between them after Angus and Ross have unknowingly fulfilled the first part of the prophecy by conferring on Macbeth the Thaneship of Cawdor. Yet Macbeth is rapt quite beyond the common understanding he has with Banquo. His extended solo asides, set against his aside conversations with his soldier–partner, constitute a privacy within a privacy, an inner state of consciousness which possesses him and which he must occupy alone.

This is the pattern in little, repeated and centrally developed in the play in Macbeth's relations with 'his dearest partner of greatness' to whom he hastens to communicate the Witches' 'All hails'. The intimacy between husband and wife as they conspire the murder together could scarcely be closer or more binding. Yet we first meet Lady Macbeth alone, standing off from the husband whose character she analyses, with superhuman effort shaping herself to shape him towards action. When they do come together there is an inalienable solitude in Macbeth which she never reaches. To the bold vista of 'sovereign sway and masterdom' which she opens up before him, he responds with apparent weak evasiveness, 'We will speak further' (I.v.68). It is a gesture he uses again in parrying Banquo's probing reminder of the Weird Sisters:

> I think not of them;
> Yet, when we can entreat an hour to serve,
> We would spend it in some words upon that business,
> If you would grant the time.
>
>   II.i.21–3

With Lady Macbeth, as with Banquo, there never will be 'a time for such a word'. The impulse to defer communication marks the consciousness of the incommunicable.

Among the many things which we do not know for certain about Shakespeare's theatre is the identity of the boy-actor for whom he created the part of Lady Macbeth – and Cleopatra – and Volumnia.[5] Shakespeare's last three tragedies set the manhood of their heroes against the strong women who, as wife, whore, mother, help define it. The thrust of Lady Macbeth's sinew-stiffening argument in I.vii is based on the appeal to manhood, playing upon all the traditional shames of *machismo*. The boastful drunkard, who cannot hold his liquor, shivers with a sick head in the morning:

> Was the hope drunk
> Wherein you dress'd yourself? Hath it slept since,
> And wakes it now to look so green and pale
> At what it did so freely?
>
>   I.vii.35–8

With drunkenness comes impotence, for, as the Porter is to point out, drink 'provokes the desire, but it takes away the performance'

(II.iii.28–9). Hence the taunting contempt of Lady Macbeth's 'From this time such I account thy love'. The root charge, though, compounding weakness of head and lack of virility, is cowardice:

> Art thou afeard
> To be the same in thine own act and valour
> As thou art in desire?
>
> I.vii.39–41

Against this Macbeth sets up the orthodox moral defence – 'I dare do all that may become a man; Who dares do more is none' – only to have it overridden by Lady Macbeth.

> When you durst do it, then you were a man;
> And to be more than what you were, you would
> Be so much more the man.
>
> I.vii.49–51

What is assumed here, in place of the man–beast antithesis, is a single continuum of manhood in which the more you dare, the more man you are. By such arguments Macbeth appears to be won over, saluting his wife with the accolade of honorary masculinity:

> Bring forth men-children only;
> For thy undaunted mettle should compose
> Nothing but males.
>
> I.vii.72–4

But in *Macbeth*, unlike *Antony and Cleopatra* or *Coriolanus*, the drama of gender is played out against an otherworld of good and evil which Lady Macbeth tries in vain to exclude or deny. The invocation to the spirits to 'unsex' her is not an appeal for man-like ruthlessness, but for a much more fundamental denaturing of the self. The unnaturalness of the will is conjured up not just as a repudiation of the feminine but of the human. That milk which Lady Macbeth calls upon the 'murd'ring ministers' to take for gall is also the 'milk of human kindness' of which Macbeth is too full. Thus the most frightening image of all, that of the violent destruction of the nursing child, is a measure of the will to break the normal bonds of the natural, in which instinctive maternal love stands type of all human interrelatedness.

The success of Lady Macbeth's strategy in I.vii is to impose upon
her husband an amoral code of masterful manhood:

> MACBETH: If we should fail?
> LADY MACBETH: We fail!
> But screw your courage to the sticking place,
> And we'll not fail.
>
>   I.vii.59–61

The argument between them is conducted in these terms on both
sides; they play the parts of strong wife invigorating reluctant
husband into renewed confidence in manly action. Yet to take on
these gendered roles is to set aside, more or less consciously,
another realm of values. It has been said that Macbeth 'never
appeals to moral considerations' in I.vii, that it is only prudential
consequences in this world which he fears in that he is prepared to
'jump the life to come'.[6] Surely this is to misread the opening
soliloquy of the scene.

'If it were done when 'tis done,' argues Macbeth, 'then 'twere
well It were done quickly.'

>   If th' assassination
> Could trammel up the consequence, and catch,
> With his surcease, success; that but this blow
> Might be the be-all and the end-all here –
> But here upon this bank and shoal of time –
> We'd jump the life to come.
>
>   I.vii.1–7

But the hypothetical premiss is denied – the consequence can *not*
be trammelled up, it will *not* be done when it is done – and the
conclusion invalidated as a result. The risk of ignoring retribution
in the next world might be worth taking if one could be guaranteed
immunity in this, but not even such limited security is possible:
'we still have judgment here'. And the 'life to come', only con-
ditionally left out, floods back into the speech with images of a Last
Judgement on Duncan's murder:

>   his virtues
> Will plead like angels, trumpet-tongu'd, against
> The deep damnation of his taking-off
>
>   I.vii.18–20

Our response to the dialogue which follows the entrance of Lady Macbeth is crucially affected by this speech. Even as she speaks of her capacity to destroy her own baby as proof of purpose, the visionary Pity, 'like a naked new-born babe striding the blast' soars indestructible above her words. Macbeth colludes with his wife in denying all that his soliloquy has expressed. In both we are shown human beings' perverse ability to block out their truest knowledge, and act instead depleted parts of man and woman.

Macbeth kills his guest, his kinsman, his king. He knows what he is doing, but he does it anyway. Why? There are too many answers and no one of them satisfactory. He murders Duncan because the Witches suggest the idea to him. But they don't, they only prophesy that he will be 'King hereafter'. He murders Duncan because he is ambitious. And yet he himself foreknows the futility of the ambition that 'o'erleaps itself and lands on th' other'; we never see passionate desire for the crown in Macbeth, certainly not with anything like a Tamburlaine's compelling 'thirst of reign'. He murders Duncan because he is persuaded to it, against his better nature, by his wife. Can we be sure, though, that, within the complex politics of the married relationship, Macbeth does not advance his weak doubts and hesitations *in order* to have them overborne by the masterfulness he can rely on in Lady Macbeth?[7] Shakespeare plausibly dramatises a series of human experiences: a dangerous idea germinating within the mind of an ambitious man; the automaton urge towards action which is ambition itself; a woman twitting her man into manliness. There are, however, interstices between, and the awareness that what is happening is more than any one sequence of human cause and event.

That awareness is manifested most of all in the invasion of the play's world by night. It is a commonplace to point out how much of the action of *Macbeth* takes place in darkness. Even I.vi, the scene of Duncan's entrance into the castle, sometimes picked out as one of the contrasting moments of sunlight, has as its opening stage direction 'Hautboys and torches' – it is twilight at earliest.[8] Yet the function of this scene is indeed contrast, and it helps to illuminate (literally) the nature of the darkness that surrounds it. Duncan's appreciation of the air which 'Nimbly and sweetly recommends itself Unto our gentle senses' (I.vi.2–3), Banquo's marvelling evocation of the 'temple-haunting martlet', stand against the vision of the King's entrance which Lady Macbeth conjured up.

> The raven himself is hoarse,
> That croaks the fatal entrance of Duncan
> Under my battlements.
>
> I.v.35–7

In place of the 'loved mansionry' of the martins, there is the symbolic bird of ill omen; instead of the evening beauty of looking up at the imagined birds' nests, there is the first of the play's several apostrophes to night, palled in 'the dunnest smoke of hell'.

Night need not be nightmarish. Banquo's domestic imagery, for example, talking with his young son Fleance, can make the black sky seem reassuringly unthreatening: 'There's husbandry in heaven; Their candles are all out' (II.i.4–5). The darkness which the Macbeths inhabit is something else again. Running through the play is a contrast between the normalities of night and sleep and the hallucinogenic night-time of evil.

> Now o'er the one half-world
> Nature seems dead, and wicked dreams abuse
> The curtain'd sleep
>
> II.i.49–51

The seeming death of nature is a suspended animation, a drugged unconsciousness – 'Good things of day begin to droop and drowse' (III.ii.52). Sleep is a frail security, whether curtained by eyelids or bedcurtains, frighteningly liable to the assault of wicked dreams. Duncan is identified with a peaceful enjoyment of the night: he goes to bed 'shut up in measureless content' (II.i.16–17). His murder goes far beyond the pathos of a defenceless old man asleep, though this is what deters Lady Macbeth from carrying it out: 'Had he not resembled My father as he slept, I had done't' (II.ii.12–13). It is the destruction of sleep itself, with all that signifies in Macbeth's great catalogue of metaphors:

> Sleep that knits up the ravell'd sleave of care,
> The death of each day's life, sore labour's bath,
> Balm of hurt minds, great nature's second course,
> Chief nourisher in life's feast.
>
> II.ii.37–40

Macbeth's act is antithetical to all that is curative and self-renewing in the natural rhythm of day and night.

The strategy of the play is to force an audience to live in complicity with the 'instruments of darkness', to apprehend more normal experience only as an innocent other. It is thus we respond to the trustfulness of Duncan, or Banquo's pleasure in the martins; so too we listen in with Macbeth to Donalbain and his unnamed room-mate (Malcolm?) woken by uneasy dreams:

> I stood and heard them;
> But they did say their prayers, and address'd them
> Again to sleep.
>
> II.ii.23–5.

Our state is that of Macbeth, unable to say 'amen', obliged to witness in guilty consciousness a trusting unawareness beyond reach. The same pattern is repeated with the murder of Banquo. As the murderers lie in wait, the first of them sketches in a genre-scene of twilight:

> The west yet glimmers with some streaks of day;
> Now spurs the lated traveller apace
> To gain the timely inn, and near approaches
> The subject of our watch.
>
> III.iii.5–8

Momentarily, the lines take us out into an ordinary world in which travellers hurry to reach their destination before nightfall, only to realise that the danger which lurks in darkness for the traveller, awaited by us/the murderers, can not be escaped.

It is most centrally through the consciousness of Macbeth that we share the dramatised experience of evil. It is a consciousness so tortured, expressed in such a densely metaphoric language, that it renders futile questions of will, motive and responsibility, whether Macbeth is agent or instrument of the horror he creates. 'Thou marshall'st me the way that I was going' (II.i.42), he says to the air-drawn dagger. The appalled imagination of murder becomes a compulsion to enact it. Hamlet's avenging mood-music – 'Tis now the very witching time of night' – is elaborated into one of the most convoluted passages of allegorical imagery in Shakespeare:

> now witchcraft celebrates
> Pale Hecate's offerings; and wither'd murder,
> Alarum'd by his sentinel, the wolf,
> Whose howl's his watch, thus with his stealthy pace,
> With Tarquin's ravishing strides, towards his design
> Moves like a ghost.
>
> II.i.51–6

With the single word 'thus', Macbeth identifies his own movements with those of the allegorised murder, of the wolf, of Tar-
quin; and yet with the final simile of the ghost he dematerialises
himself and them. This terrified participation in nightmare leads
on to the self-alienation of the period after the murder when voices
pursue him through the several titles of the Witches' salutes:

> 'Glamis hath murder'd sleep; and therefore Cawdor
> Shall sleep no more – Macbeth shall sleep no more'.
>
> II.ii.42–3

Macbeth's identity is lost, fractured and transmuted by the dark
world of which his action has made him part.

'Wake Duncan with thy knocking! I would thou couldst!' (II.ii.74),
exclaims Macbeth as the insistent knocking at the gate begins. The
prolonged night wakes up to a morning which is no morning.
Though the Porter-scene is the most famous instance of 'comic
relief' in Shakespeare, one of its functions is to withhold relief, as
the repeated failure to answer the knocking puts off the moment at
which we might expect normality to break in upon the horror-
charged atmosphere of the castle. The Porter's grotesque business
of welcoming a representative cross-section of the damned at
Hell-gate, his insistent punning on 'equivocation' (at the time of
performance a cruel jibe at the Jesuit Father Garnet's testimony in
the Gunpowder Plot trial), yields a gallows humour with no real
respite in it. There is bitter irony too in Macbeth's laconic response
to Lennox' account of the dire omens of the night before –

> Lamentings heard i' th' air, strange screams of death,

> And prophesying, with accents terrible,
> Of dire combustion and confus'd events
> New hatch'd to th' woeful time; the obscure bird
> Clamour'd the livelong night. Some say the earth
> Was feverous and did shake.
>
> II.iii.54–9

To which Macbeth can only add, with a grim understatement that is almost funny, "Twas a rough night'. No-one can really pretend, least of all Macbeth, that the night of Duncan's murder was only ordinarily rough. There is evident feeling in his expression of its consequences, hypocritical as the intent of the lines may be:

> Had I but died an hour before this chance,
> I had liv'd a blessed time; for, from this instant,
> There's nothing serious in mortality –
> All is but toys
>
> II.iii.89–92

The murder of the King disrupts time itself, destroys its significance, leaves Scotland to a timeless interim of fearful uncertainty. In the aftermath of the assassination, the Witches' curse of 'Fair is foul, and foul is fair' is visited on the characters' responses. In the effort to find adequate expressions of horror, Macduff's lines can sound as strident and forced as Macbeth's; Lady Macbeth can faint most convincingly, whereas all Malcolm can manage in reaction to the news, 'Your royal father's murder'd', is the apparently inept 'O, by whom?' In the confusion of shock, fear and suspicion, it is Banquo who speaks most authoritatively and most characteristically:

> when we have our naked frailties hid,
> That suffer in exposure, let us meet,
> And question this most bloody piece of work,
> To know it further. Fears and scruples shake us.
> In the great hand of God I stand, and thence
> Against the undivulg'd pretence I fight
> Of treasonous malice.
>
> II.iii.125–31

Here, as so often in the play, Banquo represents a norm of approved orthodoxy. At the same time, his awareness of the exposure of man's 'naked frailties', his confident yet humble dependence on God's Providence, mark him out for martyrdom as Macbeth's next victim.

In the chronicles Banquo was Macbeth's accomplice in the murder of Duncan. His exculpation by Shakespeare has always been seen as a necessary piece of authorial tact – the legendary ancestor of King James could not be shown as a party to regicide. What is more remarkable in the portrayal of Banquo is the sleight of hand by which he is characterised as both great and heroic soldier and as passive progenitor. He is linked with Macbeth as one of Duncan's two 'captains' in the battles recounted in I.ii, and is said to have 'no less deserv'd' than Macbeth in accomplishing the victory. In the reports from the battlefield, however, the acts of violent prowess such as the dispatch of Macdonwald, and the warlike epithets, 'Bellona's bridegroom', are all Macbeth's. The one passage in which Banquo is coupled with him is ambiguous in its effect, as told by the bleeding Sergeant:

> they doubly redoubled strokes upon the foe.
> Except they meant to bathe in reeking wounds,
> Or memorize another Golgotha,
> I cannot tell –
>
> I.ii.39–42

These lines may have suffered from cutting, so it is hard to be sure what is intended. But broken off as they are by the Sergeant's loss of blood – 'I am faint; my gashes cry for help' – they suggest by association suffering defence to the death as much as infinite carnage, the sacrifice on the Cross at Golgotha rather than the accumulation of skulls which gave it its name.[9] It is certainly the role of Banquo in the play to suffer rather than act, and in this scene his aggressive warriorship is masked by that of Macbeth.

Banquo has been sometimes suspected of a tacit collaboration in that he fails to act on the suspicions of Macbeth which he voices at the beginning of Act III:

> Thou hast it now – King, Cawdor, Glamis, all
> As the weird women promis'd; and I fear
> Thou play'dst most foully for't
>
> III.i.1–3

In such a reading, his willingness to attend the usurper's corona-
tion, as against Macduff's dissenting refusal, could also be put to
his discredit. But this would be to misunderstand the different
roles Banquo and Macduff are given in the play. It is the function
of Macduff to act vigorously, violently at last, to redeem the time;
Banquo's part is to wait upon events in a wise passiveness. Such is
the part wished on him by the Witches' prophecy: to be forecast as
the 'root and father of many kings' is to have nothing to strive for
oneself, everything to hope for in some unencompassable future of
one's offspring. It is also Banquo's character to be able to accept
this part. Macbeth's fear of his 'royalty of nature' is a tribute to the
quality he lacks himself:

> 'Tis much he dares,
> And to that dauntless temper of his mind
> He hath a wisdom that doth guide his valour
> To act in safety.
>
> III.i.50–3

Macbeth here glances back at that position which he advanced in
the argument with Lady Macbeth, only to abandon – 'I dare do all
that may become a man; Who dares do more is none'. Banquo has
not that impulse towards transgression which drives on Macbeth.
His courage consists in a capacity to rest within the limits of what
may be done, what may be known. Throughout the action, he
watches and understands without trying to resist what is felt to be
an irresistible current of events.

Act II is devoted to the murder of Duncan, Act III to the murder of
Banquo. The two men are linked as the fathers of future kings. In
III.i we hear from Macbeth of Donalbain and Malcolm 'bestow'd in
England and in Ireland', and in the same speech comes the
pretend-casual question to Banquo, 'Goes Fleance with you?'
(III.i.35). Though Banquo hardly has Duncan's complete trustfulness, the two are equally helpless against Macbeth's criminal
intentions. Yet neither murder can be the complete and terminal
act for which Macbeth longs. Each has consequences in the terrible
aftermath of guilt, the voices proclaiming Macbeth's murder of

sleep, the ghost of Banquo shaking its gory locks at him. More literally, it is Duncan and Banquo's issue which Macbeth fails to trammel up in the net of his murderous action. Fleance escapes as inevitably as Banquo is killed. The inevitability lies not only in the legendary historical scenario by which he had to live to father an illegitimate son on a Welsh princess, a son who was to found the Scottish royal house of Stuart. Within the pattern of the play the escape of Fleance, like that of Donalbain and Malcolm, represents the capacity of life for self-renewing survival even where it is most vulnerable and exposed. We only see Banquo and Fleance together twice for the briefest of moments; their conversation is restricted to the most ordinary exchanges about the time – 'How goes the night, boy' (II.i.1) – and the weather – 'It will be rain to-night' (III.iii.15). But the very ordinariness of these snatches carries its own special pathos. Though the companionship of father and son, just glimpsed here, is glimpsed only to be violently destroyed, the continuity which it images will remain.

It is this continuity, time itself and what it unfolds, which increasingly become Macbeth's enemy. Macbeth is remarkably without hatred, without animus against those he kills. Although he fears Banquo's 'royalty of nature', as the 'daily beauty' in Cassio's life makes Iago ugly, he has little of Iago's burning malevolence against the goodness he destroys. Murder is for him a dreaded necessity which becomes a hated chore:

> I am in blood
> Stepp'd in so far that, should I wade no more,
> Returning were as tedious as go o'er.
> III.iv.136–8

What he seeks with increasing desperation is pure present unhaunted by past or future. The craving for instantaneity, the addiction to certainty, can be traced back to the first leap towards the fixed point of the prophesied kingship. Thereafter everything fixed in prospect becomes unstable when reached, mirage succeeds mirage in the unreeling sequence of time. The ever more ruthless pursuit and execution of power is transformed into the impotence of nightmare in which even dead men won't stay dead:

> The time has been
> That when the brains were out the man would die,
> And there an end; but now they rise again,
> With twenty mortal murders on their crowns,
> And push us from our stools.
>
> III.iv.78–82

Macbeth's only recourse is to ride himself still harder, to try to regain something like the immediacy of the battlefield:

> From this moment
> The very firstlings of my heart shall be
> The firstlings of my hand.
>
> IV.i.146–8

The ghastly tragedy of Macbeth's battle with time is to watch his convulsive efforts to grasp and control a pattern which will always elude him. He killed Duncan to gain the crown, and killed Banquo to consolidate his hold on it for himself and his successors. In both cases sons and heirs of his victims escaped to represent the threat of a future displacement. When his next feared antagonist is reported as fled beyond his reach, there is a irrational rationale in his decision to destroy the whole house of Macduff:

> The castle of Macduff I will surprise,
> Seize upon Fife, give to the edge o' th' sword
> His wife, his babes, and all unfortunate souls
> That trace him in his line.
>
> IV.i.150–3

This is no vengeful act of reprisal, but like Herod's Massacre of the Innocents, an attempt to forestall the menace of the future. Macbeth's aim is not just to murder but literally to extirpate his enemies. It is an aim fated to be frustrated each time. As successors to Duncan and Banquo survive, successors such as he, Macbeth, does not have, so in the appalling annihilation of Macduff's family he creates the fit instrument of vengeance against himself, a man like himself without human ties in the world.

The painful scene of the murder of Macduff's family brings home to us the defencelessness of the normal and the natural. The smart-alec sanity of the precocious young Macduff, as he vigorously pursues the interrogation of his distracted mother, gives a robust actuality to his life which makes its violent ending all the more shocking. Lady Macduff's distressed complaint against her husband is deeply moving:

> He loves us not;
> He wants the natural touch; for the poor wren,
> The most diminutive of birds, will fight,
> Her young ones in the nest, against the owl.
>
> IV.ii.8–11

In answer to this, Ross's attempted reassurance that Macduff is 'noble, wise, judicious, and best knows the fits o' th' season' can only sound patronising and banal.

Macduff does not, in fact, lack the 'natural touch', as we see in his devastated reaction to the news of the deaths in the next scene, particularly in the quiet dignity with which he rebuffs Malcolm's conventional 'Dispute it like a man':

> I shall do so;
> But I must also feel it as a man.
> I cannot but remember such things were
> That were most precious to me.
>
> IV.iii.220–3

He goes on to take upon himself the burden of guilt.

> Did heaven look on,
> And would not take their part? Sinful Macduff,
> They were all struck for thee – nought that I am;
> Not for their own demerits, but for mine,
> Fell slaughter on their souls.
>
> IV.ii.223–7

He is not here accusing himself of failing to defend his wife and children, but is adopting the orthodox Christian attitude which reached beyond any local cause and effect and saw catastrophe as a

Providential visitation of original sin. By such irrationalist reasoning Macduff is guilty and, though innocent, Lady Macduff must suffer:

> I have done no harm. But I remember now
> I am in this earthly world, where to do harm
> Is often laudable, to do good sometime
> Accounted dangerous folly.
>
> IV.ii.73–6

The simple natural analogy of the wren that fights in defence of her young against the owl will not hold. The world of man is radically non-natural, a non-naturalness which can only be construed as the shaping of some supernatural force beyond.

From the extended conversation between Malcolm and Macduff in IV.iii, emerge the future king and hero. In this scene Shakespeare appears to have followed Holinshed with puzzlingly uninspired fidelity in dramatising Malcolm's dissimulation. It does have its point, though, apart from its theatrical function of giving Macbeth a much-needed fourth act break from the stage. Malcolm dons the mask of a more-than-Macbeth-like tyrant, something Macduff does not believe possible:

> Not in the legions
> Of horrid hell can come a devil more damn'd
> In evils to top Macbeth.
>
> IV.iii.55–7

In accusing himself of sin after sin, Malcolm succeeds in driving Macduff to indignant despair. The whole exercise is a test of loyalty – loyalty not only to the rightful king but to the principle of right he is bound to embody, the attitude exemplified by Kent in *King Lear*. This test Macduff passes in refusing to support Malcolm, however just his claim to the throne, when convinced that the Prince is not 'fit to govern! No, not to live!' (IV.iii.102–3). At this point Malcolm can 'unspeak [his] own detraction' and hail Macduff as true champion of his true cause.

One of the functions of this scene is to reaffirm the ideal of kingship associated with Duncan, though Malcolm's canny caution may appear very different from his father's trustfulness. The

emphasis here, as in the opening of the play, is on the holiness of
the King: 'Thy royal father', exclaims the scandalised Macduff to
the supposedly vice-ridden Malcolm

> Was a most sainted king; the queen that bore thee,
> Oft'ner upon her knees than on her feet,
> Died every day she liv'd.
>
> IV.iii.109–11

Even as he disclaims the possession of any of them, Malcolm gives
a remarkable catalogue of the 'king-becoming graces':

> As justice, verity, temp'rance, stableness,
> Bounty, perseverance, mercy, lowliness,
> Devotion, patience, courage, fortitude
>
> IV.iii.91–4

This was developed from Holinshed, where Malcolm enlarging on
falsehood – the third of the vices of which he stands self-indicted
and the one Shakespeare decided to omit – comments: 'there is
nothing that more becommeth a prince than constancie, veritie,
truth, and justice' (Bullough, VII, 503). The virtues that are added
in the expanded version of this represent a complete Christian
ideal, but hardly the qualities specifically required in a king.
Luther, no less than Machiavelli, took a more robustly worldly
view: 'to be qualified to rule, it is not enough to be pious. A jackass
is also pious. Ability and experience are required in order to rule.'[10]
Such was the burden of Shakespeare's own dramatisation of the
reign of Henry VI. Here in *Macbeth* it is otherwise. True kingship is
surrounded by a sacred purity remote from considerations of
strength and political skills.

   This vision is reinforced by the incident of Edward the Confessor
and his touching for the King's Evil. It seems most unlikely, as was
sometimes suggested, that this episode was included as a tribute to
Shakespeare's own monarch, as James had originally been reluctant to continue a practice he regarded as superstitious.[11] Rather,
the England ruled over by Edward where 'sundry blessings hang
about his throne That speak him full of grace' (IV.iii.158–9) is
designedly contrasted with Macbeth's Scotland. Where Edward
makes whole his 'strangely-visited people', Macbeth is the plague

that besets his country. There, according to Ross, in a speech that almost immediately succeeds Malcolm's description of Edward's healing powers,

> good men's lives
> Expire before the flowers in their caps,
> Dying or ere they sicken.
> IV.iii.171–3

It is in such a context that Malcolm's declared innocence, as naturalistically implausible as his self-slanders, is significant:

> I am yet
> Unknown to woman, never was forsworn,
> Scarcely have coveted what was mine own,
> At no time broke my faith, would not betray
> The devil to his fellow, and delight in truth
> No less than life.
> IV.iii.125–30

Malcolm here ceremonially announces himself as the antitype of the monster of depravity he had previously feigned. However hard to swallow this may be as a humanly credible speech, its effect is to constitute Malcolm the virgin boy-king who, with the hero Macduff, unborn of woman, will be the saviours of Scotland.

The scene between Malcolm and Macduff brings the beginning of a movement of recuperation, analogous to the fourth-act remobilising of the forces of goodness in *King Lear*. Following the nadir, for both Macbeth and Scotland, represented by the visit to the Witches and the subsequent murder of Macduff's family, this upward movement is experienced as both a natural and non-natural reaction to the unnaturalness of Macbeth's tyrannous reign. The extremity of Macbeth's need for his fix of future knowledge from the Witches is measured in his willingness to destroy nature itself:

> though the treasure
> Of nature's germens tumble all together,
> Even till destruction sicken – answer me

To what I ask you.

IV.i.58–61

It is appropriate, therefore, that it should be the natural world itself which takes revenge upon him, figured particularly in the forest moving in on the castle. When the Third Apparition makes the prophecy, it appears to Macbeth a natural impossibility:

> Macbeth shall never vanquish'd be until
> Great Birnam wood to high Dunsinane Hill
> Shall come against him.
> MACBETH: That will never be.
> Who can impress the forest, bid the tree
> Unfix his earth-bound root?

IV.i.92–6

For the speaker this is an unanswerable rhetorical question, assuring him that 'our high-plac'd Macbeth Shall live the lease of nature, pay his breath To time and mortal custom' (IV.i.98–100). To an audience, rather, it is an indication of Macbeth's deluded short-sightedness: there *are* powers beyond nature which may impress a forest, if need be.

The apparitions, what they say and the forms they take, are all, as might be expected of omens, riddling, ambiguous, contradictory. The armed head may be a sign of victory or defeat, the severed head of Macduff or, as it turns out, of Macbeth. The bloody child spurs Macbeth on to the ruthlessness of killing children like itself, yet it also carries as hidden meaning the violently delivered avenger ripped from his mother's womb. In the Third Apparition, however, 'a Child Crowned, with a tree in his hand' is expressed the fullest play of apparently opposite meanings. The child crowned, like the new-born babe Pity 'striding the blast', is the paradoxical conjunction of the strong and the weak.[12] In terms of orthodox political thought, a child monarch was a disaster, creating a power vacuum at the top. In the strange territory of *Macbeth* the accession of the boy-king Malcolm is to represent a triumph. The anomalous disproportion of the child that can hold a tree in his hand, with a condensation similar to that in heraldry, figures the ideas that cluster around the future in the play: the heirs that have escaped from Macbeth; the literal trees of Birnam wood that will come against him; the genealogical tree of the house of Stuart descending from Banquo, which may have been one of Shakespeare's visual sources.[13]

The fulfilment of the prophecies shapes our apprehension of Act V, as we see them happen both as a series of natural events brought about by comprehensible contingencies and as the magical conditions necessary for Macbeth's defeat. The rhythm of the action moves us between interiors and exteriors, the embattled inside of the castle and the encroaching forces without. The names of Birnam and Dunsinane come together again and again. In the army of Malcolm it is a purely casual collocation: Angus remarks that the Scots contingent will meet the English power 'near Birnam wood', Caithness reports on Macbeth: 'Great Dunsinane he strongly fortifies' (V.ii.5, 12). For an audience, though, the names generate an excitement increased by Macbeth's repetition of his charm in the next scene: 'Till Birnam wood remove to Dunsinane I cannot taint with fear' (V.iii.2–3). Malcolm and his men are innocent of what they do when at last they come to act it out. The English Siward asks 'What wood is this before us' and is told 'the wood of Birnam'. The cutting down of branches, on Malcolm's order, is a camouflage exercise to 'shadow the numbers of our host' (V.iv.5–6). Their destination is only registered as the strong point to be besieged:

> the confident tyrant
> Keeps still in Dunsinane, and will endure
> Our setting down before't.
> V.iv.8–10

But the apparently miraculous movement of the wood will drive Macbeth out of his castle to fight in open battle and be defeated.

The double vision both from within and from without, the action seen as both normal causal sequence and mysteriously determined pattern, are integral to the dramatic experience of the play's ending. We are locked inside the castle and the alienated consciousness of the Macbeths, even as we share the more ordinary vantage-point of those outside. In the murder-scenes this simultaneity was rendered in the schizoid state of Macbeth himself. As John Bayley puts it, 'Macbeth is both the consciousness of the onlooker . . . and the protagonist of an action who finds he has done something no onlooker could ever do'.[14] During the sleep-walking of Lady Macbeth the conjunction of complicity and unimplicated observation is figured in the whispered exchange between the watching Doctor and Gentlewoman:

> DOCTOR: Go to, go to; you have known what you should not.
> GENTLEWOMAN: She has spoke what she should not, I am sure of that. Heaven knows what she has known.
>
> V.i.44–7

In the sleep-walking scene, consciousness is not shared between audience and suffering mind, as it is in the intimacy of Macbeth's soliloquies. Lady Macbeth, in her somnambulistic trance, is outside the reach of consciousness, and the audience is situated rather with the gradually comprehending bystanders. But the troubled fragments of language that break from her force us to live over again the complete haunting sequence of the action: the blood-guiltiness of Duncan's murder – 'who would have thought the old man to have had so much blood in him?'; the ghost of Banquo – 'I tell you yet again, Banquo's buried; he cannot come out on's grave'; and, most disturbingly of all, the murder of Lady Macduff surfacing in the infantile sing-song of 'The Thane of Fife had a wife; where is she now?'

We may be alienated from Lady Macbeth's alienated state of mind, though what haunts her haunts us too. We remain fully involved to the end with Macbeth's damned awareness, drawn in by his capacity to imagine vividly that which he destroys and of which he feels himself deprived. This is most tellingly rendered in the first of his two great reveries of Act V where he lapses out from the restless and desperate overactivity of arming:

> My way of life
> Is fall'n into the sear, the yellow leaf;
> And that which should accompany old age,
> As honour, love, obedience, troops of friends,
> I must not look to have; but, in their stead,
> Curses not loud but deep, mouth-honour, breath,
> Which the poor heart would fain deny, and dare not.
>
> V.iii.22–8

The old age which he cannot have is the old age of Duncan, his opposite as king; his 'sear' and 'yellow leaf' are not the natural autumn which they so beautifully evoke, but another withering altogether. The totally different rhythm of time which is left to him instead is expressed in the second meditation which stands as complement to the first – 'To-morrow, and to-morrow, and to-morrow'. The flat and meaningless seriality acts as the retributive negation of the climbing pattern of time marked out by the three salutes of the Witches. But it also represents the desolate alternative to the richness of a human life and its seasons from which Macbeth is self-exiled.

'Hail, King! for so thou art.' Thus Macduff salutes Malcolm with the prize of 'Th' usurper's cursed head': 'The time is free' (V.viii.54–5). It is a moment of unalloyed triumph for the victorious army, but is not experienced as such dramatically. We cannot simply join in Malcolm's dismissive condemnation of the 'dead butcher, and his fiend-like queen' not because they do not, morally, deserve to be so described. It is rather that for so much of the play we have shared the interiority of their consciousness there is a shock in this final switch to a purely external view. There is, moreover, a broader sense that the action represents something more than a mere melodrama of evil punished and goodness reinstated. Richard Marienstras relates this to the pattern of the 'tyrant sacrificed'. 'Even as Macbeth sets himself up as tyrant, he is also setting himself up as the expiatory victim of the society he is crushing.'[15] Such a view helps to illuminate a necessary relationship in the play between Macbeth's murderous evil and the goodness to which it must ultimately give way. He is cognate to Richard III as the figure whose destruction can finally exorcise the terrible destructiveness of the society concentrated in him. But Macbeth has none of Richard's derisive contempt for the spiritual order he inverts. He takes evil within himself with a full sense of its horror, so that he is felt to suffer as well as cause the chaos that falls on Scotland.

The rhythm of redemption in *Macbeth* involves a matching of like with like, of violence with counter-violence.[16] The heroic Macbeth of I.ii is replaced by Macduff, the severed head of the rebel Macdonwald by that of the usurping king. The natural order of peace and prosperity, centered on a passive, sacred authority figure, is always vulnerable to the disequilibrium of the violent energies to which it is linked and on which it depends. There is no reassuring self-righting capacity within the natural organism of the society as such. Rather the return of normality is a movement as mysterious, in its way as terrible, as the visitation of evil it replaces. It is by means of the Caesarian Macduff, from 'his mother's womb untimely ripp'd', that the rightful king Malcolm conquers. The awe which the play generates comes from the apprehension of a world in which Macbeth is the carrier of an inescapable evil bound to run its course, before the answering magic of its opposite can be set in motion.

There are hints in the accession of Malcolm of a new dispensation, a different epoch, particularly in the decree of new English titles for the nobility:

> My Thanes and kinsmen,
> Henceforth be Earls, the first that ever Scotland
> In such an honour nam'd.
> V.viii.62–4

If the play was to any extent written to suit royal tastes, this detail, drawn from Holinshed, may have been included to suggest the coming together of the kingdoms of England and Scotland which James was so eager to promote. The transformation of native chieftainships into English titles in the sixteenth century in Ireland had been part of a policy of colonial assimilation. The metamorphosis of thanes into earls might have been seen, from a Jacobean imperial viewpoint, as the inaugural moment of an Anglicised civilisation to come. However, the play as a whole does not sustain the vision of any sort of historical progress from some prior dark age towards a new enlightenment. Although theatrical producers have often set the action in an obviously barbaric medieval Scotland, little in the text supports such a setting. At one point, in fact, Macbeth looks back to a period long before an implied present of settled society:

> Blood hath been shed ere now, i' th' olden time,
> Ere humane statute purg'd the gentle weal
> III.iv.75–6

Macbeth is without *King Lear*'s sense of the primitive or originary. The court of Duncan is ceremonious, ritually hierarchical, and it is a simulacrum of such an order which the Macbeths try to maintain in the banquet-scene, however spectacularly they fail. For all its prophetic vision of the dynasty of future Scottish kings, the play's action seems to exist outside history and the specifically historical sense of the onward movement of time. The encounter within it of order and disorder, of good and evil, natural and unnatural, is enacted instead within a mythic space and time which makes it always available, always repeatable, as tragic rhythm.

To move from *Macbeth* to *Antony and Cleopatra* or *Coriolanus* seems a shift into a different imaginative mode. The two later Roman tragedies are in history and about history, their protagonists viewed with a constant awareness of their determined place within particular historical epochs. The realm of the supernatural is almost completely absent, the sense of forces within the world beyond men's making and control which so predominates in Macbeth. The earlier Republican Rome of Coriolanus, the pre-Imperial Rome of Octavius, the Egypt of Cleopatra, are visibly human cultures shaping the identities of the characters that inhabit them. Nonetheless, the two Roman plays, so radically unlike *Macbeth* in mood and atmosphere, in imaginative milieu, are clearly concerned with similar themes and figures. All three focus on soldier heroes whose manly image is at least partly the creation of dominant women. All three explore the role of such heroes within the body politic, the relation between power and authority. The object of the following two chapters will be to look at the effect of these thematic configurations in the sceptically observed world of *Antony and Cleopatra* and *Coriolanus* as against that of the mythical, Manichaean *Macbeth*.

9

Antony and Cleopatra

Antony and Cleopatra is a play in two minds, as no other of the tragedies is, least of all *Macbeth*, written immediately before it, quite possibly in the same year 1606.[1] 'In *Macbeth* we are never in any doubt of our moral bearings. *Antony and Cleopatra*, on the other hand, embodies different and apparently irreconcilable evaluations of the central experience.'[2] It is a striking change from the spiritually polarised world of one play to the problematic moral relativism of the other: 'as we pass from *Macbeth* to *Antony and Cleopatra* we see the problem of evil suddenly lose urgency for Shakespeare'.[3] Yet this alteration need not be seen as unique, a single 'sudden' loss of urgency of the issue of good and evil, a stage beyond the tragic concerns of *Macbeth* and *King Lear*, *Othello* and *Hamlet*.

The disappearance of metaphysical absolutes from *Macbeth* to *Antony and Cleopatra* is only the final instance of the recurrent pattern of alternation between one imaginative milieu and its complementary other through the tragedies, the pattern this book has been designed to explore. The self-consciously determined Roman ethos of *Julius Caesar* is comparably distinct from the haunted universe of *Hamlet*; the ironising perspectives of *Troilus and Cressida* are equally contrasted with *Othello*'s vision of love and its damning denial. *Timon*, like *Antony and Cleopatra* derived from Plutarch, is without the order of transcendent values which is the shaping need of the characters of *King Lear*. Thus the difference of mode between *Antony and Cleopatra* and *Macbeth* is not anomalous and problematic, but representative of the dialectic doubleness of Shakespeare's tragic imagination.

In *Othello*, Shakespeare risked opening the play with a maliciously distorted vision of its hero from his most prejudiced enemy. Iago's bias, however, soon became apparent as bias. By contrast, in the opening lines of *Antony and Cleopatra*, Philo's negative view of

Antony is positively reinforced by his almost immediate entrance. For once in Shakespeare there appears to be a specified parallel between verbal and visual image. Philo has been conjuring up for Demetrius a picture of the deplorable metamorphosis of their general –

> His captain's heart,
> Which in the scuffles of great fights hath burst
> The buckles on his breast, reneges all temper,
> And is become the bellows and the fan
> To cool a gipsy's lust

– when on cue 'Flourish. Enter Antony, Cleopatra, her Ladies, the Train, with Eunuchs fanning her' (I.i.6–10). 'Look where they come!', exclaims Philo, at the spectacle so perfectly confirming his judgement. Leaving aside the question of how Shakespeare's eunuchs would have been recognisable as eunuchs in the theatre, the effect of the stage direction is deliberately to associate Antony, the metaphoric 'fan to cool a gipsy's lust', and the castrated attendants who appear literally fanning the queen.[4] Here visibly before us, as Philo suggests, is the great warrior emasculated, unmanned by his 'dotage'.

The scene that follows does indeed reveal an Antony completely in thrall to Cleopatra. One of her strategies in the display of her dominance is to taunt him with a lack of manliness. She urges him with elaborate sarcasm to give due deference to the messengers from Rome:

> Nay, hear them, Antony.
> Fulvia perchance is angry; or who knows
> If the scarce-bearded Caesar have not sent
> His pow'rful mandate to you: 'Do this or this;
> Take in that kingdom and enfranchise that;
> Perform't, or else we damn thee'.
>
> I.i.19–24

Antony is guyed as the hen-pecked husband of Fulvia, the terrified subordinate of the boy Caesar, the two constantly interlinked:

> You must not stay here longer; your dismission
> Is come from Caesar; therefore hear it, Antony.

Where's Fulvia's process? Caesar's I would say? Both?
Call in the messengers. As I am Egypt's Queen,
Thou blushest, Antony, and that blood of thine
Is Caesar's homager. Else so thy cheek pays shame
When shrill-tongu'd Fulvia scolds.

                                             I.i.26–32

Different as the tone may be, the attitude adopted by Cleopatra
here is akin to Lady Macbeth's in the crucial scene where she
persuades Macbeth back towards murder. Both women use the
spectre of unmanliness to goad their partners into being the men
they want them to be. Lady Macbeth threatens her husband that
he will 'live a coward in [his] own esteem' and in hers. Cleopatra
challenges Antony to prove that he is not the hey-you of Octavius,
the uxorious spouse of the scold Fulvia. In both scenes what we
actually see is the man dominated by the woman for whom the
image of manhood is only an instrument of domination.

The idea of sexual roles reversed recurs frequently in *Antony and
Cleopatra* and often with a heavy load of disapproval. With pursed
lips Octavius complains to Lepidus of Antony's carry-on in
Alexandria:

                    he fishes, drinks, and wastes
     The lamps of night in revel; is not more manlike
     Than Cleopatra, nor the queen of Ptolemy
     More womanly than he

                                             I.iv.4–7

From the Egyptian side, what is perceptibly the same behaviour is
the stuff of Cleopatra's reminiscences:

                    That time? O times!
     I laugh'd him out of patience; and that night
     I laugh'd him into patience; and next morn,
     Ere the ninth hour, I drunk him to his bed,
     Then put my tires and mantles on him, whilst
     I wore his sword Philippian.

                                             II.v.18–23

The image of role-swapping has been related to the story of Hercules
enslaved to Omphale, which Plutarch uses as an exemplum of

Antony's weakness: 'as we see in painted tables, where Omphale secretlie stealeth away Hercules clubbe, and tooke his Lyons skinne from him. Even so Cleopatra oftentimes unarmed Antonius' (Bullough, V, 319).[5] The violent indecorum of the comatose Antony pranked up in the robes of Cleopatra, the Queen wearing the weapon of the hero of Philippi, reinforces the idea of manhood travestied and womanised.

A Jacobean audience might well have shared Roman censoriousness of the transsexual antics of Antony and Cleopatra. Yet the play lacks the full sense of transgression attached to the overstepping of sexual roles in *Macbeth*. Lady Macbeth appeals to the forces of darkness to be unsexed – not to become manlike, but to become inhuman. When Macbeth dares do more than may become a man, he is none. Antony and Cleopatra, on the other hand, are never more human than when they give themselves up entirely to their pleasures and one another. They behave outrageously, disgracefully, indecorously. They offend against all sorts of principles and ideals: of manliness and womanliness, of responsibility and duty, of honesty and truth. But none of these offences provoke the judgement that they are wicked or sinful. The delinquencies of Antony and Cleopatra are without that perverse will to evil of the Macbeths.

Philo's opening vision of Antony, the warrior besotted by an unworthy love, 'the triple pillar of the world transform'd into a strumpet's fool', is confirmed by much that we see from the first appearance of the protagonists on. But it is also challenged from the beginning by an alternative vision, voiced in Antony's lyrical speech:

> Let Rome in Tiber melt, and the wide arch
> Of the rang'd empire fall! Here is my space.
> Kingdoms are clay; our dungy earth alike
> Feeds beast as man. The nobleness of life
> Is to do thus [*embracing*], when such a mutual pair
> And such a twain can do't, in which I bind,
> On pain of punishment, the world to weet
> We stand up peerless.
>
> I.i.33–40

The strategy here is to take on and turn inside out the conventional values by which love is judged and found wanting. 'What is a man', asked Hamlet, 'If his chief good and market of his time Be but to sleep and feed? A beast, no more!' Hamlet's was the orthodox view: man's 'godlike reason' differentiated him from the animals. Sexuality was normally thought of as one of the appetitive forces which, in overruling reason, reduced man to the bestial. Antony inverts this, proclaiming that it is in the lovers' embrace that humans transcend the dependency on 'dungy earth' which they share with their fellow animals. 'The nobleness of life is to do thus' – the phrase is a flamboyant gesture against all that nobility means to Philo and his like, manly resolution, self-discipline, self-sacrifice. Antony glorifies the erotic in the language of a heroism antithetical to it.

The provocative paradoxes here are those of Donne in 'The Sun Rising'. Antony, like Donne's lover, posits an erotocentric world, grandly dismissive of the mere realities of empire or solar system. 'She'is all states, and all princes, I. Nothing else is.' 'Here is my space. Kingdoms are clay.' But the lyric poem, unlike the drama, is inhabited only by the voice and viewpoint of the lover. When he sends the sun contemptuously about his workaday business – 'Go tell court-huntsmen, that the King will ride'[6] – there are no court huntsmen or kings there to remind us of their importance. If the poem's rhetoric implies a consciousness of its own outrageous-ness, it nonetheless invites us to share without reservation in the bravado of love. Antony's hyperboles, on the other hand, are declaimed to a public audience some of whom will be visibly scandalised. 'Let Rome in Tiber melt' is a poetic figure markedly altered by the presence of such very solid and unmelting represen-tatives of Rome as Philo and Demetrius. In other words, Antony must make good the solipsism of his love-poetry within the con-trarieties of an observed dramatic scene. There is no easy assenting to 'the nobleness of life is to do thus'. Rather the play puts before us as an open question the issue of what constitutes the nobleness of life, suspending absolute criteria of judgement by which that question might be decided.

The lack of assured moral standards in viewing the central charac-ters is compounded by the play's lack of political principles. *Antony and Cleopatra* is centrally concerned with power, no less a question than the control of the whole of the known world. The word

'world' sounds and resounds throughout, aggrandising the triumvirs, amplifying the sense of all that is at stake in the struggle
between Antony and Octavius. Given the scale of this power
struggle, there is a remarkable absence in the play of anything
which could be called a body politic. Paul Cantor has commented
that the 'world of *Antony and Cleopatra* is essentially cityless'.[7] It is
also almost peopleless. Though the stage is filled with the leaders,
their soldiers, henchmen and attendants, there is never the impression of a society dependent for its welfare on the actions of its
rulers. Certainly the triumvirs never show the slightest awareness
of the public responsibilities of their office. Their aims 'are as
personal as if they were captains of banditti'.[8]

Because *Antony and Cleopatra* is without an idea of political
legitimacy, its metaphors for the rulers are seen to be that only –
metaphors more or less apt. The image of Antony as 'triple pillar of
the world' is potent only insofar as it measures the scale of loss in
his transformation into strumpet's fool. The irony in Pompey's
tone bites as he acclaims the triumvirs as 'the senators alone of this
great world, Chief factors for the gods' (II.vi.9–10); three men by
themselves make up a whole senate, become business managers
for the deities. Poor Lepidus, never more than a shaky pillar at
best, is downed by the drink on Pompey's galley and carried off, a
pathetic 'third part of the world' (II.vii.89). With Lepidus deposed,
it is Enobarbus who provides the grimly vivid image for the
situation remaining:

> Then, world, thou hast a pair of chaps – no more;
> And throw between them all the food thou hast,
> They'll grind the one the other.
>
> III.v.13–15

Kingdoms, countries, peoples are only grist to the predatory jaws
of Antony and Octavius.

We are remote here from the monarch-centred community of
Macbeth where the body of the king is the sacred body of the state,
the 'Lord's anointed temple' sacrilegiously broken open by murder. Lady Macbeth wondered, in the haunted bewilderment of her
sleep-walking state, 'who would have thought the old man to have
had so much blood in him?' Blood, the principle of life in the
doctrine of the humours, dried up as a man grew old; so, for
instance, the aged Menenius is threatened by the sentry in the

hostile Volscian camp: 'go, lest I let forth your half pint of blood' (*Coriolanus*, V.ii.53–4). But Duncan is more than just an old man, an almost used up life: he bleeds for all Scotland. No figure of authority in *Antony and Cleopatra* can be vested with this sort of significance born of the symbolic identity of king and country. Indeed authority in its fullest sense hardly exists in the play, as power is unsupported by any sanctioning system relating ruler to ruled.

The political atmosphere of *Antony and Cleopatra*, concerned with the period of the triumvirate preceding the establishment of the Empire, was perhaps bound to be very different from that of the medieval Scotland of *Macbeth*, but it is noticeably distinct from its Plutarchan predecessor *Julius Caesar* also. Though often treated as a sequel, *Antony and Cleopatra* is imaginatively discontinuous to *Julius Caesar*, not only in the characterisation of (Mark) Antony but in the changed political ethos. Around the figure of Sextus Pompey, as M.W. MacCallum so acutely remarked, there is 'a certain afterglow of free republican sentiment'.[9] It is Pompey who is given the only detailed recollection of the events of the earlier play:

> What was't
> That mov'd pale Cassius to conspire? and what
> Made the all-honour'd honest Roman, Brutus,
> With the arm'd rest, courtiers of beauteous freedom,
> To drench the Capitol, but that they would
> Have one man but a man?
>
> II.vi.14–19

Pompey's stance here, however, is ironised and undercut by the *realpolitik* which surrounds it, and in which he joins. After the barest show of idealist defiance in this scene, he discloses that he had come to the meeting with the triumvirs prepared in advance to accept their wholly expedient deal. The inconsistent shreds of principle adhering to Pompey are merely impeding weaknesses in a catch-as-catch-can power-game. It is only a queasy conscience which causes him to turn down the pirate Menas's offer of world domination by cutting the triumvirs' throats. Hence the weight of Menas's verdict on him:

> For this,
> I'll never follow thy pall'd fortunes more.

Who seeks, and will not take when once 'tis offer'd,
Will never find it more.

II.vii.80–3

Exit Pompey – we never see him after this scene. Elsewhere in the play, the events dramatised in *Julius Caesar* are never recalled with any of the ideological colouring they had then. Philippi is remembered as a great personal triumph for Antony – hence the significance of his 'sword Philippian' donned by Cleopatra at the height of their drunken play-acting. After his death at Philippi Brutus was celebrated by Mark Antony as 'the noblest Roman of them all'. To this latter-day Antony he is recalled as 'the mad Brutus' whom he boasts he 'ended', along with the 'lean and wrinkled Cassius', while Octavius 'kept his sword e'en like a dancer' (III.xi.35–8). The battle between the libertarian conspirators and the avengers of Caesar is reduced to an occasion of individual heroics, and the issue on which they fought is forgotten.

Shakespeare seems to flatten out deliberately the historical background of *Antony and Cleopatra*, to deny its politics any sort of principled significance. The effect at times appears to be close to the satiric iconoclasm of *Troilus and Cressida*. However, it is often difficult to be sure how puncturing the irony is intended to be, as much of the action is so closely derived from the unironical Plutarch narrative. To take one minor instance, Octavius justifies his deposition of Lepidus from the triumvirate on the grounds that 'he was grown too cruel' and 'his high authority abus'd' (III.vi.32–3). Given Shakespeare's characterisation of Lepidus as the feeblest of peacemakers, it seems tempting to assume that this is intended to be evidence of the grossness of Octavius' hypocrisy. Lepidus too cruel? A likely story! But this, along with much of the rest of the scene, is taken over *literatim* from Plutarch, where there is no particular sense of the improbability of the charge against Lepidus. Octavius has come in for a good deal of critical abuse as the bloodless politician who defeats Antony by his cold-hearted single-mindedness – 'the most repellent Roman of them all'.[10] A subtler judgement is that of John Danby who sees Octavius as the last of Shakespeare's Machiavels, from whom the dramatist has 'refined away all the accidentals . . . the diabolism, the rhetoric, the elaborate hypocrisy, the perverse glamour'.[11] It may be, though, that Octavius is only incidentally so characterised, that his function in the play is to act as the neutral instrument of Antony's defeat, an antithetical foil in his tenacity, his clear purposefulness and his 'Roman' asceticism. If he cannot be taken to represent the positive ideals of Romanness associated with a Brutus, he is not necessarily designed to be condemned for lacking them.

Enobarbus, who was almost entirely Shakespeare's creation from the merest hints in Plutarch, is crucially important in defining the perspective of unillusioned scepticism which the play encourages towards its action. From his very first appearance his key-note is one of sardonic reductivism, as he snorts in reaction to the Soothsayer's fortune-telling, 'Mine, and most of our fortunes, tonight, shall be – drunk to bed' (I.ii.42–3). He has the conventional sharp cynicism of the bluff soldier, and cuts through the delicate diplomacy of the triumvirs' negotiations over a united front against Pompey:

> if you borrow one another's love for the instant, you may, when you hear no more words of Pompey, return it again. You shall have time to wrangle in when you have nothing else to do.
>
> II.ii.106–10

With his sour wit he here plots the course of what is to follow, the temporary patched-up truce between Antony and Octavius, followed by the renewal of the conflict as soon as the threat of Pompey is removed. He is hushed by Antony: 'Thou art a soldier only. Speak no more'; to which he retorts, 'That truth should be silent I had almost forgot' (II.ii.111–12).

This is a line like the Fool's in *King Lear* – 'Truth's a dog must to kennel' – and Enobarbus is, like the Fool, a truth-teller in the play. What sort of truth-teller is he, and what sort of truths does he tell? He has the role of satirical commentator of a Thersites, without Thersites' pathological need for nay-saying. He can be responsive to the glamour of Cleopatra and to the grandeur of Antony, a responsiveness which makes his detached perspective very different from the satiric tones of Thersites. Among the many figures who surround the protagonists with framing commentary, he alone carries choric weight. His loyalty to Antony, his (limited) sympathy with Cleopatra win him credit and credibility with an audience.

For this very reason, the point at which his loyalty and sympathy give out is significant. After the disgrace of Actium and the
increasing outrageousness of Antony's behaviour, Enobarbus
reasonably begins to wonder how long it makes sense to go on
following him.

> Mine honesty and I begin to square.
> The loyalty well held to fools does make
> Our faith mere folly.
>
> III.xiii.41–3

This is forceful worldly wisdom in the rationally observed world of
the play. Returning to Lear's Fool provides a point of contrast. For
when he mock-salutes Kent as fool for 'taking one's part that's out
of favour', it is an ironic praise of folly reinforcing the absolute
value of fidelity, which comes out of hiding in his later song:

> I will tarry; the fool will stay
> And let the wise man fly.
> The knave turns fool that runs away;
> The fool no knave, perdy.
>
> II.iv.80–3

Such a higher order of truth which can invert worldly standards of
folly and wisdom is unavailable to Enobarbus.

There is, all the same, a consideration which holds Enobarbus
back, at least temporarily, from the desertion which reason requires.

> Yet he that can endure
> To follow with allegiance a fall'n lord
> Does conquer him that did his master conquer,
> And earns a place i' th' story.
>
> III.xiii.43–6

This is the best that the world of *Antony and Cleopatra* can offer, 'a
place i' th' story'. All the characters in Shakespeare's classically
derived tragedies inhabit stories which are more or less laid down

for them. They live up to or fall short of reputations which are pre-established. Julius Caesar plays the part of the Olympian Caesar, 'constant as the northern star' until the knives of the conspirators cut him short. Brutus and Cassius enact a bloody drama to be repeated down the ages, though in a spirit they little foresee. Troilus and Cressida swear themselves into the stereotypes they are to become. Even the less well-known Timon lives out the afterlife of his own legend as idealist turned misanthrope. But in *Antony and Cleopatra* there is a special scrutiny of the story of the protagonists and the roles they play in it. History itself hardly gives them their significant meaning. Though the play is built round the contrasting image systems of Rome and Egypt, it is not in any real sense a conflict between the values of East and West. No compelling political necessity drives towards the victory of Octavius which is expected as mere inevitability. Instead the focus is almost entirely on Antony and Cleopatra's capacity to imagine identities for themselves, to create and sustain their parts in the story in the face of the ironies and disbelief which surround them.[12]

A myth of Antony haunts the play which is partly, but only partly, the myth of his past. Philo, in the opening lines, conjures up the superhuman warrior of former battles, 'like plated Mars' himself. The deplorable metamorphosis of that hero into the 'strumpet's fool', Philo yet tries to excuse as a temporary lapse:

> sometimes when he is not Antony,
> He comes too short of that great property
> Which still should go with Antony.
>
> I.i.56–9

Antony, it seems, is something other than the person he happens to be: he is, or ought to be, the 'great property' which belongs to his name. Enobarbus uses the same figure when Lepidus urges him to 'entreat your captain to soft and gentle speech' in the negotiations with Octavius:

> I shall entreat him
> To answer like himself. If Caesar move him
> Let Antony look over Caesar's head
> And speak as loud as Mars.
>
> II.ii.3–6

Once again the ideal Antony is Mars-like, out-topping the puny
Octavius; but once again also, it is an Antony used as Antony's
own super-ego.

This heroic warrior-image casts a huge shadow in the play. Its
reality, though, is called in question by the Antony we actually see
in action, or more often in inaction, who only intermittently if at all
resembles his alleged self. He excuses his Egyptian lethargy to
Octavius as a time 'when poisoned hours had bound me up From
mine own knowledge' (II.ii.94–5); the return visit to Rome represents a vigorous shaking of himself awake. But within stage
minutes of his good resolutions to his newly married wife Octavia
– 'I have not kept my square; but that to come Shall all be done by
th' rule' (II.iii.6–7) – the Roman rule-book is once again abandoned:

> I will to Egypt;
> And though I make this marriage for my peace,
> I' th' East my pleasure lies.
>
> II.iii.39–41

The imperial magnificence of Antony depends largely on his heroic
warriorship. This is ironically called in question not only by his
Egyptian backslidings, but by the damaging little scene of Ventidius in Parthia. Though the substance of this scene is derived from
Plutarch, its very extraneousness to the action draws attention to
it, making the effect more pointed. Ventidius who has triumphed
over the Parthians – something, according to Plutarch, no other
Roman general ever did – refrains from pushing home his victory
for fear of arousing Antony's jealousy. Instead the good lieutenant
will, in his dispatches to Antony,

> humbly signify what in his name,
> That magical name of war, we have effected.
>
> III.i.30–1

'*His* name . . . *we* have effected': the disjunction of pronouns helps
to expose satirically the totemic idea of Antony 'the greatest soldier
of the world'.

In the later parts of the play, there are glimpses of something like
the reported Antony of old. They are, though, only glimpses, and
in being something like actually show their unlikeness. After
Actium, Antony oscillates between a shame-struck, paralysed defeatism, and bursts of blustering rodomontade. In one of the latter

veins, he sends his personal challenge to Octavius to 'answer me declin'd, sword against sword, Ourselves alone' (III.xiii.27–8). Enobarbus' aside underscores the absurdity of the gesture:

> Yes, like enough high-battled Caesar will
> Unstate his happiness, and be stag'd to th' show
> Against a sworder!
>
> III.xiii.29–31

No-one doubts that Antony is the stronger soldier, but the imperial power is not a heavyweight boxing championship. Octavius' contemptuous reply to the challenge strips Antony of all his titles: 'Let the old ruffian know I have many other ways to die' (IV.i.4–5). 'I am Antony yet', he shouts as he calls up what remaining attendants he has to whip the messenger of Octavius. This, though, is no Senecan proclamation of continuing integrity, '*Medea super est*'; it is a hollow attempt to reassure himself as 'authority melts' from him. Antony is granted a kind of warrior's grandeur as he prepares for the last fight in Alexandria, a grandeur we have hardly seen anywhere else in the play. He dignifies himself and the joy of battle he evokes to Cleopatra:

> O love,
> That thou couldst see my wars to-day, and knew'st
> The royal occupation! Thou shouldst see
> A workman in't.
>
> IV.iv.15–18

This last arming, however, and the glory that briefly plays about him as he comes home at the end of the day in triumph, is only a prelude to the final despair:

> Unarm, Eros; the long day's task is done,
> And we must sleep.
>
> IV.xiv.35–6

As far as the heroic Roman warrior Antony is concerned, it might seem that, after a temporary return to energetic resolution in Act II, the action of the play is one long slide down to defeat. Yet the identity of the character is complicated by the partly antithetical, partly overlapping, image of Cleopatra's Antony. For just as Antony challenges the Roman ideal of the 'nobleness of life' in the opening scene, he posits a self not betrayed but sustained by his love. Cleopatra has pretended to disbelieve his absolute assurances of devotion; still, she says

> I'll seem the fool I am not. Antony
> Will be himself.
> ANTONY: But stirr'd by Cleopatra.
>   I.i.42–3

What Antony affirms here is that his true self, which Cleopatra professes to think is dishonest, is only true and only itself as she inspires it. This interdependence of self recurs through the play, as each feels bound to live up to the imagined majesty of the other. 'Since my lord Is Antony again, I will be Cleopatra' (III.xiii.186–7), the Queen declares after the reconciliation following the quarrel over her suspiciously kind reception of Octavius' messenger. Cleopatra has relatively little difficulty being herself, that highly volatile self whose very essence seems to be its shape-shifting. The identity of Antony, on the other hand, which is dependent on Cleopatra for validation, remains unstable; he can never be assuredly himself against the assault of doubt about her truth.

Ernest Schanzer says of Antony that 'instead of being "with himself at war", like Brutus, or Macbeth, or Othello, he is like a chronic deserter, forever changing sides in the struggle, and this emotional pattern mirrors and underlines the structural pattern of the entire play'.[13] Even if Brutus' internal conflict is limited to the period before he decides to murder Caesar, Schanzer's statement helps to illuminate an essential difference between the tragedy of Antony and that of Othello, Macbeth or, he might have added, Lear and Hamlet. In all four tragedies, there is an implosion of identity of the central figure bound up with a profound dislocation of the worlds in which they exist. The madness of Hamlet and of Lear, the frenzied anguish of Othello and Macbeth, originate in a fragmentation of the self which mirrors, precipitates, amplifies out into, the convulsions of their dramatic environment. With Antony, by contrast, there is a constant movement between alternative selves, a fluctuating to and fro of belief and disbelief in the potential identities available. Rome and Egypt are states of mind which he can occupy by turns. Antony's world is not destroyed by his self-division nor he by its; rather both hero and context are the constructs of imagination liable to arbitrary dissolution and reconstruction.

'Dissolution' is a key word. The importance of ideas of melting in the play, the commonness of the vocabulary of liquefaction including unique coinages such as 'discandy', have often been pointed out.[14] The omnipresence of such images makes Antony's meditation on defeat especially significant.

> ANTONY: Eros, thou yet behold'st me?
> EROS: Ay, noble lord.
> ANTONY: Sometimes we see a cloud that's dragonish;
> A vapour sometime like a bear or lion,
> A tower'd citadel, a pendent rock,
> A forked mountain, or blue promontory
> With trees upon't that nod unto the world
> And mock our eyes with air. Thou hast seen these signs;
> They are black vesper's pageants.
> EROS: Ay, my lord.
> ANTONY: That which is now a horse, even with a thought
> The rack dislimns, and makes it indistinct,
> As water is in water.
> EROS: It does, my lord.
> ANTONY: My good knave Eros, now thy captain is
> Even such a body. Here I am Antony;
> Yet cannot hold this visible shape, my knave.
>
>   IV.xiv.1–14

Antony's mood of bewildered self-alienation is figured in the very movement of this passage. Sharing the intimacy of Antony's personal attendant Eros, we can only give tentative gestures of assent to the speech which so slowly reveals its direction. There seems at first a complete disjunction between the opening question 'thou yet behold'st me?' and the extended evocation of the cloud-world that follows. Perhaps, with the suggestiveness of 'signs' and 'black vesper's pageants', it may appear momentarily that it is with omens of coming death that Antony is preoccupied. At last the straying consciousness settles back on the person which, in straying away, it has emptied out of substance. Eros's 'captain', a word of armoured definiteness, has become a thing as 'indistinct, As water is in water'. It is Cleopatra who has left Antony thus dematerialised, the Queen 'whose heart I thought I had, for she had mine'. Her imagined betrayal denies Antony reality and makes of the world itself no more than an illusory cloud-drift.

Contrast the Macbeth of 'To-morrow, and to-morrow, and to-morrow'. In Macbeth's speech, there is a horror, an indignation at life's meaninglessness, absent from Antony's cloudscape. Antony yields himself up to a dissolving world in which his own separate identity is dissolved, whereas for Macbeth individual consciousness continues as the unending finality of despair. 'I gin to be aweary of the sun', says Macbeth, 'And wish th' estate o' th' world were now undone'. For him there is no escaping the 'estate o' th' world': he must arm for his last fight, an empty effigy of the heroic warrior he once was, whose violent death in battle will renew the kingdom. Antony, unarmed, slips protractedly down towards a death dependent for its significance, as his life was, on the imagination of Cleopatra.

'I dreamt there was an Emperor Antony', says Cleopatra after his death. The word 'dream' accepts the imaginative, possibly fictive, element in the conception, while the very grandeur of the phrase 'an Emperor Antony' and the extraordinary cosmic vision of him which follows, defiantly proclaim their own reality. Cleopatra throughout the play is both the source and the object of a hyperbolic imagination which lives always with the actualities it attempts to transcend. The mock catechism of her very first exchanges with Antony sets the pace:

CLEOPATRA: If it be love indeed, tell me how much.
ANTONY: There's beggary in the love that can be reckon'd.
CLEOPATRA: I'll set a bourn how far to be belov'd.
ANTONY: Then must thou needs find out new heaven, new earth.

I.i.14–17

The pretence of establishing limits is only a stimulant to urge love on beyond itself into the infinite. Her constant changes of mood and changes of role, part natural, part tactical, are a means of resisting definition. She takes on and lives out the expected images of herself, but by setting one against another constantly challenges them.

Cleopatra is both queen and whore: Enobarbus' famous tribute to her in the description of her first meeting with Antony at Cydnus is an appreciation of both. The set-piece evocation of the scene – 'The barge she sat on like a burnish'd throne Burn'd on the water' – represents the erotic raised to the power of majesty. At the same time, there is a coarse and reductive voyeurism in the Roman Agrippa's reaction:

> Royal wench!
> She made great Caesar lay his sword to bed.
> He plough'd her, and she cropp'd.
>
> II.ii.230–2

Even Enobarbus' final judgement, often quoted as the supreme accolade to Cleopatra's eternal attractiveness, is also a tribute to the superwhore:

> Age cannot wither her, nor custom stale
> Her infinite variety. Other women cloy
> The appetites they feed, but she makes hungry
> Where most she satisfies; for vilest things
> Become themselves in her, that the holy priests
> Bless her when she is riggish.
>
> II.ii.239–44

Here, and recurrently through the play, Cleopatra's sexuality is imagined in terms of consumption. 'He will to his Egyptian dish again' (II.vi.121) Enobarbus says of Antony when in less lyrical mood. Even more disgustedly reductive is Antony's own repudiation of Cleopatra in the scene with Octavius' messenger:

> I found you as a morsel cold upon
> Dead Caesar's trencher. Nay you were a fragment
> Of Cneius Pompey's, besides what hotter hours,
> Unregist'red in vulgar fame, you have
> Luxuriously pick'd out
>
> III.xiii.116–20

This is close to the mood of *Troilus and Cressida* – Troilus' revulsion at the 'fragments, scraps, the bits, and greasy relics' of Cressida's 'o'er-eaten faith'. The words of Troilus, though, reflect a once-and-for-all disillusionment reducing idealised love to a nauseating physicality. Antony's abusiveness is one end of an emotional spectrum which will take him back to devoted faith within the scene. What is more, Cleopatra can see herself as edible sex-object without any sense of degradation:

> Broad-fronted Caesar,
> When thou wast here above the ground, I was
> A morsel for a monarch; and great Pompey
> Would stand and make his eyes grow in my brow;
> There would he anchor his aspect and die
> With looking on his life.
>
> I.v.29–34

So far from regarding her sexual past with shame, she proclaims with pride the vitality which has survived the great conquerors she has conquered. This list of lovers is headed by the sun-god himself, as she transmutes her age and her complexion into the most daring image of all. 'Think on me', she enjoins the absent Antony,

> That am with Phoebus' amorous pinches black,
> And wrinkled deep in time.
>
> I.v.27–9

The grotesque is outfaced here in an exultant sexuality extended on to a cosmic scale.

Cleopatra can take such risks and bring them off because she is queen as well as whore. If the idea of Antony is amplified by his position as triumvir, 'triple pillar of the world', Cleopatra has an answering magnificence as monarch of Egypt. She can prepare for death as for an enthronement, making her suicide an act 'fitting for a princess Descended of so many royal kings' (V.ii.324–5). Stricken after Antony's death, she sets aside the titles, 'Royal Egypt, Empress!', with which Iras tries to recall her to herself:

> No more but e'en a woman, and commanded
> By such poor passion as the maid that milks
> And does the meanest chares.
>
> IV.xv.73–5

Even when she affirms the ordinariness of her humanity, it is with the grace of magnanimity only possible in the great. She is named as Egypt in the formal synecdoche of king for kingdom: 'I made these wars for Egypt' says Antony; 'I am dying, Egypt, dying'. All that is strange, exotic, luxurious in the imagination of Egypt, as well as what from a Roman viewpoint is sinister and decadent, all this inheres in Cleopatra. She is her country, though not as its mystical centre for good or ill of the monarchical system as conceived in *Hamlet* or *Macbeth*. There is even less sense of Egypt as a body politic than there is of Rome. Rather, there is a constant identification of Cleopatra with things Egyptian, the Nile with its fertilising fluidity, its serpents and its crocodiles, a world of spontaneous generation.

The grandeur of Antony and Cleopatra is central to the play's imaginative expansiveness. The protagonists are not only monarchs, imperial rulers; in their own imagination and that of those around them, they are enlarged to the dimensions of gods or demigods. The exceptionally high number of legendary and mythological allusions in the play has often been noted. Cleopatra is associated with the goddesses Isis and Venus, Antony with Hercules and Mars; the two of them as lovers are analogues of Dido and Aeneas.[15] Yet throughout they remain the images of a purely human imagination straining towards transcendence. When Antony is imagined 'like plated Mars', or Cleopatra 'o'erpicturing that Venus where we see the fancy outwork nature', these are larger than life projections of heroic strength and beauty. The amplitude lent by images of pagan gods and heroes has very little of its potential allegorical significance – War versus Love – and even less of the resonance of the numinous. In *Antony and Cleopatra*, 'the "divine" manifests itself – if at all – only in the forms and processes of nature'.[16]

No gods govern the world of *Antony and Cleopatra*, it is not felt to move by the action of forces beyond itself. In the second scene the tragic fates of the attendants of Cleopatra are laid down in the prophecies of the Soothsayer. He is given a sombre dignity in his modest indication of his limited powers:

> In nature's infinite book of secrecy
> A little I can read.
>   I.ii.9–10

That blank verse dignity, however, is almost overwhelmed by the atmosphere of heedless prose which surrounds it. The solemnity of the seer, shaping a tragic course ahead, is subverted by the frivolous jokes of Charmian and Iras. 'You shall outlive the lady whom you serve', he tells Charmian. 'O, excellent!', she exclaims, 'I love long life better than figs' (I.ii.30–1). The prophecy will be ironically fulfilled in the last scene when Charmian dies minutes after Cleopatra; figs, with their sexual innuendo here, are to become the vehicle for death, which Charmian will finally prefer to a long life outliving her mistress. Iras and Charmian are cast by the Soothsayer for the high tragic parts they will eventually play in attendance on Cleopatra's suicide, even though in this scene they appear the dramatic stuff of comedy, irresponsible, lubricious, silly. The mixed tone brings out in how comic a world the tragedy of Antony and Cleopatra must make its way.

In the second scene where the Soothsayer appears, to warn Antony of the dangers of Octavius to him, though the effect is fully serious, the sense of the supernatural is again limited. Antony asks the Soothsayer 'Whose fortunes shall rise higher, Caesar's or mine?':

> Caesar's.
> Therefore, O Antony, stay not by his side.
> Thy daemon, that thy spirit which keeps thee, is
> Noble, courageous, high, unmatchable,
> Where Caesar's is not; but near him thy angel
> Becomes a fear, as being o'erpow'r'd.
>
> II.iv.17–23

The ascendancy of Octavius over Antony is short of a full fatality; it is a localised operation of luck or fortune. It was this idea from Plutarch which Shakespeare had in mind when he gave Macbeth the lines about Banquo:

> under him
> My Genius is rebuk'd, as it is said
> Mark Antony's was by Caesar.
>
> III.i.54–6

But Banquo's superiority, and Macbeth's awareness of it, involved a true 'royalty of nature' feared by a usurper. No such co-ordinates of good and evil, no such concept of ultimate destiny, define Antony's lucklessness against Octavius.

The victory of Octavius over Antony is inevitable, not only as a known historical fact, the event which finally initiated the principate but, in the influential vision of Virgil's *Aeneid*, the Providential goal to which all Roman history had been working. To this sort of inevitability *Antony and Cleopatra* bears little witness. The defeat of Antony is accomplished by a slow and eddying drift of fortune rather than by any driven forces of necessity. Even such a key event as the decision to fight by sea at Actium, against all advice, is given as an oddly blank and unmotivated resolution on Antony's part. He is not persuaded to it by Cleopatra, though she approves the decision and there is a strong feeling that it represents a commitment to the Egyptian element of water rather than the Roman firmness of land. There remains a pitch-and-toss arbitrariness in the strategic move which is to determine the control of the whole world. The succession of large numbers of very brief scenes which make up Acts III and IV contributes to the impression of a desultory rather than directed movement to the action. No defeat seems quite definitive beyond the possibility of a recovery of fortunes; the erratic ebbing and flowing of Antony and Cleopatra's confidence in themselves overlays any clear pattern of catastrophe.

One scene only grants a visionary dimension to Antony's coming doom. Shakespeare makes of an omen recorded in Plutarch the lovely IV.iii in which the soldiers, posted on sentry duty the night before battle, hear 'music of the hautboys under the stage'.

> 2 SOLDIER: Peace, what noise?
> 3 SOLDIER: List, list!
> 2 SOLDIER: Hark!
> 3 SOLDIER: Music i' th' air.
> 4 SOLDIER: Under the earth.
> 5 SOLDIER: It signs well, does it not?
> 4 SOLDIER: No.
> 3 SOLDIER: Peace, I say!
> What should this mean?
> 2 SOLDIER: 'Tis the god Hercules, whom Antony lov'd,
> Now leaves him.
>   IV.iii.12–17

It is moment of mystery unparalleled elsewhere in the play, a

mystery enhanced by the bewildered awe the music provokes in
the sentries, and the strange certainty with which the Second
Soldier stills their speculation as to its meaning. It is, however, a
curiously unominous omen, in its beauty closer to the spirit of the
bewitching unearthly music of *The Tempest* than to the signs which
presage the death of Julius Caesar, much less those before the
assassination of Duncan. It is noticeable that it does not provoke
panic or desertion among the soldiers. In fact, such is the dislocation of omen from event that what follows immediately after is not
the defeat of Antony but his last unexpected victory.

When Antony is finally defeated and his death announced to
Octavius, it is experienced as anticlimax in its very lack of the signs
which should have attended it:

> The breaking of so great a thing should make
> A greater crack. The round world
> Should have shook lions into civil streets,
> And citizens to their dens. The death of Antony
> Is not a single doom: in the name lay
> A moiety of the world.
>
> V.i.14–19

In *Antony and Cleopatra* the age of miracles is past; no lion appears
on the city streets as it did the night before the Ides of March.
Though in his name 'lay a moiety of the world', Antony's death
brings none of that universal cataclysm entailed by a monarch's
'cease of majesty'.

Cleopatra nonetheless contrives to make of Antony's death a
moment of transcendent significance:

> O wither'd is the garland of the war,
> The soldier's pole is fall'n! Young boys and girls
> Are level now with men. The odds is gone,
> And there is nothing left remarkable
> Beneath the visiting moon.
>
> IV.xv.64–8

Arnold Stein perceptively remarks that this 'is made of the same
stuff, and partly of the same language, as Macbeth's lament for the
death of Duncan. But that is a different scene, and language

always imagines its reality in a scene.'[17] Macbeth's words, for all
their surface hypocrisy, tell a truth supported by the play's whole
experience: 'renown and grace *is* dead', their source in Duncan
killed by Macbeth. With Cleopatra, rather, we can see 'language
imagining its reality in a scene', a scene which she creates and
dominates.

Cleopatra's re-imagination of Antony's greatness after his death
she acknowledges as fictive. Her marvellous rhapsodic elegy of the
fifth act is conceived in a reverie from which Dolabella tries vainly
(and comically) to recall her to reality.

> His legs bestrid the ocean; his rear'd arm
> Crested the world. His voice was propertied
> As all the tuned spheres, and that to friends;
> But when he meant to quail and shake the orb,
> He was as rattling thunder. For his bounty,
> There was no winter in't; an autumn 'twas
> That grew the more by reaping. His delights
> Were dolphin-like: they show'd his back above
> The elements they liv'd in. In his livery
> Walk'd crowns and crownets; realms and islands were
> As plates dropp'd from his pocket.
>   V.ii.82–92

This bears some resemblance to the Antony of the play: the
Colossus-like image of the 'triple pillar of the world', the 'mine of
bounty' whose magnanimous generosity broke the tough-minded
Enobarbus' heart, the exuberant sensuality of the lover with his
'dolphin-like' delights. Yet clearly no such person ever existed
except as the utmost limit of hyperbole. Dolabella cannot well give
any other reply than he does to Cleopatra's question:

> CLEOPATRA: Think you there was or might be such a man
> As this I dreamt of?
> DOLABELLA: Gentle madam, no.
>   V.ii.93–4

Cleopatra's vehement repudiation of this deferential common
sense is followed by a much more hypothetical argument of con-
ditionals and subjunctives:

> You lie, up to the hearing of the gods.
> But if there be nor ever were one such,
> It's past the size of dreaming. Nature wants stuff
> To vie strange forms with fancy; yet t' imagine
> An Antony were nature's piece 'gainst fancy,
> Condemning shadows quite.
>
> V.ii.95–100

It is almost as if, like Descartes justifying the existence of God in the *Meditations*, Cleopatra is claiming reality for her idea of Antony by virtue of her very capacity to conceive of something so far beyond the scale of anything merely imagined.

It is in such a mood of exaltation that she can go further and imagine an afterlife and a celestial reunion with Antony in it. Antony himself, when he contemplated suicide believing Cleopatra dead, had conjured up an Elysian future for them:

> Where souls do couch on flowers, we'll hand in hand,
> And with our sprightly port make the ghosts gaze.
> Dido and her Aeneas shall want troops,
> And all the haunts be ours.
>
> IV.xiv.51–4

As many commentators have pointed out, this is a strangely distorted view of the classical Elysium, not least in making Dido and Aeneas very unVirgilian reunited lovers. Where all the other inhabitants of the underworld are disembodied ghosts, ethereal souls couching on flowers, Antony and Cleopatra with their 'sprightly port' seem more substantial than mere sprites. It is an equally physical, equally tangible, world beyond death to which Cleopatra looks forward, as she imagines Iras, who dies before her, getting a head start in the race to reunion:

> If she first meet the curled Antony,
> He'll make demand of her, and spend that kiss
> Which is my heaven to have.
>
> V.ii.299–301

The imagination of the protagonists' afterlife is exceptional among the tragedies. On the whole, 'Shakespeare is . . . totally unconcerned with extrapolating the lives of his creatures beyond the stage and into a future estate of blessedness or damnation'.[18] In the case of Antony and Cleopatra the afterlife is so obviously imagined that there is no question of a theological judgement on blessedness or damnation. Janet Adelman usefully contrasts Othello's lines to the dead Desdemona, 'When we shall meet at compt, That look of thine will hurl my soul from heaven'.

> This is no mere poetic assertion of the impossible . . . it is a statement about the highest reality which is terrifying precisely in its literalness. But in *Antony and Cleopatra*, there is no context which demands that we believe in the literal possibility of the afterlife.[19]

What we witness at Cleopatra's suicide is a pure histrionicism which defies disbelief and succeeds in imposing upon an audience a dream of apotheosis.

Antony and Cleopatra, with its lack of absolutes of faith or feeling, seems in some ways a strikingly modern play. A Hollywood-like glamour plays about the protagonists, their grandeur being no less grand for its artificial amplification or the awareness of its rackety meretriciousness. The tragedy does not attack the fraudulence of human pretensions to the heroic as polemically as *Troilus and Cressida*. Instead heroism is dramatised as the collaborative creation of the human imagination, in its potential for authentic greatness, in its vulnerability to doubt, in its measure of inherent factitiousness. It is a completely secular world from which, according to John Danby, Shakespeare has 'deliberately excise[d] the Christian core of his thought'.[20] That is to make the assumption that the core of Shakespeare's thought is Christian, whereas the aim of this book has been to show alternative non-Christian perspectives as integral to his tragic imagination. But *Antony and Cleopatra* does suspend the vision of a transcendent scheme of things which might give significance to the tragic action. The action must work itself out amid the relativising human evaluations of love and glory.

The play, with its close fidelity to Plutarch, is grounded in history. The battle of Actium, the defeat of Antony and Cleopatra, were the crucial events in establishing the principate, the Roman

Empire of the following 400 years. 'The time of universal peace is near', promises Octavius as Antony's defeat is in sight.

> Prove this a prosp'rous day, the three-nook'd world
> Shall bear the olive freely.
>
> IV.vi.5–7

These words would have had an extra dimension of significance for a Christian Renaissance audience because it was during the reign of Augustus that Christ was to be born, initiating the true 'time of universal peace'.[21] Yet this historical dimension to *Antony and Cleopatra* is never given the prominence we might expect. Octavius' words, for example, quoted above, come almost incidentally in a brief transition passage, in a scene where the main dramatic focus is on the unhappy renegade Enobarbus, looking back towards his deserted master Antony. As so often in the play, Octavius is the dramatically inert lay figure who supplies a fabric of historical narrative against which the protagonists are defined. His victory is not registered as an epochal moment in the history of the world, in the establishment of the Roman Empire or the coming inauguration of the Christian era. These are concepts notionally available but not dramatically realised in Shakespeare's play.

The secular historicity of the action of *Antony and Cleopatra* is felt only in relative contrast to the mythic mode of *Macbeth*. The restoration of Malcolm and the beheading of the tyrant Macbeth are experienced within a rhythmic cycle of the perpetual war of good and evil in the world. Octavius wins, Antony and Cleopatra lose, in something much more like mere historical continuum. In such a context, however, the story of the lovers is dramatised, personalised, to the point where it seems no more significantly historical than that of Romeo and Juliet. Antony and Cleopatra are what they make themselves rather than what history made them, or at least they play out with their own wilfulness the parts in which history has cast them. From this autogenesis of the heroic in *Antony and Cleopatra*, Shakespeare was to turn in *Coriolanus* to the figure of the hero in a far more determined world, a determinism of the historical, the political and the psychological.

10
Coriolanus

Most of this book has been concerned with loosely paired pairs of plays: *Julius Caesar* and *Hamlet*, *Troilus and Cressida* and *Othello*, *Timon of Athens* and *King Lear*. With *Coriolanus*, Shakespeare completed something like a triptych, the other two panels being *Macbeth* and *Antony and Cleopatra*. All three focus on soldier heroes and are studies in the relation of personal power to political authority; in all three masculine heroism is partially defined by a female vision of it.[1] *Coriolanus*, though, stands in contrast to both its companion tragedies, and is significantly itself in its difference from both. It belongs with *Antony and Cleopatra* in its lack of the visionary supernatural which so shapes the action of *Macbeth*. The gods are much invoked in *Coriolanus* but never for more than formal rhetorical emphasis; they do not even vivify the language of the play with the sort of high colour and amplifying intensity of the mythic allusions in *Antony and Cleopatra*. Omitting such supernatural omens as he found in Plutarch's *Life of Coriolanus*, Shakespeare created a world of human force against force rather than good against evil. In *Coriolanus*, as in *Antony and Cleopatra*, cause and event in character and action are dramatised with analytic clarity where in *Macbeth* they are experienced in their hiddenness as a source of dread.

At the same time, *Coriolanus* is as different from *Antony and Cleopatra* as it is from *Macbeth*. The Roman play was strangely unpreoccupied with politics. The vast arena of power in which Antony and Cleopatra came to defeat, Octavius to victory, seemed little more than a defining context within which the protagonists imagined themselves and one another. By contrast the story of Coriolanus, an unimportant episode in the early history of the Roman Republic, is made to appear a key paradigm of political process. The imagination of the heroic in *Antony and Cleopatra* played upon the real, evaded it, transmuted it. In *Coriolanus* the concept of the hero, like everything else in the play, is shaped by a reality which is basic, often brutal, and immutable. In the last of Shakespeare's tragedies, we watch a hero made and unmade with

249

a precise and clear-eyed attention to what in his environment make and unmake him. Coriolanus is more nearly a creature of context than any other of the tragic protagonists – more nearly, but not completely. For the dramatisation of heroic identity in *Coriolanus* escapes from that text-book understanding of politics and psychology which it appears so much to illustrate. In the most austere and stringently analytic embodiment of tragic action, without the metaphysics of a *Macbeth* or the imaginative expansiveness of *Antony and Cleopatra*, Shakespeare yet continues to evoke a drama beyond the merely determined.

In *Macbeth* the body politic is metaphor for the state, a body in desperate need of treatment according to Macbeth's grimly playful remarks to the Doctor in Act V:

> If thou couldst, doctor, cast
> The water of my land, find her disease,
> And purge it to a sound and pristine health,
> I would applaud thee to the very echo
>
> V.iii.50–3

For the usurper the disorder he himself has caused is terminal; but we can see the country struggling convulsively to cure itself, with the Anglo-Scottish army appearing as the 'med'cine of the sickly weal'. The body politic of *Coriolanus* is much more literally embodied, in Menenius' shaping fable of the first scene, and in the human bodies which as soldiers or citizens incorporate the community. In *Macbeth* the traditional microcosm–macrocosm equation is fully metaphorical with the mystical life of the state vested in the true king's body. The dominant linguistic mode in *Coriolanus* is metonymy, and all the figures we see, from the First Citizen, that 'great toe', on up, are but constituent members of some larger physical whole.[2] For all the efforts of Coriolanus to imagine the people as animally unRoman –

> I would they were barbarians, as they are,
> Though in Rome litter'd; not Romans, as they are not,
> Though calved i' th' porch o' th' Capitol.
>
> III.i.238–40

– Rome is the aggregation of his body and theirs.

We start with hunger and its urgency. The Midlands Insurrection of 1607 may well have provided a topical background for the
play's emphasis on famine, prompting Shakespeare to stress this
rather than the other grievances of the people cited in his
authorities.[3] In Livy and Plutarch it was the oppressions of taxes
and usury which led to the people's secession from the city, and
required Menenius' fable of the belly and the members to conciliate
them; the corn riots belonged to a later period. Shakespeare's
adaptation makes for a different effect. Where originally the revolt
of the body's members was intended as a very specific analogy for
the people's secession, in the play the allegory of the belly takes on
a new sort of immediacy by meeting directly the literal and basic
need to eat. It is designed by Menenius as a pacifying rhetorical
strategy, a soothing model of paternalism – 'I tell you, friends,
most charitable care Have the patricians of you' (I.i.63–4) – and that
is to some extent the way it operates. The First Citizen, chief
spokesman for the militants, is wrong-footed by Menenius'
shrewd handling. But the fable acts not merely as an expedient to
divert the crowd from their mutinous purposes; it implicitly grants
their claim to be regarded as full members of the body politic and
acknowledges that as such they must be provided for.

Menenius' emollient approach to the citizens is often admiringly
contrasted with the rebarbitiveness of Marcius in the first scene.[4]
However, they share a basic attitude of patrician contempt. Here
too, Shakespeare's rearrangement of his source material produces
a complex dramatic effect which resists easy analysis. In Livy,
Menenius Agrippa was chosen as the Senate's mediator with the
people because he was 'welbeloved among the commons, for that
he was from them descended' (Bullough, V, 497). His mediation
led directly to the institution of the tribunate and at his death, 'this
truchman, this mediator for civile attonement' was so popular that
he was buried at the cost of the commons (Bullough, V, 499). In
Plutarch's account, also, the tribunate is part of the deal between
Senate and people which Menenius negotiates. In neither Livy nor
Plutarch is there any special link between Menenius and Marcius;
in fact Menenius' death is recorded in the year Marcius took
Corioli. Shakespeare evidently decided to build up the character of
Menenius, and to give him an integral dramatic part as honorary
father to Marcius. This may have been the motive for some of the
rearrangement of the narrative in the first scene. To this end

Menenius and Marcius needed to be shown belonging to the same patrician cadre, even if Menenius' tactics with the plebeians might be more diplomatic. The diplomacy in Shakespeare, however, does not actually lead anywhere. It notably does *not* lead to the concession of the tribunate, which is granted offstage to another group of rebellious citizens and announced by the disgusted Marcius. "Sdeath!' he exclaims, 'The rabble should have first unroof'd the city Ere so prevail'd with me' (I.i.215–7).

The result of Shakespeare's recasting of his source material in the first scene is that there is no simple contrast between an admirably conciliatory Menenius producing 'civile attonement', and an aggressive Marcius exacerbating civil strife. There is equally no direct correlation between the ideal of social harmony represented by the fable of the belly and the democratisation of instituting the tribunate. Instead we see the polis dramatised as the clash of violent energies at best only just held in check. On the one hand, there is the surging force of the hungry people 'resolv'd rather to die than to famish' (I.i.3–4); on the other, the terrifying military threat of Marcius:

> Would the nobility lay aside their ruth
> And let me use my sword, I'd make a quarry
> With thousands of these quarter'd slaves, as high
> As I could pick my lance.
>
> I.i.195–8

The tribunate is a compromise wrung from the Senate facing the prospect of civil war. Although the mutineers assembled at the start of the scene are deflected and dispersed, and it might not have been politically possible on a Jacobean stage to show popular agitation directly bringing about constitutional change, yet that is effectively what takes place discreetly offstage. Internal class war is suspended only with the external threat of war with the Volscians in which the force of Marcius comes into its own. He comments with vicious exultation on the news of war: 'I am glad on't; then we shall ha' means to vent Our musty superfluity' (I.i.223–4). Jeeringly, he taunts the unsoldierlike Citizens, preparing to 'steal away', with their recent demands for food:

> The Volsces have much corn: take these rats thither
> To gnaw their garners.
>
> I.i.247–8

The first scene of *Coriolanus* is a daunting display of the unstable physics of the state of Rome.

The prospect of the complete destruction of Rome visualised by Marcius as an alternative to compromise – 'The rabble should have first unroof'd the city' – is to be repeated again and again in the play as an urgently possible reality. Even before the avenging Coriolanus returns as an apparently unstoppable destroyer in Act IV, the consul Cominius has raised the spectre of mass destruction to try to stop the Tribunes' agitation in the Senate:

> That is the way to lay the city flat,
> To bring the roof to the foundation,
> And bury all which yet distinctly ranges
> In heaps and piles of ruin.
>
> III.i.204–7

We are far here from the metaphoric grandiloquence of Antony – 'Let Rome in Tiber melt, and the wide arch Of the rang'd empire fall'. Antony's is pure figure of speech, Cominius' an all too real and likely vision of apocalypse now.

As the play exposes more directly than anywhere else in Shakespeare the convulsive powers of political process, so it dramatises with a uniquely immediate ferocity the soldiership of its soldier hero. We hear of Macbeth on the battlefield doing violent execution upon Macdonwald, but it is through a style of epic report which allegorises his valour. Antony before his last victorious battle wishes Cleopatra present:

> That thou couldst see my wars today, and knew'st
> The royal occupation! Thou shouldst see
> A workman in't.
>
> IV.iv.16–18

But neither Cleopatra nor the audience are afforded the opportunity of seeing Antony at work, and his warrior's reputation remains an aureole of reflected glory. Coriolanus, alone among Shakespeare's tragic heroes, is actually shown on stage physically making good his claim to heroism. It is a frightening and exhilarating sight. As Marcius execrates his cowardly troops who draw back, charges

alone into the enemy city, emerges bloody but victorious only
anxious lest he miss the other half of the battle where he can find
Aufidius, we are reminded of his mother's imposing vision of him
as 'a harvest-man that's task'd to mow Or all or lose his hire'
(I.iii.36–7). No hire can reward Marcius, he is entirely self-tasked,
but he is driven by an all or nothing need to be the one man sent to
mow. 'O me alone!' he calls out to the soldiers who chair him aloft
on the battlefield, 'Make you a sword of me' (I.vi.76).[5] He is like an
ever-moving force of nature, while yet the manifestation of the
very intensity of an individual human will, never more vividly
characterised than in battle.

The momentum which bears Marcius onward against the Volscians very nearly carries him to the consulship. The force he
generates on the battlefield is translated into the mounting en-
thusiasm first of the army's acclamations, and then of the hero's
welcome home to Rome conjured up by the disgruntled Brutus:

> stalls, bulks, windows,
> Are smother'd up, leads fill'd and ridges hors'd
> With variable complexions, all agreeing
> In earnestness to see him.
>
> II.i.200–3

This is a man with a city at his back, and Sicinius, dismayed, sees
where that must necessarily lead: 'On the sudden I warrant him
consul' (II.i.211–12). It is not even that Coriolanus seeks the consulship. There is no doubting the authenticity of his declaration to
his mother, so arrogant in its humility,

> I had rather be their servant in my way
> Than sway with them in theirs.
>
> II.i.193–4

But he is borne along, at times literally kicking and protesting, by a
tidal movement which his action has set in motion.

The drama of *Coriolanus* is built on rhythms of surge and
counter-surge in which the individual energies of the hero are
placed within the dynamics of a political system. In the scene of
Coriolanus' ritual appearance in the market-place we see the previously forward-driving movement begin to falter and stall. The
crowd is no longer a crowd, the war-hero no longer a war-hero;

instead we have a sequence of timid and uncertain people, fum-
blingly trying to make human contact with a man paralysed with
distaste at his own *mauvaise foie*. It is a non-event at once touching
and acutely embarrassing. As a moment of inertia it becomes a
starting-point for the resisting action organised by the Tribunes
which will expel Coriolanus.

With smoothly operating management skills, Sicinius and Brutus
proceed to undo what looks like the *fait accompli* of the election.
Detecting unease among the citizens, pouncing on the technicality
of Coriolanus' failure to show his wounds, they rehearse once
again the arguments which the people should have used against
him:

> Could you not have told him –
> As you were lesson'd – when he had no power
> But was a petty servant to the state,
> He was your enemy; ever spake against
> Your liberties and the charters that you bear
> I' th' body of the weal; and now, arriving
> A place of potency and sway o' th' state,
> If he should still malignantly remain
> Fast foe to th' plebeii, your voices might
> Be curses to yourselves?
>
>   II.iii.173–82

Such words, unspoken to Coriolanus, become as though spoken,
and the Citizens are marshalled to revoke their 'ignorant election'.
With transparent dishonesty, the Tribunes supply the people not
only with the arguments against Coriolanus' consulship, but elaborate defences of him to be falsely ascribed to themselves. Though
this is obvious manipulation, Sicinius' final comment to Brutus,
when they are left alone, suggests what is there to be manipulated:

> To th' Capitol, come.
> We will be there before the stream o' th' people;
> And this shall seem, as partly 'tis, their own,
> Which we have goaded onward.
>
>   II.iii.257–60

'As partly 'tis': the Citizens did have a real if inarticulate sense of
dissatisfaction with Coriolanus' behaviour to them, justifiably so.

It is the function of the Tribunes to give purpose and direction to the 'stream o' th' people' and harness the force that is in them.

The forcefulness of that force is measured in Act III against the power of Coriolanus himself. The opposition of the Tribunes, exactly as they expected, drives him into a rage from which he launches a series of tirades as unstoppable as his assaults upon the Volscians. Nothing in the play is more brilliantly contrived than the bifocal effect of this scene. Coriolanus is at his most magnificent in the unguarded integrity of his denunciation of the Tribunes' power to the Senate. This is no mere angry harangue, but a passionately reasoned anti-democratic argument. For Coriolanus there cannot be, there must not be, power-sharing between the classes: 'you are plebeians', he tells the patricians, 'if they be senators' (III.i.101–2). The result can only be chaos:

> and my soul aches
> To know, when two authorities are up,
> Neither supreme, how soon confusion
> May enter 'twixt the gap of both and take
> The one by th' other.
>
> III.i.108–12

In 'soothing' the plebs, 'we nourish 'gainst our Senate The cockle of rebellion, insolence, sedition' (III.i.69–70). The tribunate was a concession made under duress and should now be abrogated:

> In a rebellion,
> When what's not meet, but what must be, was law,
> Then were they chosen; in a better hour
> Let what is meet be said it must be meet,
> And throw their power i' th' dust.
>
> III.i.166–70

Coriolanus' vision is consistent, relentless and massively true to itself.

But of course utterly impossible in context. Whatever the earnestness and monolithic sincerity of Coriolanus, we can see yawning gaps opening up around him. On the one side, stand the horrified senators trying vainly to hold him back; on the other, the Tribunes genuinely scandalised, perhaps, by what their intrigue has brought out into the open. In the space of some 150 lines the

about-to-be consul has transformed himself into an arraigned
traitor. Coriolanus thinks that he is upholding a pristine ideal of
the 'fundamental part of the state' which can be restored by
removing the dangerous innovation of the tribunate. He cannot
understand that, the tribunate once granted in whatever circumstances, the people's representatives are legal magistrates of the
state, and that in proposing to rescind their rights, it is indeed he
who is the 'traitorous innovator'. The political status quo, however
reached, has the sanctity of law. All this – Coriolanus' complete
failure to understand that what he is saying is the politically
unspeakable, the senators' dismay, the Tribunes' outrage – would
be funny if it were not so deadly serious.

It is striking to compare Coriolanus' tirade in this scene with
Ulysses' 'degree' speech in *Troilus and Cressida*. The rhetoric of
Ulysses was ironised in so far as it was perceptibly in excess of its
object, the tactical effort to stiffen discipline in the Greek camp.
Yet, for all its ironic context, it remained an articulation of orthodox
Renaissance political/social theories commanding at least theoreti-
cal assent. Coriolanus' insistence on authoritarian politics too
might have had its supporters in a Jacobean audience, including
James himself.[6] The political situation represented in the play,
though, shows not only the impracticability but the disastrousness
of such a theory. Even if we accord an awed respect to the integrity
of the man who voices it, its tone and substance are visibly
unacceptable. In *Coriolanus* Shakespeare eliminates even a notionally ideal vision of the state with which to contrast the actuality.
Absolutist ideals, such as they are, are creations of the actual
which must live with their actual political consequences.

The consequences for Coriolanus are instantaneous. As headlong as his onslaught against the Tribunes is the movement they
lead towards his expulsion. They seize the initiative with a summary sentence of death on him for treachery and, with a show of
law, order his execution by the lynch-mob of plebeians. His armed
resistance in the Capitol itself, though it may mean for the moment
that 'the Tribunes, the Aediles, and the People are beat in', makes
it even harder for Coriolanus' supporters to defend his conduct.
Menenius as peace-maker, having succeeded in bundling Coriolanus off the stage, has to struggle even to win him a further
hearing. The Tribunes, from the tactically strong bargaining position of insisting on his immediate execution, seem to be yielding
ground in allowing him to 'answer by a lawful form, In peace, to

his utmost peril'. Poor Menenius must have to swallow hard at the insolent graciousness of Sicinius who invests him with the authority of a 'people's officer' to go and arrest his friend and fellow-patrician Coriolanus.

The momentum working for the Tribunes in III.i is to continue to the end of the act. Between the two public scenes of anger and conflict comes the pivotal interior III.ii, the dead centre of the play, in which Coriolanus' friends urge him to temporise with the people. This is a crucial scene, particularly as Volumnia's successful pleading to her son in it provides the pattern for her later all-important intercession. But in terms of the outcome to be expected in III.iii, it can change nothing. Coriolanus is most unlikely to abide by his promise of temperance, however often he is schooled by Menenius in that word so unfamiliar in his vocabulary, 'mildly'. In the event, Sicinius has only to name the charge of 'traitor to the people' and he is beside himself with fury again. The Tribunes are never going to let slip the advantage they have over him by now, or reduce the head of political steam that has been built up in III.i. They cannot be stopped, as they orchestrate the people's voices to echo whatever may be their verdict. The scene ends inevitably with Coriolanus' banishment; his isolation is completed in the toweringly contemptuous declaration of unilateral independence, 'I banish you'.

Coriolanus is a play of juggernaut movements, forward and back. After the banishment, there is to be the sweeping destructive force of the Volscians only stayed at the gates of Rome, and the counter-swing to that which will culminate in the violent assassination of the hero. It is a rhythm quite unlike the drift and eddy of action in *Antony and Cleopatra* so aptly evoked in the image of the 'vagabond flag upon the stream' which 'goes to and back, lackeying the varying tide, to rot itself with motion'. Menenius, in the first scene, provides a corresponding key-note for *Coriolanus*. 'You may as well', he tells the rebellious plebeians,

> Strike at the heaven with your staves as lift them
> Against the Roman state; whose course will on
> The way it takes, cracking ten thousand curbs
> Of more strong link asunder that can ever
> Appear in your impediment.

I.i.65–70

Locally, this is a standard rhetorical tactic of authoritarian politics, identifying the patricians, against whom the people are in
revolt, with the state, and the state with heaven, majestically
inviolable. Yet his words evoke also a prophetic vision of Rome's
imperial destiny stretching ahead, a historical vision which has
been construed in very different ways. John Velz, for example, has
argued that Shakespeare, like Virgil, 'had a strongly teleological
view of history' and that it is 'Coriolanus's tragedy . . . to become
an anachronism in his own time and to be crushed, bewildered, by
the ineluctable momentum of history'.[7] Against this positive idea
of the play's political and historical vision, there are those who
regard it as much bleaker. 'In *Coriolanus*', according to Norman
Rabkin, 'Shakespeare . . . comes closer than ever before to our
least illusioned sense of what political reality may be. No modern
dramatist has written a more despairing or a more convincing play
about man and the state.'[8] The fact that both positions can be
consistently and convincingly argued testifies to what Coleridge
called 'the wonderful philosophic impartiality in Shakespeare's
politics'.[9] In *Coriolanus* political energies seem governed by principles as fixed as the Newtonian laws of motion, and it is in such a
context that the interaction of hero and polis is neutrally observed.

Coriolanus is defined by his political situation more obviously
than any other of Shakespeare's tragic protagonists. But equally he
is shown to be the product of psychological conditioning. As
Lawrence Danson points out, 'we learn more about the *childhood* of
this insistently heroic man than we do about the childhood of any
other of Shakespeare's tragic heroes'.[10] His precocious deeds of
valour are rehearsed both by his mother – 'When yet he was but
tender-bodied . . . to a cruel war I sent him, from whence he
return'd his brows bound with oak' (I.iii.5–15) – and formally by
Cominius – 'His pupil age Man-ent'red thus, he waxed like a sea'
(II.ii.96–7). As in no other Shakespeare tragedy, the very specific
circumstances of Marcius' youth and upbringing are shown as the
necessary conditions shaping the adult we see. The cue for this
was supplied by Plutarch who commented with unironical sententiousness at the beginning of his Life:

Caius Martius, whose life we intend now to write, being left an
orphan by his father, was brought up under his mother a
widowe, who taught us by experience, that orphanage bringeth

many discommodities to a childe, but doth not hinder him to become an honest man, and to excell in virtue above the common sorte.

(Bullough, V, 505–6)

Indeed. But there are possible 'discommodities' of orphanage which Plutarch did not envisage. These Shakespeare developed from the suggestion of a later passage:

Martius thinking all due to his mother, that had bene also due to his father if he had lived; dyd not only content him selfe to rejoyce and honour her, but at her desire tooke a wife also, by whom he had two children, and yet never left his mothers house therefore.

(Bullough, V, 508)

From such hints came the formidable figure of Volumnia (who appears in Plutarch only at the point of her *in extremis* embassy) and the power by which she dominates son and household.

The identification of mother and son is established from her very first appearance. She imagines him on the battlefield:

Methinks I see him stamp thus, and call thus:
'Come on, you cowards! You were got in fear,
Though you were born in Rome'.
I.iii.32–4

This is the authentic idiom of Marcius who, in the very next scene, we see excoriating his cowardly troops just so:

All the contagion of the south light on you,
You shames of Rome! . . . You souls of geese
That bear the shapes of men, how have you run
From slaves that apes would beat!
I.iv.30–6

We can read this identity two ways. Marcius can be seen as his mother's clone, mouthing her words, enacting her disdain. Alternatively, it may be Volumnia who projects on to her son a fantasy of violence, what is a fantasy only for her, but a lived reality for him. Either way, Volumnia clearly speaks a central truth of the play when she proclaims to her son, 'Thy valiantness was mine, thou suck'dst it from me' (III.ii.129).

How far is this relationship and its effect intended to be seen as psychopathological? Coriolanus, with his mother dependence, has been an obvious case for psychoanalytic treatment. One of the fullest and most complex accounts has been Janet Adelman's, who detects in Coriolanus' aggressive hatred of the people and his rejection of their need for food, the behaviour of a threatened elder sibling undernourished by the mother who proclaims 'anger's my meat'.[11] Both Coppelia Kahn and Linda Bamber, exploring Shakespeare's definition of sexual roles, link *Coriolanus* with *Macbeth*. 'A paradox of sexual confusion lies at the heart of these two plays', Kahn argues:

> Their virile warrior-heroes, supreme in valour, are at the same time unfinished men – boys, in a sense, who fight or murder because they have been convinced by women that only through violence will they achieve manhood.[12]

Bamber, who discerns in the rest of Shakespeare an antithesis between masculine Self and feminine Other, distinguishes *Macbeth* and *Coriolanus* by the absence of the latter. 'Lady Macbeth and Volumnia are the heroes' collaborators or stage managers rather than independent centers of self-interest. There is no dialectic between the masculine Self and the feminine Other in these plays because the primary representatives of the feminine are not Other to the hero.'[13]

Some distinctions need to be made here between the cases of Coriolanus and Macbeth. Lady Macbeth's retrospective threat to her nursing baby is often compared with, equated to, Volumnia's harsh aesthetic of blood:

> The breasts of Hecuba,
> When she did suckle Hector, look'd not lovelier
> Than Hector's forehead when it spit forth blood
> At Grecian sword, contemning.
>
> I.iii.40–3

Kahn, whose chapter on the two plays is entitled 'The Milking Babe and the Bloody Man in *Coriolanus* and *Macbeth*', sees an identical moral in both: 'In each play, the single striking image of a nursing babe defines [a] disrupted relationship between men and women'.[14] This may be to override essential differences of context, differences in what is implied as normative in the imaginative world of _Coriolanus_ as against _Macbeth_. Lady Macbeth's lines are a conscious exercise in horror, a terrorist tactic for herself as well as for Macbeth. The violence of the will is felt as profoundly un-natural, and not only as it offends the principle of maternal femi-ninity. The association of Lady Macbeth's imagined infanticide with Macbeth's earlier 'naked new-born babe', the personified Pity, makes of her speech a deliberate and knowingly perverse assault on the very idea of the sacred which the ethos of the play as a whole sustains.

The Romanness of Volumnia produces a different effect. In her exaltation of manliness, she speaks for the highest ideal of her culture. In an often-quoted passage, Plutarch comments on the moral climate in which Coriolanus grew up:

> Now in those days, valliantnes was honoured in Rome above all other vertues: which they called _Virtus_, by the name of vertue selfe, as including in that generall name, all other speciall vertues be-sides. So that _Virtus_ in the Latin, was asmuche as valliantnes.
>
> (Bullough, V, 506)

It is this all-encompassing _virtus_ which Volumnia instills in her son, and which Shakespeare dramatises in the play. With the phrase 'in those days', Plutarch marks off the (already for him historically) remote period of the early Roman Republic as a time of primitive moral austerity. Shakespeare follows his lead in making the Rome of _Coriolanus_ a distanced arena for a particular kind of heroic endeavour.[15] In this perspective, Volumnia shows not as a denatured woman, such as the witchlike Lady Macbeth: it is of Virgilia, most improbably, that this sort of language is used, and then only by the cowardly Tribunes wilting under the force of her anger after Coriolanus' banishment. 'Are you mankind?' (IV.ii.16) says the berated Sicinius. Volumnia instead is characterised as the type of Roman motherhood, fierce, self-sacrificing, utterly commit-ted to an ideal of manly honour.

The ideas of manhood which the two plays construct are not identical. Coriolanus defends to Volumnia his uncompromising stand against the Tribunes as a necessary truth to his manly self:

> Would you have me
> False to my nature? Rather say I play
> The man I am.
>
> III.ii.14–16

Volumnia responds drily:

> You might have been enough the man you are
> With striving less to be so
>
> III.ii.19–20

This is in marked contrast to Lady Macbeth.

> When you durst do it, then you were a man;
> And to be more than what you were, you would
> Be so much more the man.
>
> I.vii.49–51

Both women urge their men to act against their sense of manhood. But where Lady Macbeth's urging is to overstep the limits that Macbeth sets up, Volumnia's is for understatement, a temporising with the fullness of the man's conception of himself. What is missing from the scheme of things in *Coriolanus* is the absolute moral imperative of Macbeth's definition, 'I dare do all that may become a man Who dares do more is none'. That is spoken as the unquestioned truth of which Lady Macbeth's argument is a perverse denial. The text places her undifferentiated upward extension of manhood on a scale of willed daring as the futile, self-cancelling launching into nothingness of 'Vaulting ambition, which o'erleaps itself And falls on th' other'. In the Roman play, how a man should project himself admits of real debate; the insistence of Coriolanus on uncompromising integrity has a sort of value, but it has to be weighed against the political shrewdness of his mother's counter-arguments.

Because of the informing Roman ethos, the broader relationship between sexuality and aggression may be displayed for observation rather than the disapproval it often receives from modern critics. It is Volumnia who provides the first of a series of images which celebrate the martial at the expense of the erotic. 'If my son were my husband', she tells the gentle Virgilia (an all too suggestive hypothesis for post-Freudian readers), 'I should freelier rejoice in that absence wherein he won honour than in the embracements of his bed where he would show most love' (I.iii.2–4). For Marcius himself, on the field of battle, the exultant strength of comradely feeling for Cominius is equated with marital consummation:

> O! let me clip ye
> In arms as sound as when I woo'd, in heart
> As merry as when our nuptial day was done,
> And tapers burn'd to bedward.
>
> I.vi.29–32

Most strikingly of all, there is Aufidus' joyful salutation at the offer of friendship from his former enemy.

> Know thou first,
> I lov'd the maid I married; never man
> Sigh'd truer breath; but that I see thee here,
> Thou noble thing, more dances my rapt heart
> Than when I first my wedded mistress saw
> Bestride my threshold.
>
> IV.v.113–18

There need not be anything covert or suspect about the homoeroticism of passages such as these.[16] Instead they are used to evoke a code of values in which the sexual element in masculine warriorship is quite unabashedly identified, and the tenderness of lovemaking subordinated to it. Subordinated but not denied. Conventionally in the Renaissance Honour was to be preferred to Love, though in necessary relation to it – Tamburlaine's speech 'What is beauty, saith my sufferings then' is one of the most eloquent statements of the principle. The force of Marcius' or Aufidius' declarations is the truth and depth of their feelings of wedded love which martial joy equals or outpasses.

It is noticeable that it is specifically wedded love. After the magnificent lubriciousness of sexuality in *Antony and Cleopatra*, love in *Coriolanus* is centred in marriage and disciplined to a severely Roman ideal of chastity. Menenius, the only character in the play much given to pleasures of the flesh, is limited to those of eating and drinking. What would be a routine sexual innuendo in another Shakespeare play –

3 SERVANT: . . . Do you meddle with my master?
CORIOLANUS: Ay; 'tis an honester service than to meddle with
thy mistress.
IV.v.46–8

– seems astonishingly off-key here because so uncharacteristic of
Coriolanus and *Coriolanus*. Once again, however, we should perhaps be wary of a modern view of deformations and repressions
here. Coriolanus' relationship with Virgilia, his 'gracious silence',
has seemed to many to indicate the capacity for a normal loving
marriage stunted, almost atrophied, by the dominant masculinism
of his mother. He greets Virgilia at their reunion in Act V with 'a
kiss Long as my exile, sweet as my revenge' and a quite remarkable
asseveration of male chastity:

> Now, by the jealous queen of heaven, that kiss
> I carried from thee, dear, and my true lip
> Hath virgin'd it e'er since.
> V.iii.44–8

A note that is almost comic has been detected in this, and in the
'astonishingly operatic address' to Valeria which follows.[17]

> The noble sister of Publicola,
> The moon of Rome, chaste as the icicle
> That's curdied by the frost from purest snow,
> And hangs on Dian's temple – dear Valeria!
> V.iii.64–7

Times have changed and tastes with them since 1912, when Bradley
cited this admiringly as probably the most often quoted passage in
the play, indicating Coriolanus' sensitivity to a finely chivalrous
ideal.[18] Our contemporary distrust of the hero's chilly rhetoric of
sexual purity may be as inappropriate as Bradley's complacently
patriarchal raptures.

How then are we to view the complete collapse of Coriolanus' male
self-sufficiency before the female embassy of Valeria, Virgilia and
Volumnia? Is it the proof that he is no more than what Aufidius

later calls him, a 'boy of tears', an unfinished man in his continued dependence on his mother?

> I'll never
> Be such a gosling to obey instinct, but stand
> As if a man were author of himself
> And knew no other kin.
>
> V.iii.34–7

Even as he speaks the lines, their futility is evident, a hopeless attempt to resist the emotional tide already acknowledged – 'I melt, and am not of stronger earth than others' (V.iii.28–9). This failure can be interpreted positively, as Coriolanus' recognition of human interrelatedness, tragic only in that it comes too late. '*Coriolanus* is a tragedy in that its protagonist does finally learn certain necessary truths about the world in which he exists, but dies before he has any chance to rebuild his life in accordance with them.'[19] Yet it is hard to see any signs in the Coriolanus who returns to face death in Antium/Corioli that he has learned anything significant, or might be in a position to rebuild his life if he continued to have one. The capitulation to Volumnia surely represents some sort of defeat for him, however glorious a victory for her and Rome.

One way to look at the emotional crux represented by this scene is to trace it back to Volumnia's position as single parent. She is both father and mother to her son. With her assumption of the masculine role of father/super-ego, she has bred him to be all man; and yet she retains her maternal part as the source and object of love and retains her power to withdraw it. It is significantly the same tactic with which she wins her way both in the earlier persuasion-scene (III.ii) and in the final climax. The first time round, she seems to succeed by relying on his need for approval:

> I prithee now, sweet son, as thou hast said
> My praises made thee first a soldier, so,
> To have my praise for this, perform a part
> Thou hast not done before.
>
> III.ii.107–10

Coriolanus agrees reluctantly – 'Well, I must do't' – but then works himself up into a lather of indignation in which he mutinies again:

> I will not do't,
> Lest I surcease to honour mine own truth,
> And by my body's action teach my mind
> A most inherent baseness.
>
> III.ii.120–3

Volumnia's lessons in honour have been all too well learned. It is at this moment that the last weapon is used. 'At thy choice then . . .'

>   Let
> Thy mother rather feel thy pride than fear
> Thy dangerous stoutness; for I mock at death
> With as big heart as thou. Do as thou list.
>
> III.iii.123–8

Approval is withdrawn, the mother mimes the pathos of being cast off – this is the fine flower of emotional blackmail. Coriolanus succumbs instantly with a wry boyishness:

>   Pray be content.
> Mother, I am going to the market-place;
> Chide me no more.
>
> III.ii.130–2

The strategy is similar in the later scene. After all the forceful eloquence of Volumnia's appeals to her son's sense of honour, reputation, patriotism, it is the turning away that finally precipitates his yielding:

>   Come, let us go.
> This fellow had a Volscian to his mother;
> His wife is in Corioli, and his child
> Like him by chance.
>
> V.iii.177–80

For all the scene's drama, there is a whiff of cool comedy in the way this is observed. It raises once again the unease with *Coriolanus* as tragedy which has led so many critics to try to re-categorise it as history, satire, debate.[20] For to see the hero revealed quite so clearly and certainly as mother's boy, just as to watch his progress

as a function of political mechanism, seems to represent an un-
tragic stripping-down of the nexus of character and situation.
Recurrent efforts have been made to place the way in which
Coriolanus is unsatisfactorily unlike other tragic protagonists, his
lack of an inner life – 'he has no more introspection in him than a
tiger'[21] – or the knee-jerk inevitability of his reactions: 'As Antony
is the most unpredictable, Coriolanus is the most predictable of
men. He is . . . the Coriolanus doll: wind him up and he rages.'[22]
The comparison with Antony is an interesting one because it
highlights Coriolanus' deficiencies as an actor. Antony's is one of
the most supremely histrionic of Shakespeare's tragic roles, only
equalled or surpassed by Cleopatra herself. Antony enacts with
true actorly commitment whatever part he is currently playing,
devoted lover, tough political bargainer, warrior general, with
minimal awareness of their potential incompatibility. Coriolanus,
by contrast, can only 'play the man I am' (III.ii.15–16). It is not only
that he has contempt, a true Platonist's disdain, for the 'harlot's
spirit' of acting. He is no good at it, and he knows it, as we see
most acutely in the gown of humility scene in the market-place. If
Shakespeare's virtuoso actors, Richard III, Hamlet, Antony, gain
grace and glamour as stage parts from their very actorliness, then
Coriolanus' anti-histrionicism may be felt as a limitation.

Coriolanus more than any other of the tragedies seems to ask for
diagnosis, what is wrong with the hero or with the state that expels
him. Here, perhaps more than in the other Roman tragedies, the
evaluative format of Plutarch's *Lives*, weighing vice with virtue,
assessing the shape of a career, pinpointing the 'solitarines' that is
Coriolanus' fundamental defect, shapes the play that results. Yet
Coriolanus, however tough-minded, is not radically different in
kind from the other tragedies. Wilbur Sanders, in countering the
Bradleyan view of Coriolanus' inadequate innerness, articulates
the play's tragic matrix: 'he knows as much about himself as he
profitably can, and if he comes to disaster it is less out of "self-
ignorance" – which would make a homiletic tale -- than out of a
fundamental contradiction in the constitution of things, to which
he is subject, and to which he will not bow – and that makes a
tragedy'.[23] What distinguishes *Coriolanus* is the severe clarity with
which this 'fundamental contradiction in the constitution of things'
is set out and the hero's part in it dramatised.

Norman Rabkin remarks that 'Like Lear, Macbeth, Brutus and
Hamlet, Coriolanus makes us realise how much the hero is created
by what he has accomplished, defined by the events through
which he has passed.'[24] In fact this is much truer of Coriolanus
than it is of the other tragic heroes cited, because we actually see
him being so created. The issue of identity is central in all the
tragedies, what shapes, what feeds, what destroys the protagonists' sense of self, nowhere more than in *Antony and Cleopatra*. In
Coriolanus Shakespeare returns for a last time to a heroic persona
which represents the fullest and most extreme occupation of the
self, and examines with a new sort of attention how it is consti-
tuted. Caius Marcius Coriolanus is someone made by his mother,
by his city, by his 'deed-achieving honour'; the very process of this
making is laid bare. Yet he is also the hero who resists the forces
that shape and validate his being in the extremity of his commitment to an absolute idea of selfhood.

For Coriolanus any notion of reward for what he does, whether
it be a special share of battle-spoils or the people's votes for consul,
traduces the authenticity of the action. He winces away from
praise as it makes a public guy of the self. He will not stay in the
Senate to hear his 'nothings monster'd' (II.ii.75). Even Volumnia's
approval is painful to him:

> my mother,
> Who has a charter to extol her blood,
> When she does praise me grieves me.
> I.ix.13–15

How much more grotesque then is it for him to have to play the
war-hero in the market-place, to stage a show of the privateness of
his wounded body to win the voices of those he despises. The one
honour which he receives more or less graciously is the horse
given him by Cominius, and the name that goes with it:

> Therefore be it known,
> As to us, to all the world, that Caius Marcius
> Wears this war's garland; in token of the which,
> My noble steed, known to the camp, I give him,
> With all his trim belonging; and from this time,
> For what he did before Corioli, call him
> With all th' applause and clamour of the host,

> Caius Marcius Coriolanus.
> Bear th' addition nobly ever!
>
> I.ix.58–66

For once public praise does not drive him into a tantrum of disclaimers.

> I will go wash;
> And when my face is fair you shall perceive
> Whether I blush or no. Howbeit, I thank you;
> I mean to stride your steed, and at all times
> To undercrest your good addition
> To th' fairness of my power.
>
> I.ix.68–73

The horse he can accept as the soldierly honour it is, given by his respected general. But the name too seems acceptable as it defines him by the purest moment of action he has ever achieved, a deed both purely action and purely his own.

The nearest parallel in the tragedies to Marcius' new name is the new title conferred on Macbeth. He becomes Cawdor, as Marcius becomes Coriolanus, by what he has achieved for his country on the battlefield. But in *Macbeth* the source for such honours is an unquestioned legitimating authority to which all service is owed and from which all rewards come. The situation in *Coriolanus* is very different. There is in Rome no severing gap between the fighting power of the individual hero and the embodiment of the state in government. Consequently the sequence Marcius, Coriolanus, Consul, is a perfectly plausible development, whereas Glamis, Cawdor, King is a radically unnatural progression.

But the Rome for which the hero fights is a problematic entity, only partly the true state to which he can give allegiance. So, in so far as his identity is not self-created but dependent upon a mixed community of others, it is always vulnerable, always liable to instability. Marcius' individual aggressiveness is always on the point of being turned on his own, of naming as alien or enemy what claims to be on his side. The cowardly Roman soldiers on the battlefield are threatened thus:

> He that retires, I'll take him for a Volsce,
> And he shall feel my edge. . . .

> Mend and charge home,
> Or, by the fires of heaven, I'll leave the foe
> And make my wars on you.
>
> I.iv.28–40

Sicinius puns aptly when he calls Coriolanus 'this viper That would depopulate the city and Be every man himself (III.i.263–5). 'Depopulate' already meant 'to deprive wholly or partly of inhabitants' (OED 2), something Coriolanus seems all too willing to attempt. At the same time Sicinius implies that he aspires to a city-state of just one in which he would become what the people actually are: 'What is the city but the people?' (III.i.199). Coriolanus cannot understand when even his mother, who has taught him to be what he is, advises him to seem other than he is in order to win power, a power he does not want if it is to be gained by such self-betraying means. There is a moment of fierce joy when, under sentence of banishment, he can again define himself in pure opposition to the city which casts him out.

What sort of self, though, is left to a Coriolanus without family or city? He presents himself in Antium initially as the man from nowhere – 'Where dwell'st thou?' 'Under the canopy.' 'Where's that?' 'I' th' city of kites and crows' (IV.v.36–42). When he reveals himself to Aufidius it as the hated Coriolanus: 'Only that name remains' of all he has done for his country. In the alliance with the Volscians, he is bent on making himself entirely anew at the expense of his ungrateful people. As Cominius reports in Act V,

> 'Coriolanus'
> He would not answer to; forbad all names;
> He was a kind of nothing, titleless,
> Till he had forg'd himself a name i' th' fire
> Of burning Rome.
>
> V.i.11–15

But the Caius Marcius Romanus which he aims to become is ultimately an impossible projection of the self. The embassy of women forces him to recognise an identity of mother and motherland which would make the annihilation of Rome profoundly self-destructive rather than self-renewing. He can only return to the Volscians and re-live, in the exhilarating freedom of a suicidal gesture, his eponymous moment:

> If you have writ your annals true, 'tis there
> That, like an eagle in a dove-cote, I
> Flutter'd your Volscians in Corioli.
> Alone I did it.
>
> V.vi.114–17

Coriolanus, according to Bradley, is 'what we call an impossible person'.[25] It is a beautifully judged phrase, reflecting the combination of outraged irritation and admiring understanding that the figure evokes. But all Shakespeare's tragic protagonists are, more or less, impossibilists, in the insistence of the demands they make upon the world and the intractability of the world in meeting them. Coriolanus is exceptional only in the extent to which we see this conflict from without rather than within. He is given no speech equivalent to Macbeth's 'My way of life Is fall'n into the sear, the yellow leaf', or Antony's cloud-reverie, in which the desolation or the dissolution of the inner landscape is conveyed. Yet surely we need not regard such inwardness as a *sine qua non* of tragedy and the tragic protagonist. A wordless cracking of the self may be just as powerful and as significant: 'He holds her by the hand, silent'.

The tragic hero in Shakespeare acts as a focal point of energy and consciousness for the surrounding collective context. In *Macbeth*, *Antony and Cleopatra* and *Coriolanus*, the hero pushes the sense of what it is to be a man to its limit and beyond. In all three it is specifically a gendered sense of manhood, underwritten or undermined by women, defined by and against the feminine. In the spiritual universe of *Macbeth* the overstepping of limits is a knowing transgression into an abyss of evil which provides the simultaneous understanding of its opposite in an absolute sanctity. The amoralism of *Antony and Cleopatra* allows for the pursuit of a will o' the wisp idea of greatness sustained only in so far as the collaborative imagination of protagonists and audience can sustain it. Coriolanus comes much closer to be being defined by the collectivities that surround him, the hero understood as a certain sort of culturally conditioned figure, necessary to the state and yet as necessarily to be alienated from it. It can be seen as Shakespeare's final and most comprehensive secularising of tragedy, making of the tragic action a dramatic sequence within an exclusively human world of perceived cause and event. This is not to define it as something other

than tragedy, to rule it out as anomalous according to some
prescriptive idea of the form; in the context of this book, rather,
Coriolanus stands as a culminating development of one tendency
within Shakespeare's essentially multiple tragic imagination.

11
Sacred and Secular

This book started with a reading experience. Reading and re-reading Shakespeare's tragedies, I sensed in sequent plays a pattern of related themes and situations dramatised in sharply different, even opposed, imaginative milieus. I looked for origins of this pattern, for the evolution of alternative ways of imagining, in the English histories. In analysing the nine plays in the tragic mode from *Julius Caesar* to *Coriolanus*, my aim was to consider how they appeared within the scheme of contrasted interrelationship, to bring out the distinctiveness of each by showing its likeness and unlikeness to its neighbouring tragedies. I am left with the question of where that brings me out. Why might there be such an imaginative dialectic in the tragedies, or what might it signify?

'Tragedy is born in the West each time that the pendulum of civilisation is halfway between a sacred society and a society built around man.'[1] Camus here links the Renaissance with the period of Greek tragedy as the two such moments of historical shift. The context of the English Renaissance, with its swing from the God-centred to the man-centred, has been variously invoked to account for the nature of Shakespeare's tragedies. So, for example, in John Danby's *Shakespeare's Doctrine of Nature*, the two competing ideologies of *King Lear* are associated with the conflict between an older order of Providential nature, voiced by Hooker and Bacon, and the emergent naturalism of Hobbes.[2] The disappearance of transcendental certainties, guaranteed by Christianity, has equally been diagnosed as the source of tragedy in *Hamlet*: Philip Edwards, for instance, has characterised the world of *Hamlet* as one in which God may be hidden, but may be simply absent, and has argued that the play's tragic balance rests on this inscrutable and unresolved doubt.[3] C.L. Barber and Richard P. Wheeler's account places the tragedies generally within 'the new cultural moment of the Renaissance and Reformation': they 'dramatize the post-

Christian situation, shaped by some of the expectations and values of Christianity, but without God and the Holy Family, with only the human family'.[4]

The perspective of this book has not been to focus on such historical and cultural contexts, though they may well have provided the necessary conditions for the creation of the tragedies. Rather, what I have tried to highlight within the texts themselves is the predominance of the secular in the tragedies with classical sources, the contrasting imagination of the sacred which continued to be available in the non-classical tragedies. This is not a distinction between Christian and pagan. Shakespeare's most self-consciously sustained pagan setting in the tragedies is *King Lear* which is yet closer akin to *Hamlet, Othello* and *Macbeth,* than it is to the other pagan plays. It is not that one group of the tragedies was informed by a system of Christian *belief* supported by the *beliefs* of the original audiences, whereas the others dramatised an alien culture to be viewed with ironic detachment. *Hamlet* and *King Lear* do not embody any more absolutely assured values, may be as ontologically uncertain as *Troilus and Cressida* or *Antony and Cleopatra.* The sense of the sacred in Shakespeare's tragedies, in so far as it is there in some of the plays and felt to be lacking in others, cannot be simply identified with the presence or absence of a shared Christian code of meaning.

Part of what differentiates the classically-derived tragedies is a distinctive attitude towards history and legend, which had its origins in the narrative materials from which they were created. Against the (more or less) sacred history of the English chronicles with their teleological shaping, Plutarch supplied stories cast to quite other ends. The very conception of the parallel *Lives* made them comparative, evaluative, relativising. Each life of a noble Grecian or Roman was to be studied always with an eye to its companion life, as the illustration of moral issues arising out of character in action. Plutarch afforded Shakespeare the opportunity to reach out imaginatively to a given historical situation and to dramatise within it the connections of personality and context. The analytic mode of the original, its distance in time and culture, made it possible for the dramatist to conceive a non-mythic version of history.

All three of the main Plutarchan plays are creations of the historical imagination. The characters of *Julius Caesar, Antony and Cleopatra, Coriolanus,* are shaped and conditioned by the specifically Roman ethos in which they are conceived. It is not the same Roman ethos from play to play: in the late Republic of *Julius Caesar* the backward-looking political ideals of Brutus still command respect, doomed as they are; by *Antony and Cleopatra* they are phantoms of the past; *Coriolanus* returns to the early city-state to dramatise a code of Romanness in its origins. What defines the historicity of these plays is not so much their awareness of historical process, of political and social change and development. Such awareness, though there in the Roman plays, is limited. The perspective of the Plutarchan tragedies is historical in that its protagonists are creatures of the cultural place they occupy, a cultural place marked off in time.

The narratives inherited from the classical world were used constantly by Renaissance writers as exemplifying history and legend. As such, Plutarch's reflective, analytic *Lives* were especially attractive, and Shakespeare's quarrying of them for drama characteristic of his period. But the case of *Timon of Athens* suggests that there were limits to the uses to be made of the Plutarchan classical setting. The small inset legend of Timon, a life invoked only to illustrate one incident in Plutarch's *Life of Antony*, was probably too slight a source for Shakespeare (and Middleton) to build into a complex dramatic structure equivalent to that of the Roman plays. The story of Timon yielded little of the vivifying substance, the wealth of narrative lights and sidelights on character and situation which the *Lives* of Brutus, Antony or Coriolanus afforded. Instead *Timon of Athens* was conceived as a fable that blanked out such specifics of time and place, an ahistorical parable of idealism and disillusionment, ingratitude and misanthropy. Yet the strain within the play towards a visionary or mythic universality did not accord with the legendary/emblematic nature of the story and its classical origins. This strain could only find expression in the mythopoeic imaginative space of *King Lear*.

Even in the classical narrative which appeared most to offer the grandeur of myth, the mythic was resisted in Shakespeare. The effect of *Troilus and Cressida* is to demythologise the heroes of the Trojan War, to turn the archetypal tragedy of the fall of Troy, the doomed love of the lovers, into iconoclastic, satiric history. The characters try unsuccessfully to live up to their epic reputations, struggle to sustain the transcendent orders of meaning which they are meant to embody. The fatedness of Homer, the controlled narrative design of Chaucer, turn into a tragedy of arbitrary event and determined contingencies.

Troilus and Cressida, with its radical scepticism and its element of the burlesque, is an extreme case. But all of the classically derived tragedies, more or less, reflect an awareness of their historical status, the fact that they are inherited as familiar history by a latter-day audience. Hence the ironic effectiveness of Brutus and Cassius enacting as mimic play the assassination which they have just staged, or Troilus and Cressida naming themselves in some inconceivable future as the legendary by-words which in the audience's time they have become. So the full march of imperial history lives within Menenius' vision of 'the Roman state'

> whose course will on
> The way it takes, cracking ten thousand curbs.

Antony and Cleopatra as royal lovers magnificent in defeat, even Timon as misanthrope, all have roles to play predetermined by the stories in which they are cast. These tragedies are based on the interaction of their known pastness, Shakespeare and his audience looking back towards the ancient world where they are located, and the present immediacy of their dramatic re-creation.

The storystuffs used in the classical tragedies are relatively homogeneous in comparison with those on which *Hamlet*, *Othello*, *King Lear* and *Macbeth* are based. The latter range eclectically from legendary pseudohistory and romance, through medieval chronicle, to nearly contemporary novella. Within any one individual text the imaginative location may be unstable. *Hamlet*, for instance, portrays a Renaissance court convincingly of its time into which a theatrical troupe from Elizabethan London can, not implausibly, wander. Yet the remembered reign of the warrior King Hamlet, only two months dead, suggests some primal era of heroic endeavour haunting the degenerate present. The tragedies are hospitable to anachronism, even when they are set in consciously remote periods. So the Porter in *Macbeth* can allude easily to the topicalities of the Gunpowder Plot trials; Poor Tom mimics the language of Bedlam beggars, borrows devils from the polemic pamphlets of Samuel Harsnett, future Archbishop of Canterbury, without disturbing the fiction of *King Lear*'s primitive pre-Christian world. Contrarily, where in *Othello* the historical setting is close to the

audience's present, Shakespeare makes little of the events which
might have fixed the action at a remembered moment of the
relatively recent past. *Othello* is a play which elects *not* to be about
the Battle of Lepanto.

Though none of them have the status of fiction, indeterminacy
of time helps these tragedies to escape from history. *King Lear* is set
back in something like an originary time, the *in illo tempore* of
primitive myth.[5] *Macbeth* is not thus outside a historical continuum, in so far as it dramatises events from the chronicles of
Scotland involving the legendary ancestor of Shakespeare's reigning
monarch. But for all the sideshow of the line of kings stretching out
to the crack of doom, the play does not enact a given scene from
the country's story of itself, as the English histories do. The
Providential narrative which brought James to the throne of Scotland and England is marginal in the magical rhythm of action
which defeats Macbeth and restores Malcolm.

Who knows, who cares what sort of King of Denmark Fortinbras
will prove, or what are the implications for the future of a Norwe-
gian take-over of the kingdom? All our attention is given to the
death of Hamlet, as it represents the consummation of the tragedy
in the belated and catastrophic accomplishment of revenge. It is
the characteristic closure of the tragic form to end thus on a still
contemplation of the protagonist's death rather than the consideration of what may flow from it. In this sense, the restricted significance of the ending of *Othello* may be less anomalous than it has
sometimes been thought. Certainly the deaths of Othello and
Desdemona may not affect their society like the destruction of the
whole royal house of Denmark, or the reinstatement of the legitimate heir to the Scottish throne. But the 'tragic loading' of the
wedding-bed may be no less momentous in its significance. Each
of these four tragedies is invested with its own visionary meaning
which is not dependent on a broader framework of historical
causality.

Barbara Everett stresses the uniqueness of *Othello*'s source in
novella: 'Shakespeare . . . took every other tragedy he wrote, even
including *Romeo and Juliet*, from historical materials, or from materials that passed in the Renaissance for historical'.[6] But *Othello* is
more closely cognate to *Hamlet*, *King Lear* and *Macbeth*, than these
three are to the other tragedies based on 'history', because none of
the four is apprehended as historical. It is true that Renaissance
audiences were quite catholic in what they were prepared to

receive as history. Still, even for them, the reigns of a King Lear or a King Macbeth, a Hamlet Prince of Denmark, in their relative obscurity, must have had a different standing from the narratives inherited from antiquity. The assassination of Julius Caesar, the victory of the future Augustus over Antony and Cleopatra, the Trojan War, were among the most often-rehearsed events of world history. Even with lesser known episodes such as the life of Coriolanus, or the legend of Timon of Athens, their location within a classical milieu brought an established cultural context. In *Hamlet*, *King Lear* and *Macbeth*, by contrast, Shakespeare was free to create an autonomous time and space for each tragedy, unconstricted by expectations bound up with the story's origins. Denmark, Scotland, prehistoric Britain were their own places, peopled according to the demands of each drama in its uniqueness. This imaginative independence *Othello* could share, for all its difference from the others as a novella story in a present setting. What *Hamlet*, *King Lear*, *Macbeth* and *Othello* have in common is that they are not answerable to other versions of their stories, do not need the support of being known as history.

The sense of the sacred in these four tragedies to be contrasted with the secularity of the others, I have argued, is not to be equated with the opposition of Christian and pagan. What sense of the sacred is it, then? And how is it manifested in the plays, how differentiated from the secularity of the secular? The 'sacred' tragedies include the resources of Christian belief and iconography without making Christianity their determining meaning. *Hamlet* is explicitly Christian in setting, its drama drawing upon the theology of supernatural phenomena, of sin and guilt, salvation and damnation. Yet older, more atavistic orders of pollution and retribution co-exist in the play with orthodox Christian concerns. Co-exist, not conflict. *Hamlet* ought to be about the struggle of a creed of love and forgiveness against a pre-Christian code of vengeance and honour, or at least about the moral dilemma of the avenger which in *The Spanish Tragedy* is centred on the Biblical injunction 'Vindicta mihi'. Whose is vengeance – the avenger's or God's? *Hamlet* ought to dramatise such a conflict of systems of belief, has often been treated as though it did, but it doesn't. Instead Hamlet is prompted to his revenge by heaven *and* hell, he must be scourge *and* minister to the kingdom of Denmark. The Ghost's command, coming from an extra-Christian imaginative realm, is the play's categorical imperative which Hamlet has to obey, though to do so is to risk perdition.

'Of all the tragic heroes Othello is the most emphatically Christian. He is a soldier in the war against the Turks. . . . His language is rich with allusion to Christian eschatology . . . his love for Desdemona is a version of Christian faith.'[7] A version of Christian faith is precisely what it is, but a heterodox one. Shakespeare does indeed build into his play the Christian grand design of believer against infidel, though he complicates and challenges the simplicity of that design by making his Christian hero a Moor. More importantly, the traditional opposition of *eros* and *agape* is denied by integrating the erotic into the ideal of loving faith which the tragedy affirms. The effect of the non-classical tragedies is to subsume Christian images within other less specific adumbrations of the sacred. Thus the traditional dispute over Christian or non-Christian interpretations of *King Lear* is to a large extent a pseudocontroversy. Cordelia is not a Christ figure, although her martyrdom for truth and her self-sacrificial love are Christ-like qualities. The tragedies invert the normal priorities of the Christian scheme of things by which all human experiences derive their meaning from the primary truths of revealed religion. Such truths become, rather, one set of images in a laicised drama of the sacred. This is so even in *Macbeth*, where the conflict between good and evil seems most securely based in an orthodox Christian metaphysic. The equivocal status of the Witches, the obscure origins of evil in the drama, the strange sense of Macbeth as victim as well as villain, make the tragedy something other than a homiletic morality-play of transgression, punishment and redemption.

The 'secular' tragedies are secular in that they are without the vision of the sacred which, in its various forms, animates *Hamlet*, *Othello*, *King Lear* and *Macbeth*. The progressive elimination of the supernatural is one dimension of this secularity. In *Julius Caesar* unearthly omens are represented and the ghost of Caesar does appear, though in nothing so theatrically embodied or dramatically significant a form as the Ghost in *Hamlet*. But in *Troilus and Cressida* allusions to the gods are strictly *pro forma*. When Agamemnon talks about 'the protractive trials of great Jove', Jove is a figure of speech for nothing in particular. In Shakespeare's play, it is inconceivable that the gods should appear on the battlefield to aid this hero and frustrate that, as they do in Homer. With *Timon of Athens*, the apparatus of overseeing gods to be found in Lucian was dismantled; equally in *Coriolanus*, the providential phenomena recounted by Plutarch in his *Life* were all removed. ''Tis the god Hercules, whom Antony lov'd, Now leaves him.' This one exceptional moment in *Antony and Cleopatra* seems to stand for some more final departure of all the gods from the world of the classical plays. They depart, but not to be replaced by some truer God, as in Milton's 'Nativity Ode'. In these plays men and women are finally on their own.

It is, though, not just a lack of the numinous which makes the secular tragedies secular. The drama resists the ritualisation of the sacred where it is attempted. The conspirators, inspired by Brutus, try to make a rite of the killing of Caesar. The assassination is to be a sacrifice and not a butchery; from the dead Caesar 'great Rome shall suck reviving blood'; after the murder, the liberators anoint themselves in a blood-bath of purification. These images are cognate not only to the Christian mystery of sacrificial redemption, but to more primitive sacral patterns of the king who must die. However the effect of *Julius Caesar* is to turn these potentially ritual acts and images into would-be rituals. The body of Caesar is no more than a 'bleeding piece of earth' after all; the remains of 'the noblest man that ever lived in the tide of times', perhaps, but also of the believably weak, superstitious, self-important old man we have seen other men adulate and envy. The idea of the assassination is seen to be just that, an idea that does not work, can not impose itself on the reality of what takes place on stage. How different from the murder of old king Hamlet whose body poisoned in the secret garden poisons the body of the state, or of Duncan when 'most sacrilegious murder hath broke ope The Lord's anointed temple, and stole thence The life o' th' building'.

The difference here is a difference between a sacred concept of kingship, as it was symbolically represented in the Renaissance, and the kingless state of Rome. In *Hamlet*, in *Macbeth*, to a lesser extent in *King Lear*, the mystical identity of king and country is an imaginative datum. *Julius Caesar* turns on the radical resistance in Roman ideology to the claim of any one man to be more than one man. In *Antony and Cleopatra* the triumvirs are 'triple pillars of the world' as a rhetorical fiction merely. It is not only the Tribunes but the very action of *Coriolanus* which thwart his desire to 'depopulate the city and be every man himself'. The microcosm/macrocosm analogy is fundamentally different within a conception of the polis in which all its citizens, down to its great toe, are members of one another, and a state where one person, one body, symbolically incorporates the life of everybody.

With differences in the political construction of the world, there are broader differences in the way it is represented in language. To a large extent, the tragedies were made from linguistic whole cloth. In some degree, a consciously Roman style was cultivated for the Roman plays, but very frequently we find the same rhetorical tropes recurring from play to play, whatever the setting. So it is, for instance, with the conventional association of celestial disorders and human disasters. In *Julius Caesar*, as in *Hamlet*, 'The heavens themselves blaze forth the death of princes'; in *King Lear* 'these late eclipses of the sun and moon portend no good to us'. Man pins his faith on love, and its failure is the collapse of the universe: for Troilus, 'The bonds of heaven are slipp'd, dissolv'd, and loos'd'; for Othello, 'chaos is come again'. The death of one person destroys the possibility of meaning in the latter-day world in which the survivor is left. Macbeth on Duncan:

> from this instant,
> There's nothing serious in mortality –
> All is but toys.

Cleopatra on Antony:

> The odds is gone,
> And there is nothing left remarkable
> Beneath the visiting moon.

Even for Shakespeare, the stock-in-trade of figures of speech to express dramatically the extremities of human emotion was limited, and he redeployed them at need throughout the tragedies.

Yet these same figures differ strikingly in effect from instance to instance, depending on whether the context does or does not admit a transcendent order of absolutes. Thus, for Macbeth, 're-nown and grace is dead' with the death of Duncan. That death, his deed, has truly emptied the world and his words of significance. The concepts of renown and grace have a sovereignty matching the sovereignty of kingship itself. It is otherwise with Cleopatra. 'O wither'd is the garland of the war, The soldier's pole is fall'n'.

Even as we yield to the beautiful pathos of the lines, this is felt to be the hyperbolic elegy it is. Antony cannot be the type of all soldiers as Duncan can embody kingship, because the play has revealed the imagined element in his or anyone's image as soldier-hero.

The figurative language of the secular tragedies characteristically draws attention to itself, offers perspectives which place its figurativeness. In the tragedies of the sacred, the imagination climbs towards truths beyond itself, their authenticity guaranteed by the very struggle to conceive them. Metaphor in such a context can be fully metamorphic. Chaos *is* come again, the play's world is unmade, when Othello loses faith in Desdemona. By contrast, though our hearts may go out to Troilus in the pain of his disillusionment, the watching comments of Thersites and Ulysses cut into his rhetoric: 'Will 'a swagger himself out on's own eyes?' 'May worthy Troilus be half-attach'd With that which here his passion doth express?' Troilus' speech has to be seen as the expression of passion to be distinguished from the realities it tries to transmute. Such a withholding of poetic faith, the refusal to suspend disbelief, belong with a scepticism very differently valued in plays founded upon belief and those founded on irony. So Cicero's comment in *Julius Caesar* on the omens, 'men may construe things after their fashion Clean from the purpose of the things themselves', seems a normative neutrality, a wise detachment. By comparison, the sardonic sneer of Edmund, 'an admirable evasion of whoremaster man, to lay his goatish disposition on a star', bespeaks a polemic atheism which redounds against itself. This is not just a contrast of dramatic context. The lines in *Julius Caesar* are representative of a prevailing doubt in the secular tragedies about the human tendency to invest the world with meaning through language, whereas in *King Lear*, as in the other sacred tragedies, to deny that tendency is to deny the informing purpose and value of life itself.

The plays with a classical setting are without a transcendent metaphysic extending outward the significance of their characters' lives. Equally, they are without the full interiority of the protagonists in the other tragedies. Soliloquies are crucial to the dramatic experience of *Hamlet*, *Othello*, *King Lear* and *Macbeth*, though in the case of Lear they are often apostrophes, mad meditations, rather than conventional soliloquies. In each case, an audience is implicated in the inner life of the hero, a life adrift from the social world that surrounds it. The madness of Hamlet or Lear, the metamorphosis of Othello, the distracted 'raptness' of Macbeth, focus attention on the separateness of their dislocated and fractured selves. The self-reflexive inwardness of these heroes is largely missing from the classical tragedies.

In the case of Brutus, the orchard soliloquy does appear to give private access to the troubled mind within. But for the rest of the play he remains unswervingly committed to his public Roman personhood. Even visitation by Caesar's spirit before Philippi provokes none of the anguished self-examination that Richard III must go through in *his* tent, after the appearance of *his* ghosts, on the eve of the battle of Bosworth. Brutus' stoical integrity commands the respect due to its ideal Romanness; it is not displayed for censure as a suppression of the inner life. The self in the secular tragedies is socially constructed. 'There is a world elsewhere', exclaims Coriolanus in injured anger turning his back on the Rome that has expelled him. But there isn't. Rome has made him and there can be no self for him outside the city. The ultimate in self-annihilation for an Antony is imaged as liquidation: 'here I am Antony; Yet cannot hold this visible shape'. The visible shape, the identity validated by others' eyes, this is the only self which the Roman heroes have to lose, and its loss is tragic catastrophe. By contrast, to escape selfhood in just such a way is what Hamlet longs for: 'O that this too too solid flesh would melt'. In comparison with the torments that inhabiting the self inflicts in the sacred tragedies, the burden of consciousness for Hamlet, the degrading fantasies of Othello, Lear's crazed imagination, Macbeth's haunted aloneness, release into non-being would be release indeed.

The soliloquising innerness of these four heroes is not there primarily to *characterise* them, to bring them before us as more fully individual human beings. Almost the opposite is true. There is more vivid individuation in the little detail of Coriolanus on the battlefield attempting, and failing, to remember the name of his poor Coriolan host whom he wants released, than in the great soliloquies of Hamlet or Macbeth. One self, inside itself, feels much like another. In soliloquy distinguishing particulars of character, which are the marks of outer notedness, fall away, and the movements of the mind are experienced as generic, representative. 'To be or not to be' puts the question at its most fundamental, hence its problematic relation to its dramatic context – is Hamlet thinking about suicide or revenge, why does the speech come where it does in the action? Soliloquy is both a withdrawal into selfhood and a lapsing out from its specificities. As such it makes possible the expression of a drama beyond the bounds of character and situation.

Throughout *Hamlet*, *Othello*, *King Lear* and *Macbeth*, inner and outer interchange and interpenetrate. The vision of the in-turned hero, shut out from his social environment, can nonetheless impose itself upon the dramatic world the play creates. We are not able confidently to diagnose Hamlet as neurotic, to place his mental condition as pathological, because his diseased and death-obsessed imagination of Denmark as a prison makes it a prison for us too. 'There is nothing either good or bad, but thinking makes it so.' This should be no more than the trite commonplace of a complacently sceptical relativism, but in *Hamlet* it is not. Hamlet's self-nausea authenticates a tragic universe. It is similar with Othello, Lear and Macbeth. Even where, as in the case of Othello, we can see how completely he is deluded, we are committed to his vision of what love and its betrayal need to mean. Lear is childish, absurd, has been played as senile already in the first scene of the play. Yet can any audience or reader honestly set aside his outraged imagination of apocalypse as the temper-tantrums of second childhood? Why, we may wonder, can we not simply assent to Malcolm's perfectly accurate final description of Macbeth and his wife as 'this dead butcher, and his fiend-like queen'. Not merely because we have identified with them emotionally and feel for their destruction, physical and moral, but because to identify with them was to share the play's deepest imaginative apprehension of the world.

In this mutuality of inner and outer, the spiritual supports the sacred. The travail of the spirit in the tragedies does not bring the hero to the assurance of a certain providential order in the end. Rather, the very bafflement of the soul enforces an awed awareness of what it fails to understand. 'There are more things in heaven and earth, Horatio, Than are dreamt of in your philosophy.' The nature of the numinous is not doctrinally specific, not Christian, nor pagan, nor pagan standing in for Christian. The sacred is intuited instead in the soul's need for it, in the disturbance of the self struggling for a self-transcendent vision. By contrast, in the secular tragedies both self and world are constructed and seen to be constructed. In this their lack of interiority and of a metaphysical dimension is linked. The characters in these plays define themselves as they belong within a city, a culture, a social community. There are no other selves for them to be. The destruction of the self, its tragic impossibility, derives in the secular tragedies from the fiction of the self's autonomy. The best the protagonists can do is to endeavour to be true to that fiction. The personality can not fissure and collapse inward into that nothingness which, in the sacred tragedies, allows the imagination of a corresponding infinite.

I have called this book *Shakespeare's Tragic Imagination* – there was a case for calling it *Shakespeare's Tragic Imaginations*. One of the main aims of my argument has been to stress that Shakespeare's tragic imagination is not single but (at least) double. The tragedies do not conform to one pattern, do not support one view of the world. Historically, it may well be that the co-existence in the Renaissance of different conceptions of man in the universe made possible the alternation of a sacred with a secular tragic vision. In Shakespeare's texts it appears to have been a creative development growing from the encounter with the historical perspectives of the classical world, alternating with other mythic or visionary modes of imagination. The two groups of plays that resulted are quite startlingly different in language, in atmosphere, in dramatic effect. A bias towards the modernity of the secular tragedies, with their awareness of the cultural createdness of human lives, should not lead us to misread the mysterious givenness of things in the sacred tragedies. In spite of this doubling of the tragic imagination in Shakespeare, however, I decided to keep the title of my book singular. Because, in the end, that imagination, so extraordinary in its capacity to tenant apparently antithetical or incompatible ways of seeing, is one and is Shakespeare's.

Notes

PREFACE

1. Vivian Thomas, *Shakespeare's Roman Worlds* (London and New York, 1989), p. 4.
2. Kenneth Muir, *Shakespeare's Tragic Sequence* (Liverpool, 2nd edn, 1979), p. 12.

1   FROM THE HISTORIES TO THE TRAGEDIES

1. Quotations from Shakespeare here, and throughout, are from Peter Alexander (ed.), *The Complete Works* (London, 1951).
2. See particularly John Wilders, *The Lost Garden* (London, 1978).
3. See Philip Edwards's illuminating analysis of the 'rex absconditus' in *Threshold of a Nation* (Cambridge, 1979), pp. 110–30.
4. E.M.W. Tillyard, *Shakespeare's History Plays* (London, 1944).
5. Arthur Sewell, *Character and Society in Shakespeare* (Oxford, 1951), pp. 77, 80.
6. J.L. Simmons, *Shakespeare's Pagan World: the Roman Tragedies* (Brighton, 1974).
7. This is the date assigned to it by the editors of the 1986 Oxford *Complete Works*, who also ascribe a share of its authorship to Middleton. See Chapter 6 for a fuller discussion of the question.

2   *JULIUS CAESAR*

1. See particularly Geoffrey Bullough, *Narrative and Dramatic Sources of Shakespeare* (London and New York 1964), Vol. V, pp. 4–35. References for source material quoted from Bullough's collection throughout the book are given parenthetically in the text.
2. Bernard Shaw, *Collected Plays with their Prefaces* (London, 1971), Vol. II, p. 39.
3. Ernest Schanzer, *The Problem Plays of Shakespeare* (London, 1963), pp. 32–3.
4. J.E. Phillips Jr., *The State in Shakespeare's Greek and Roman Plays* (New York, 1940), p. 172.
5. Schanzer, *Problem Plays of Shakespeare*, p. 51.
6. René Girard, *Violence and the Sacred*, trans. Patrick Gregory (Baltimore, 1977).
7. See, for example, Leo Kirschbaum, 'Shakespeare's Stage Blood and its Critical Significance', *PMLA* 64 (1949), 524, and Maurice Charney,

Shakespeare's Roman Plays (Cambridge, Mass., 1961), p. 49, both of whom stress the shock effect of the scene's bloodiness. Ernest Schanzer, however, is of a different opinion, suggesting that 'we feel towards [the assassination] more as we do towards "The Murder of Gonzago" than the murder of Duncan'. See Schanzer, *Problem Plays of Shakespeare*, p. 66.

8. Brents Stirling, *Unity in Shakespearean Tragedy* (New York, 1956), p. 49.
9. Stirling, *Unity in Shakespearean Tragedy*, p. 50.
10. Simmons, *Shakespeare's Pagan World*, p. 68.
11. Nicholas Brooke, *Shakespeare's Early Tragedies* (London, 1968), p. 143.
12. Schanzer, *Problem Plays of Shakespeare*, p. 37.
13. For a succinct summary of the question, see Arthur Humphreys (ed.), *Julius Caesar* (Oxford, 1984), V.i.111n.
14. For a detailed treatment of the subject see Rowland Wymer, *Suicide and Despair in the Jacobean Drama* (Brighton, 1986).
15. Charney, *Shakespeare's Roman Plays*, p. 16.
16. Reuben A. Brower, *Hero and Saint: Shakespeare and the Graeco-Roman Heroic Tradition* (Oxford, 1971), p. 226.

3 HAMLET

1. For discussion of the question of dating see E.A.J. Honigmann, 'The Date of *Hamlet*', *Shakespeare Survey* 9 (1956), 24–34.
2. See Harold Jenkins (ed.), *Hamlet* (London, 1982), III.ii.103n.
3. Philip Edwards (ed.), *Hamlet* (Cambridge, 1985), p. 6.
4. John Dover Wilson, *What Happens in Hamlet* (Cambridge, 3rd edn, 1951), pp. 52–86.
5. Eleanor Prosser, *Hamlet and Revenge* (Stanford, 1967).
6. Compare Peter Mercer's comments on the 'doubleness of the structure of revenge tragedy' in his excellent book, Hamlet *and the Acting of Revenge* (London, 1987), p. 14.
7. G. Wilson Knight, *The Wheel of Fire* (London, 4th edn, 1949), p. 33.
8. Wilson Knight, *The Wheel of Fire*, p. 33.
9. Wilson Knight, *The Wheel of Fire*, pp. 34, 35.
10. Jenkins, *Hamlet*, I.v.93n.
11. See Edwards, *Hamlet*, p. 14 and I.iv.17–38n.
12. Reuben Brower reads this speech as wholly admiring of Fortinbras, *Hero and Saint: Shakespeare and the Graeco-Roman Heroic Tradition* (Oxford, 1971), p. 303. I find G.K. Hunter's analysis of the mixed tone of the speech much more convincing. See 'The Heroism of Hamlet', in *Dramatic Identities and Cultural Tradition* (Liverpool, 1978), pp. 235–6.
13. OED cites this passage as the first recorded instance of 'relative', *adj.* 3, 'having relation to the question or matter in hand: pertinent, relevant'.
14. Ernest Jones's fullest study is the book-length *Hamlet and Oedipus* (London, 1949). For a more recent psychoanalytic analysis of the play, see C.L. Barber and Richard P. Wheeler, *The Whole Journey: Shakespeare's Power of Development* (Berkeley, Los Angeles and London, 1986), pp. 237–81.

15. L.C. Knights, 'An Approach to *Hamlet*', in *'Hamlet' and other Shakespearean Essays* (Cambridge, 1979), p. 45.
16. Wilson Knight, *The Wheel of Fire*, p. 32.
17. Hamlet glances at the doctrine of the king's two bodies in his riddling antics after the murder of Polonius: 'The body is with the King, but the King is not with the body' (IV.ii.26–7). Rosencrantz enunciates a traditional exposition of the organic interrelation of king and kingdom, III.iii.15–23.
18. Gilbert Murray, 'Hamlet and Orestes', in *The Classical Tradition in Poetry* (Cambridge, Mass., 1927).
19. Wilson, *What Happens in Hamlet*, p. 267.
20. Harley Granville Barker, *Prefaces to Shakespeare* (London, 1958), Vol. I, p. 139.
21. Brower, *Hero and Saint*, p. 310.
22. See, for example, Martin Dodsworth's analysis of the graveyard-scene in *Hamlet Closely Observed* (London, 1985), pp. 236–51.
23. 'Fighting' in the heart is used as the same sort of semi-physiological sign of premonition in *Arden of Faversham*, Scene 9, 1, ed. K. Sturgess (Harmondsworth, 1969).
24. See, for example, Edwards, *Hamlet*, p. 58: 'There is no doubt of the extent of Hamlet's failure. In trying to restore "the beauteous majesty of Denmark" he has brought the country into an even worse state, in the hands of a foreigner.'
25. In one production, directed by Michael Bogdanov (Dublin, 1983), heavily influenced by memories of the Falklands War, Fortinbras' entry was a massive paratroop assault on the stage; the 1988 Renaissance Theatre Company version had an even more sinister militaristic *coup d'état*, with the words 'Go bid the soldiers shoot' an order for immediate political liquidations, starting with Horatio.
26. D.G. James, *The Dream of Learning* (Oxford, 1951), p. 36.
27. C.S. Lewis, '*Hamlet*: the Prince or the Poem', reprinted in *Shakespeare's Tragedies: an Anthology of Modern Criticism*, ed. Laurence Lerner (Harmondsworth, 1963), p. 75. See also Philip Edwards, 'Tragic Balance in *Hamlet*', *Shakespeare Survey* 36 (1983), 43–52.

4 TROILUS AND CRESSIDA

1. G.K. Hunter, '*Troilus and Cressida*: a tragic satire', *Shakespeare Studies* (Tokyo) 13 (1977), 1–23.
2. See the interesting debate between T. McAlindon and Mark Sacharoff on 'Language, Style and Meaning in *Troilus and Cressida*', *PMLA* 87 (1972), 90–9, arising out of an original article by McAlindon in *PMLA* 84 (1969).
3. See, for example, Gayle Greene, 'Language and Value in Shakespeare's *Troilus and Cressida*', *Studies in English Literature 1500–1900*, 21 (1981), 271–85.
4. See Peter Alexander, '*Troilus and Cressida*, 1609', *The Library* (4th series) IX (1928), 267–86.

5. See Kenneth Palmer (ed.), *Troilus and Cressida* (London, 1982), p. 47, n. 2.

6. See, for example, Hamish F.G. Swanston, 'The Baroque Element in *Troilus and Cressida*', *Durham University Journal*, XIX (N.S.) (1957–8), 14–23, or Greene, 'Language and Value in Shakespeare's *Troilus and Cressida*', 285.

7. *Troilus and Criseyde*, Book III, 1776–78, *The Complete Works of Geoffrey Chaucer*, ed. F.N. Robinson (Oxford, 2nd edn, 1974).

8. A.J. Smith, *Literary Love* (London, 1983), p. 33.

9. *Troilus and Criseyde*, Book IV, 152–4.

10. Oscar J. Campbell, *Comicall Satyre and Shakespeare's Troilus and Cressida* (San Marino, California, 1938), pp. 212, 213.

11. Kenneth Muir (ed.), *Troilus and Cressida* (Oxford, 1982), III.ii.11n.

12. See Palmer (ed.), *Troilus and Cressida*, III.ii.11n.

13. Campbell, *Comicall Satyre*, p. 212.

14. See Ann Thompson, *Shakespeare's Chaucer* (Liverpool, 1978), pp. 133, 141.

15. John Bayley, *The Uses of Division* (London, 1976), p. 205.

16. See Carolyn Asp, 'In Defense of Cressida', *Studies in Philology*, 74 (1977), 406–17, or Gayle Greene, 'Shakespeare's Cressida: "A kind of self"', in *The Woman's Part: Feminist Criticism of Shakespeare*, eds Carolyn R.S. Lenz, Gayle Greene and Carol T. Neely (Urbana, Illinois, 1980), pp. 133–49.

17. Miguel de Cervantes Saavedra, *The Adventures of Don Quixote*, trans. J.M. Cohen (Harmondsworth, 1950), p. 108.

18. Bernard Shaw, *Collected Plays with their Prefaces* (London, 1970), Vol. I, p. 29.

19. Jonathan Dollimore, *Radical Tragedy* (Brighton, 1984), pp. 40–50.

20. Rosalie Colie, *Shakespeare's Living Art* (Princeton, 1974), p. 351.

21. Elizabeth Freund suggests that in future the play may come to be regarded not as a unique oddity in the Shakespeare canon but a paradigmatic Renaissance text in its simultaneous awareness of and challenge to its classical precursors. See '"Ariachne's broken woof": the rhetoric of citation in *Troilus and Cressida*', in *Shakespeare and the Question of Theory*, eds Patricia Parker and Geoffrey Hartman (New York and London, 1985), pp. 19–36.

22. Jane Adamson, *Troilus and Cressida* (Brighton, 1987), p. 164.

5 OTHELLO

1. See G.M. Matthews, '*Othello* and the Dignity of Man', in *Shakespeare in a Changing World*, ed. Arnold Kettle (London, 1964), pp. 123–45.

2. This is the hypothesis of Emrys Jones, '*Othello*, *Lepanto* and the Cyprus Wars', reprinted from *Shakespeare Survey* in *Aspects of Othello*, eds Kenneth Muir and Philip Edwards (Cambridge, 1977), pp. 61–6.

3. 'The Lepanto', lines 10–11, *The Poems of James VI of Scotland*, ed. James Craigie (Edinburgh and London, 1955), Vol. I, p. 202.

4. Such was the suggestion of Eduard Engel, cited in Bullough, VII, 195.

5. *Poems of James VI*, Vol. I, p. 198.
6. G.K. Hunter, 'Othello and Colour Prejudice', in *Dramatic Identities and Cultural Tradition* (Liverpool, 1978), pp. 31–59.
7. A point made by Helen Gardner in '*Othello*: a Retrospect, 1900–67', reprinted from *Shakespeare Survey* in *Aspects of Othello*, pp. 1–11.
8. Terry Eagleton, *William Shakespeare* (Oxford, 1986), p. 68.
9. Wilson Knight, *The Wheel of Fire*, p. 107. Those who have argued for the broader significance of the play in various ways include John Bayley in *The Characters of Love* (London, 1960), and Jane Adamson in *Othello as Tragedy: some problems of judgment and feeling* (Cambridge, 1980).
10. The whole issue of rank in the play is well discussed by Paul Jorgensen in *Shakespeare's Military World* (Berkeley and Los Angeles, 1956), pp. 100–18.
11. See Kenneth Muir (ed.), *Othello* (Harmondsworth, 1968), I.i.66n.
12. Stephen Greenblatt, *Renaissance Self-Fashioning: From More to Shakespeare* (Chicago, 1980), p. 242.
13. Helen Gardner, 'The Noble Moor', *Proceedings of the British Academy* 41 (1955), 192.
14. Norman Sanders (ed.), *Othello* (Cambridge, 1984), III.iii.91–2n.
15. William Empson, *The Structure of Complex Words* (London, 1951), p. 219.
16. *Haec-Vir: or The Womanish Man* (London, 1620), sig. B2v. Interestingly, on the same page of this anonymous pamphlet, it is said that 'the Venetians kisse one another ever at the first meeting'.
17. Lawrence Stone in *The Family, Sex and Marriage in England 1500–1800* (London, 1977), pp. 520–1, in commenting on the English custom of kissing in his chapter on 'Upper-class attitudes and behaviour' in relation to sex, and in his statement that 'sexual modesty was a characteristic of the lower-middle-class' (*Family, Sex and Marriage*, p. 522), seems to imply that the practice was thus class-specific, though he doesn't actually say so. Further evidence is provided by the passage in Middleton's *Women Beware Women*, where the bourgeois Leantio's mother welcomes her new aristocratic daughter-in-law Bianca:

> MOTHER: Gentlewoman, thus much is a debt of courtesy
>   [*Kisses her.*]
> Which fashionable strangers pay each other
> At a kind meeting

Women Beware Women, I.i.111–13, in Thomas Middleton, *Five Plays*, eds Bryan Loughrey and Neil Taylor (London, 1988).
18. Eagleton, *William Shakespeare*, p. 68.
19. For Iago's Vice ancestry see Bernard Spivack, *Shakespeare and the Allegory of Evil* (New York, 1958). Leah Scragg argues persuasively, against Spivack, that Iago is related to stage presentations of the Devil rather than the Vice in 'Iago – Vice or Devil?', reprinted from *Shakespeare Survey* in *Aspects of Othello*, pp. 48–59.
20. Jane Adamson, in *Othello as Tragedy*, p. 146, suggests the term crisis-scene instead.

21. See T.R. Henn, *The Living Image* (London, 1972), pp. 17–18, for commentary on this image.
22. Michael Long, *The Unnatural Scene: a Study in Shakespearean Tragedy* (London, 1976), p. 58.
23. See Martin Elliott's interesting analysis of this passage in *Shakespeare's Invention of Othello* (London, 1988), p. 70.
24. Pointed out by David Kaula, 'Othello Possessed: Notes on Shakespeare's Use of Magic and Witchcraft', *Shakespeare Studies* 2 (1966), 112–32.
25. This is the view of, among others, S.L. Bethell, 'Shakespeare's Imagery: the Diabolic Images in Othello', reprinted from *Shakespeare Survey* in *Aspects of Othello*, pp. 29–47. The whole issue of whether Othello is to be seen as saved or damned is well discussed by Rowland Wymer, *Suicide and Despair in Jacobean Drama*, p. 90ff.
26. Mark Rose, 'Othello's Occupation: Shakespeare and the Romance of Chivalry', *English Literary Renaissance* 15 (1985), 306.
27. According to Rowland Wymer, it has more words of Christian significance than in any other Shakespeare play apart from *Richard III*, *Suicide and Despair in the Jacobean Drama*, p. 90.
28. Robert Hapgood, 'Othello', in *Shakespeare*, Select Bibliographical Guides, ed. Stanley Wells (Oxford, 1973), p. 166.
29. See Jane Adamson on the importance of the suicide as it conditions our reading of the last speech: *Othello as Tragedy*, p. 296.

6 TIMON OF ATHENS

1. I am accepting the dating of the editors of the Oxford Shakespeare as 1604–5, after *Othello* and immediately before *King Lear*, even though the evidence is largely conjectural; nearly as good a case can be made for assigning it to a later date, between *Antony and Cleopatra* and *Coriolanus*. See *William Shakespeare, The Complete Works: Compact Edition*, general editors, Stanley Wells and Gary Taylor (Oxford, 1988), p. 883, and Stanley Wells and Gary Taylor, with John Jowett and William Montgomery, *William Shakespeare: a Textual Companion* (Oxford, 1987), p. 127. I am also convinced, as the Oxford editors are, by the arguments of R.V. Holdsworth that Middleton collaborated with Shakespeare in *Timon*; see R.V. Holdsworth, *Middleton and Shakespeare: the Case for Middleton's Hand in* Timon of Athens (PhD, University of Manchester, 1982). In any such collaboration, though, Shakespeare would have been the senior partner – Middleton, in his mid twenties at the conjectured time of composition, was still near the beginning of his playwriting career. Even allowing for Middleton's hand in the play, therefore, and for the generally agreed unfinished nature of the text, it still seems to me to remain, in substance, an authentic work of the Shakespearean imagination. In what follows, I comment on Middleton's presumed share in the play only where it appears outstandingly distinct in tone or theme.
2. See A.D. Nuttall, *Timon of Athens* (New York, London, etc., 1989), pp. xi, xviii–xix.

3. See Willard Farnham's useful analysis of the various versions of the Timon legend in *Shakespeare's Tragic Frontier* (Berkeley, 1950, repr. Oxford, 1973), pp. 50–68.
4. The references to Judas and the Eucharist at I.ii.38–47, echoed in III.ii.64–5, commented on below, come in scenes ascribed to Middleton by Holdsworth and the Oxford editors. Similarly the allusion to the Sermon on the Mount in Flavius' speech at IV.iii.464–5 –

   How rarely does it meet with this time's guise,
   When man was wish'd to love his enemies

   – is part of a section accounted definitely Middletonian. See Wells, Taylor, Jowett and Montgomery, *William Shakespeare: a Textual Companion*, p. 127, for a complete listing of the passages ascribed by Holdsworth to Middleton.
5. Emrys Jones, *The Origins of Shakespeare* (Oxford, 1977), p. 73.
6. Farnham, *Shakespeare's Tragic Frontier*, p. 57.
7. *The Revenger's Tragedy*, III.v.79–80, in Thomas Middleton, *Five Plays*, ed. Loughrey and Taylor. In the battle over the authorship of *The Revenger's Tragedy*, the Middletonians seem to be winning, and the speech of Apemantus quoted is from a Middleton scene of *Timon*. The similarity between the two passages is hardly surprising if they are both by the same author.
8. Knights, *'Hamlet' and other Shakespearean Essays*, p. 104.
9. As Lesley W. Brill does in 'Truth and *Timon of Athens'*, *Modern Language Quarterly* 40 (1979), 28–9.
10. See, for example, the influential views of Muriel Bradbrook, in *Shakespeare the Craftsman* (Cambridge, 1969): 'The piece describes an arc – a double rainbow or solar year; the rising half is divided into scenes which are set in opposition with the falling half', p. 145.
11. Knights, *'Hamlet' and other Shakespearean Essays*, p. 111.
12. L.C. Knights is provoked to censorious disapproval – 'Timon, in becoming nastier, has become sillier', *'Hamlet' and other Shakespearean Essays*, p. 114. R.P. Draper also finds the speech disturbing, coming near 'to what Lawrence calls "doing dirt" on life', *'Timon of Athens'*, *Shakespeare Quarterly* VIII (1957), 197.
13. *Tamburlaine*, Part I, II.vii.18–20, *The Complete Works of Christopher Marlowe*, ed. Fredson Bowers (Cambridge, 1973), I.
14. Farnham, *Shakespeare's Tragic Frontier*, pp. 65–7.
15. This scene, and the whole part of Flavius, are confidently attributed to Middleton by Holdsworth on the basis of his battery of technical authorship tests. Formally and stylistically, however, the role of the Steward is well integrated into the text.
16. See David Grene, *Reality and the Heroic Pattern* (Chicago, 1967), pp. 154–66.
17. John Dover Wilson, *The Essential Shakespeare* (Cambridge, 1932), p. 131.

7 *KING LEAR*

1. G.K. Hunter (ed.), *King Lear* (Harmondsworth, 1972), p. 7.
2. See Wilfrid Perrett, *The Story of King Lear from Geoffrey of Monmouth to Shakespeare* (Berlin, 1904), pp. 1–28.
3. Quoted by Perrett, *The Story of King Lear*, p. 7, from the 1695 edition of Camden's *Britannia*. The full Latin text ran as follows: 'Quod nomen Romanis temporibus gesserit Leicestria, non coniicio. *Caer Lerion* in Nennii Catalago vocari existimo, sed Leirum fabulosum Regem construxisse, per me, credat qui velit.' William Camden, *Britannia* (London, 1600).
4. Quotation in this chapter, for consistency with the rest of the book, is from the Alexander text, but in the light of the major textual controversy over the play in recent years, and the strenuous arguments put forward by the Oxford editors and others against the traditional conflated text, I have checked First Quarto (Q) and Folio (F) variants throughout and have noted these where they seem to make a crucial difference in sense.
5. Janet Adelman comments that the play's opening 'seems . . . to insist on its distance from contemporary political concerns by introducing the alarming spectacle of a king about to divide his kingdom and then making it clear that the king's noblemen and counsellors do not find the spectacle alarming'. See Janet Adelman (ed.), *Twentieth Century Interpretations of King Lear* (Englewood Cliffs, NJ, 1978), p. 6.
6. See Bullough, VII, 337–402, for a full text of *The True Chronicle Historie of King Leir*.
7. See Harry V. Jaffa, 'The Limits of Politics: *King Lear*, Act I, scene i' in Allan Bloom with Harry V. Jaffa, *Shakespeare's Politics* (New York, 1964).
8. *Locrine* (London, 1595, repr. Tudor Facsimile Texts, Edinburgh and London, 1911), B3.
9. *Coleridge's Shakespeare Criticism*, ed. Thomas Middleton Raysor (London, 1930), Vol. I, pp. 60–1.
10. As William R. Elton concludes in the fullest and most systematic study of the subject, 'Shakespeare seems deliberately striving for fidelity to heathen life and experience as the Renaissance could have understood them'. *King Lear and the Gods* (Lexington, Kentucky, 2nd edn, 1988), p. 254.
11. See Kenneth Muir (ed.), *King Lear* (London, 1950, repr. 1985), pp. xviii–xix for discussion of this.
12. Extracts printed in Bullough, VII, 414–20.
13. Ann Thompson, 'Who Sees Double in the Double Plot?', in *Shakespearian Tragedy*, eds Malcolm Bradbury and David Palmer (London, 1984), pp. 47–75.
14. *Coleridge's Shakespeare Criticism*, Vol. I, p. 61.
15. Kathleen McCluskie, 'The Patriarchal Bard: Feminist Criticism and Shakespeare: *King Lear* and *Measure for Measure*', in *Political Shakespeare*, eds Jonathan Dollimore and Alan Sinfield (Manchester, 1985), p. 106.
16. Elton, *King Lear and the Gods*, pp. 147–70.

17. See Lily B. Campbell, *Shakespeare's Tragedies: Slaves of Passion* (Cambridge, 1930), pp. 175–207.
18. Jonas A. Barish and Marshall Waingrow, '"Service" in *King Lear*', *Shakespeare Quarterly* 9 (1958), 349.
19. *The Canterbury Tales*, X, 538, Robinson (ed.) *Complete Works of Geoffrey Chaucer*, p. 244.
20. In Peter Brook's 1970 film, based on his famous theatre production of the 1960s, Goneril had plenty of reason for complaint against Lear's hundred knights who were visibly the 'disorder'd rabble' she claimed them to be; a close-up of Irene Worth (playing Goneril) showed her suffering through the terrible curse of sterility invoked on her by her father.
21. Maynard Mack, *King Lear in Our Time* (Berkeley and Los Angeles, 1965), p. 49.
22. Paul Jorgensen, *Lear's Self-Discovery* (Berkeley and Los Angeles, 1967), p. 73.
23. Maynard Mack, 'The Jacobean Shakespeare', in *Jacobean Theatre*, Stratford-upon-Avon Studies 1, eds J.R. Brown and Bernard Harris (London, 1962), pp. 17–18.
24. The title-page is reproduced in full in Muir (ed.), *King Lear*, p. xviii.
25. Stephen Greenblatt, 'Shakespeare and the Exorcists', in *Shakespeare and The Question of Theory*, eds Patricia Parker and Geoffrey Hartman (New York and London, 1985), p. 177. This essay appears in revised form in Greenblatt's *Shakespearean Negotiations* (Oxford, 1988), pp. 94–128.
26. 'According to the traditional irascible-concupiscible distinction, Lear's intellectual error of anger receives the conventional punishment of madness (*ira furor brevis*), and Gloucester's physical sin of lechery the conventional retribution of blindness.' W.R. Elton, *King Lear and the Gods*, p. 270.
27. Janet Adelman, however, in one of the most illuminating analyses of the figure of Edgar, makes a persuasive case for regarding him 'not merely as a succession of roles, but as a full character who expresses himself through these roles'. Adelman, *Twentieth Century Interpretations of King Lear*, p. 16.
28. *Luke* 2, 49. The quotation is from the 1562 Geneva *Bible*, which would have been familiar to Shakespeare, and is even closer to Cordelia's words than the later Authorised Version: 'wist ye not that I must be about my Father's *businesse*'.
29. C.L. Barber and Richard P. Wheeler, *The Whole Journey*, p. 293.
30. W.K. Wimsatt Jr (ed.), *Samuel Johnson on Shakespeare* (London, 1960), p. 97.
31. This was strenuously argued by Wilfrid Perrett in 1904, *The Story of King Lear*, pp. 243–5, but it has largely been ignored by subsequent scholars and critics.
32. John Reibetanz, *The Lear World* (Toronto, 1977), p. 114.
33. For this pattern, much remarked on in modern criticism, see particularly, Stephen Booth, *King Lear, Macbeth, Indefinition and Tragedy* (New Haven and London, 1983).
34. This is particularly true of F's deletion of Edgar's substantial account of Kent's offstage appearance after the death of Gloucester (V.iii.204–21).

This speech may have seemed necessary in the first place to bring the long absent and inactive Kent back into the story, but it retards the action intolerably and it may well have been felt actually to weaken Kent's subsequent entrance.

35. Jan Kott, *Shakespeare Our Contemporary*, trans. Boleslaw Taborski (London, 2nd edn, 1967), p. 116.
36. Greenblatt, 'Shakespeare and the Exorcists', p. 177.
37. Ibid., p. 181.

8 MACBETH

1. I.ii is one of the (many) scenes in the play pronounced unShakespearean in the past; it benefited from the reintegrating movement of the mid-twentieth century which reclaimed so much of the supposedly spurious in the canon as authentic, only to be again called in question by a contrary swing-back in scholarly fashion. The Oxford editors who ascribe *Macbeth* to 'William Shakespeare, adapted by Thomas Middleton' do not definitely give the scene to Middleton but point to renewed suspicions cast on its authorship by R.V. Holdsworth's work on *Timon of Athens*. See Wells and Taylor *et al.*, *William Shakespeare: a Textual Companion*, p. 129. However, without substantial evidence, such as there is for the Hecate scenes, that it is not original Shakespeare, it seems reasonable to assume that it is integral to the play's design.
2. See Bullough, VII, 511–13. The effect of compression may have been accentuated by cuts in the text: see Kenneth Muir (ed.), *Macbeth* (London, 1951), I.ii notes.
3. Wilbur Sanders, *The Dramatist and the Received Idea* (Cambridge, 1968), p. 257.
4. For the importance of this 'mark', see Keith Thomas, *Religion and the Decline of Magic* (London, 1971), p. 530.
5. T.W. Baldwin assigned all three parts to the very shadowy apprentice John Edmans, but on highly conjectural evidence. See *The Organization and Personnel of the Shakespearean Company* (Princeton, 1927), p. 277 and charts III and IV facing p. 229.
6. Muir (ed.), *Macbeth*, V.i.34n. Frederick Turner also denies that Macbeth 'shows much moral sensitivity to his crime: he is concerned . . . with the physical consequences of his actions and their effect on his own interests', *Shakespeare and the Nature of Time* (Oxford, 1971), p. 129.
7. This, at least, is one way of playing the scene going back to Irving. See Marvin Rosenberg, *The Masks of Macbeth* (Berkeley, Los Angeles, London, 1978), p. 267.
8. See A.C. Bradley, *Shakespearean Tragedy* (London, 1904), p. 334, and Muir (ed.), *Macbeth*, I.vi.S.D.n. G.K. Hunter (ed.), *Macbeth* (Harmondsworth, 1967), in his note on the scene thinks it is set in daylight and conjectures that the 'torches' refer to attendants who would normally act as torch-bearers.
9. For commentary on the ambiguous effect of this passage, see M.J.B.

Allen, 'Toys, Prologues and the Great Amiss: Shakespeare's Tragic Openings', in *Shakespearian Tragedy*, Stratford-upon-Avon Studies, 20, eds M. Bradbury and D. Palmer (London, 1984), p. 7.

10. Quoted by Roland Mushat Frye, *Shakespeare and Christian Doctrine* (Princeton, 1963), p. 196.

11. H.N. Paul examines the background of the King's attitude towards 'touching', his reluctant agreement to continue the traditional ceremony under pressure from his English advisers, and concludes, ingeniously if hardly convincingly, that 'the king's councillors wished help in their efforts to bring the king to their way of thinking concerning the royal touch. . . . The dramatist of the King's Company knew of their wishes and respected them.' *The Royal Play of Macbeth* (New York, 1950), p. 385.

12. An effect first commented on by Cleanth Brooks, 'The Naked Babe and the Cloak of Manliness', in *The Well Wrought Urn* (London, 1949), p. 45.

13. Reproduced from John Leslie's 1578 *De Origine, Moribus, et Rebus Gestis Scotorum* in Bullough, VII, plate 2, facing 517.

14. John Bayley, *Shakespeare and Tragedy* (London, Boston, etc., 1981), p. 192.

15. Richard Marienstras, *New Perspectives on the Shakespearean World*, trans. Janet Lloyd (Cambridge and Paris, 1985), p. 79.

16. Marienstras analyses interlaced systems of reference in the play to the honourable and the sacrilegious shedding of blood. *New Perspectives on the Shakespearean World*, p. 94.

9 *ANTONY AND CLEOPATRA*

1. The most recent Shakespeare chronology, by the Oxford editors, assigns both plays to 1606. See Wells and Taylor *et al.*, *Textual Companion*, pp. 127–8.

2. L.C. Knights, *Some Shakespearean Themes* (London, 1959), p. 144.

3. Farnham, *Shakespeare's Tragic Frontier*, p. 203.

4. The stage direction is likely to be authorial, given that it appears in the Folio text, generally taken to derive from Shakespeare's own manuscript.

5. The analogy is made by Maurice Charney, *Shakespeare's Roman Plays* (Cambridge, Mass., 1961), p. 130. For commentary on this passage see also Janet Adelman, *The Common Liar: an Essay on Antony and Cleopatra* (New Haven and London, 1973), p. 91.

6. Quotations are from John Donne, *The Complete English Poems*, ed. A.J. Smith (Harmondsworth, 1971).

7. Paul Cantor, *Shakespeare's Rome: Republic and Empire* (Ithaca, NY, 1976), p. 205.

8. A.C. Bradley, *Oxford Lectures on Poetry* (London, 2nd edn, 1909, repr. 1959), p. 291.

9. M.W. MacCallum, *Shakespeare's Roman Plays* (London, 1910), p. 374.

10. Julian Markels, *The Pillar of the World* (Ohio, 1968), p. 43.

11. John F. Danby, *Poets on Fortune's Hill* (London, 1952), p. 144.
12. See David Grene, *The Actor in History: a Study in Shakespearean Stage Poetry* (University Park, Pa, and London, 1988), pp. 13–35.
13. Schanzer, *Problem Plays of Shakespeare*, p. 145.
14. See, among many others, Charney, *Shakespeare's Roman Plays*, p. 140.
15. See Janet Adelman, *The Common Liar*, Chapter 2, 'The Common Liar: Tradition as Source in *Antony and Cleopatra*' for a skilful analysis of the multiple interpretive possibilities, both positive and negative, which these mythological figures afforded to a Renaissance audience.
16. S.L. Goldberg, 'A Tragedy of the Imagination: a Reading of *Antony and Cleopatra*', *Melbourne Critical Review* 4 (1961), 43.
17. Arnold Stein, 'The Image of Antony: Tragic and Lyric Imagination', *Kenyon Review* 21 (1959), 600.
18. Roland Mushat Frye, *Shakespeare and Christian Doctrine*, p. 51.
19. Adelman, *The Common Liar*, p. 166.
20. Danby, *Poets on Fortune's Hill*, p. 149.
21. See Andrew Fichter, '*Antony and Cleopatra*: The Time of Universal Peace', *Shakespeare Survey* 33 (1980), 99–111.

10 CORIOLANUS

1. See D.W. Harding's suggestive article, 'Women's Fantasy of Manhood: a Shakespearian Theme', *Shakespeare Quarterly* 20 (1969), 245–53.
2. On the metonymic character of the play's language, see Lawrence Danson, *Tragic Alphabet: Shakespeare's Drama of Language* (New Haven and London, 1974), p. 143*ff.*
3. See Bullough, V, 456–9.
4. See, for example, Brower, *Hero and Saint*, p. 361, or Bullough, V, 459.
5. The emphasis and punctuation are in doubt here. The Folio text gives 'Oh me alone, make you a sword of me.' The Alexander edition renders this as 'O, me alone! Make you a sword of me?' Other editors reassign the line to the soldiers: see, for example, Philip Brockbank (ed.), *Coriolanus* (London, 1976).
6. One modern monograph has argued that the play represents support for James's increasing absolutism against his Parliamentary adversaries, whom he called 'tribunes of the people'. See Clifford Chalmers Huffman, *Coriolanus in Context* (Lewisburg, 1971).
7. John W. Velz, 'Cracking Strong Curbs Asunder: Roman Destiny and the Roman Hero in *Coriolanus*', *English Literary Renaissance* 13 (1983), 60, 66.
8. Norman Rabkin, *Shakespeare and the Common Understanding* (New York and London, 1967), p. 120.
9. Raysor (ed.), *Coleridge's Shakespeare Criticism*, Vol. I, p. 89.
10. Danson, *Tragic Alphabet*, p. 152.
11. Janet Adelman, '"Anger's My Meat": Feeding, Dependency, and Aggression in *Coriolanus*', in *Shakespeare: Pattern of Excelling Nature*, eds David Bevington and Jay L. Halio (Newark, Delaware and London, 1978), pp. 108–24.

12. Coppelia Kahn, *Man's Estate: Masculine Identity in Shakespeare* (Berkeley, Los Angeles, London, 1981), p. 151.
13. Linda Bamber, *Comic Women, Tragic Men: A Study of Gender and Genre in Shakespeare* (Stanford, 1982), p. 92.
14. Kahn, *Man's Estate*, p. 153.
15. See Cantor, *Shakespeare's Rome: Republic and Empire* for an interpretation of the specifically Republican ethos of the play.
16. 'I do not hear Shakespeare the therapist tut-tutting from behind the couch', comments Wilbur Sanders. See 'An Impossible Person: Caius Martius Coriolanus', in Wilbur Sanders and Howard Jacobson, *Shakespeare's Magnanimity: Four Tragic Heroes, their Friends and Families* (London, 1978), p. 166.
17. See Adrian Poole, *Coriolanus* (New York, London, etc., 1988), p. 102.
18. A.C. Bradley, 'Coriolanus', *Proceedings of the British Academy* (1911–12), 472–3.
19. Anne Barton, 'Livy, Machiavelli, and Shakespeare's *Coriolanus*', *Shakespeare Survey* 38 (1985), 128.
20. This sort of unease is commented on by Brower, *Hero and Saint*, p. 354.
21. Bradley, 'Coriolanus', 466.
22. Michael Goldman, *Shakespeare and the Energies of Drama* (Princeton, 1972), p. 110.
23. Sanders and Jacobson, *Shakespeare's Magnanimity*, p. 164.
24. Rabkin, *Shakespeare and the Common Understanding*, p. 132.
25. Bradley, 'Coriolanus', 463.

11 SACRED AND SECULAR

1. Albert Camus, 'Lecture Given in Athens on the Future of Tragedy', in *Selected Essays and Notebooks*, ed. and trans. Philip Thody (Harmondsworth, 1979), p. 199.
2. John F. Danby, *Shakespeare's Doctrine of Nature: a Study of 'King Lear'* (London, 1949).
3. Philip Edwards, 'Tragic Balance in *Hamlet*', *Shakespeare Survey* 36 (1983), 43–52.
4. Barber and Wheeler, *The Whole Journey*, pp. 1, 38.
5. See Mircea Eliade, *Myths, Dreams and Mysteries*, trans. Philip Mairet (London, 1968), p. 23.
6. Barbara Everett, *Young Hamlet* (Oxford, 1989), pp. 39–40.
7. Rabkin, *Shakespeare and the Common Understanding*, p. 63.

Bibliography

Adamson, Jane, *Othello as Tragedy: some problems of judgment and feeling* (Cambridge, 1980).

Adamson, Jane, *Troilus and Cressida* (Brighton, 1987).

Adelman, Janet, '"Anger's My Meat": Feeding, Dependency, and Aggression in *Coriolanus*', in D. Bevington and J.L. Halio (eds), *Shakespeare: Pattern of Excelling Nature* (Newark, Delaware and London, 1978), pp. 108–24.

Adelman, Janet, *The Common Liar: an Essay on Antony and Cleopatra* (New Haven and London, 1973).

Adelman, Janet, (ed.), *Twentieth Century Interpretations of King Lear* (Englewood Cliffs, NJ, 1978).

Alexander, Peter, (ed.), *The Complete Works of William Shakespeare* (London, 1951).

Alexander, Peter, 'Troilus and Cressida, 1609', *The Library* (4th series) IX (1928), 267–86.

Allen, M.J.B., 'Toys, Prologues and the Great Amiss: Shakespeare's Tragic Openings', in M. Bradbury and D. Palmer (eds), *Shakespearian Tragedy*, Stratford-upon-Avon Studies, 20 (London, 1984), pp. 3–30.

Asp, Carolyn, 'In Defense of Cressida', *Studies in Philology* 74 (1977), 406–17.

Baldwin, T.W., *The Organization and Personnel of the Shakespearean Company* (Princeton, 1927).

Bamber, Linda, *Comic Women, Tragic Men: a Study of Gender and Genre in Shakespeare* (Stanford, 1982).

Barber, C.L. and Wheeler, Richard P., *The Whole Journey: Shakespeare's Power of Development* (Berkeley, Los Angeles, London, 1986).

Barish, Jonas A. and Waingrow, Marshall, '"Service" in *King Lear*', *Shakespeare Quarterly* 9 (1958), 347–55.

Barton, Anne, 'Livy, Machiavelli, and Shakespeare's *Coriolanus*', *Shakespeare Survey* 38 (1985), 115–29.

Bayley, John, *The Characters of Love* (London, 1960).

Bayley, John, *Shakespeare and Tragedy* (London, Boston, etc., 1981).

Bayley, John, *The Uses of Division* (London, 1976).

Bethell, S.L., 'Shakespeare's Imagery: the Diabolic Images in Othello', in K. Muir and P. Edwards (eds), *Aspects of Othello* (Cambridge, 1977), pp. 29–47.

Bevington, David and Halio, Jay L. (eds), *Shakespeare: Pattern of Excelling Nature* (Newark, Delaware and London, 1978).

Bloom, Allan with Jaffa, Harry V., *Shakespeare's Politics* (New York, 1964).

Booth, Stephen, *King Lear, Macbeth, Indefinition and Tragedy* (New Haven and London, 1983).

Bowers, Fredson (ed.), *The Complete Works of Christopher Marlowe* (Cambridge, 1973).

Bradbrook, Muriel, *Shakespeare the Craftsman* (Cambridge, 1969).

Bradbury, Malcolm and Palmer, David (eds), *Shakespearian Tragedy*, Stratford-upon-Avon Studies, 20 (London, 1984).

Bradley, A.C., 'Coriolanus', *Proceedings of the British Academy* (1911–12), 457–73.

Bradley, A.C., *Oxford Lectures on Poetry* (London, 2nd edn, 1909, repr. 1959).

Bradley, A.C., *Shakespearean Tragedy* (London, 1904).

Brill, Lesley W., 'Truth and *Timon of Athens*', *Modern Language Quarterly* 40 (1979), 17–36.

Brockbank, Philip, (ed.), *Coriolanus* (London, 1976).

Brooke, Nicholas, *Shakespeare's Early Tragedies* (London, 1968).

Brooks, Cleanth, *The Well Wrought Urn* (London, 1949).

Brower, Reuben A., *Hero and Saint: Shakespeare and the Graeco-Roman Heroic Tradition* (Oxford, 1971).

Bullough, Geoffrey, *Narrative and Dramatic Sources of Shakespeare* (London and New York, 1957–75), 8 vols.

Camden, William, *Britannia* (London, 1600).

Campbell, Lily B., *Shakespeare's Tragedies: Slaves of Passion* (Cambridge, 1930).

Campbell, Oscar J., *Comicall Satyre and Shakespeare's Troilus and Cressida* (San Marino, California, 1938).

Camus, Albert, *Selected Essays and Notebooks*, ed. and trans. Philip Thody (Harmondsworth, 1979).

Cantor, Paul, *Shakespeare's Rome: Republic and Empire* (Ithaca, NY, 1976).

Cervantes Saavedra, Miguel de, *The Adventures of Don Quixote*, trans. J.M. Cohen (Harmondsworth, 1950).

Charney, Maurice, *Shakespeare's Roman Plays* (Cambridge, Mass., 1961).

Colie, Rosalie, *Shakespeare's Living Art* (Princeton, 1974).

Craigie, James (ed.), *The Poems of James VI of Scotland* (Edinburgh and London, 1955).

Danby, John F., *Poets on Fortune's Hill* (London, 1952).

Danby, John F., *Shakespeare's Doctrine of Nature: a Study of 'King Lear'* (London, 1949).

Danson, Lawrence, *Tragic Alphabet: Shakespeare's Drama of Language* (New Haven and London, 1974).

Dodsworth, Martin, *Hamlet Closely Observed* (London, 1985).

Dollimore, Jonathan, *Radical Tragedy* (Brighton, 1984).

Dollimore, Jonathan, and Sinfield, Alan (eds), *Political Shakespeare* (Manchester, 1985).

Draper, R.P., 'Timon of Athens', *Shakespeare Quarterly* VIII (1957), 195–200.

Eagleton, Terry, *William Shakespeare* (Oxford, 1986).

Edwards, Philip (ed.), *Hamlet* (Cambridge, 1985).

Edwards, Philip, *Threshold of a Nation* (Cambridge, 1979).

Edwards, Philip, 'Tragic Balance in *Hamlet*', *Shakespeare Survey* 36 (1983), 43–52.

Eliade, Mircea, *Myths, Dreams and Mysteries*, trans. Philip Mairet (London, 1968).

Elliott, Martin, *Shakespeare's Invention of Othello* (London, 1988).

Empson, William, *The Structure of Complex Words* (London, 1951).

Elton, William R., *King Lear and the Gods* (Lexington, Kentucky, 2nd edn, 1988).

Everett, Barbara, *Young Hamlet* (Oxford, 1989).

Farnham, Willard, *Shakespeare's Tragic Frontier* (Berkeley, 1950, repr. Oxford, 1973).

Fichter, Andrew, '*Antony and Cleopatra*: The Time of Universal Peace', *Shakespeare Survey* 33 (1980), 99–111.

Freund, Elizabeth, '"Ariachne's broken woof": the rhetoric of citation in *Troilus and Cressida*', in P. Parker and G. Hartman (eds), *Shakespeare and the Question of Theory*, (New York and London, 1985), pp. 19–36.

Frye, Roland Mushat, *Shakespeare and Christian Doctrine* (Princeton, 1963).

Gardner, Helen, 'The Noble Moor', *Proceedings of the British Academy* 41 (1955), 189–205.

Gardner, Helen, '*Othello*: a Retrospect, 1900–67', in K. Muir and P. Edwards (eds), *Aspects of Othello* (Cambridge, 1977), pp. 1–11.

Girard, René, *Violence and the Sacred*, trans. Patrick Gregory (Baltimore, 1977).

Goldberg, S.L., 'A Tragedy of the Imagination: a Reading of *Antony and Cleopatra*', *Melbourne Critical Review* 4 (1961).

Goldman, Michael, *Shakespeare and the Energies of Drama* (Princeton, 1972).

Granville Barker, Harley, *Prefaces to Shakespeare*, I (London, 1958).

Greenblatt, Stephen, *Renaissance Self-Fashioning: From More to Shakespeare* (Chicago, 1980).

Greenblatt, Stephen, 'Shakespeare and the Exorcists', in P. Parker and G. Hartman (eds), *Shakespeare and The Question of Theory* (New York and London, 1985), pp. 163–87.

Greenblatt, Stephen, *Shakespearean Negotiations* (Oxford, 1988).

Greene, Gayle, 'Language and Value in Shakespeare's *Troilus and Cressida*', *Studies in English Literature 1500–1900* 21 (1981), 271–85.

Greene, Gayle, 'Shakespeare's Cressida: "A kind of self"', in C.R.S. Lenz, G. Greene and C.T. Neely (eds), *The Woman's Part: Feminist Criticism of Shakespeare* (Urbana, Illinois, 1980), pp. 133–49.

Grene, David, *The Actor in History: a Study in Shakespearean Stage Poetry* (University Park, Pa, and London, 1988).

Grene, David, *Reality and the Heroic Pattern* (Chicago, 1967).

Haec-Vir: or The Womanish Man (London, 1620).

Hapgood, Robert, '*Othello*', in S. Wells (ed.), *Shakespeare*, Select Bibliographical Guides, (Oxford, 1973), pp. 159–70.

Harding, D.W., 'Women's Fantasy of Manhood: a Shakespearian Theme', *Shakespeare Quarterly* 20 (1969), 245–53.

Henn, T.R., *The Living Image* (London, 1972).

Holdsworth, R.V., *Middleton and Shakespeare: the Case for Middleton's Hand in Timon of Athens* (PhD, University of Manchester, 1982).

Honigmann, E.A.J., 'The Date of *Hamlet*', *Shakespeare Survey* 9 (1956), 24–34.

Huffman, Clifford Chalmers, *Coriolanus in Context* (Lewisburg, 1971).

Humphreys, Arthur (ed.), *Julius Caesar* (Oxford, 1984).

Hunter, G.K., *Dramatic Identities and Cultural Tradition* (Liverpool, 1978).

Hunter, G.K. (ed.), *King Lear* (Harmondsworth, 1972).

Hunter, G.K. (ed.), *Macbeth* (Harmondsworth, 1967).

Hunter, G.K., 'Troilus and Cressida: a tragic satire', *Shakespeare Studies* (Tokyo) 13 (1977), 1–23.

James, D.G., *The Dream of Learning* (Oxford, 1951).

Jenkins, Harold (ed.), *Hamlet* (London, 1982).

Jones, Emrys, *The Origins of Shakespeare* (Oxford, 1977).

Jones, Emrys, 'Othello, Lepanto and the Cyprus Wars', in K. Muir and P. Edwards (eds), *Aspects of Othello* (Cambridge, 1977), pp. 61–6.

Jones, Ernest, *Hamlet and Oedipus* (London, 1949).

Jorgensen, Paul, *Lear's Self-Discovery* (Berkeley and Los Angeles, 1967).

Jorgensen, Paul, *Shakespeare's Military World* (Berkeley and Los Angeles, 1956).

Kahn, Coppelia, *Man's Estate: Masculine Identity in Shakespeare* (Berkeley, Los Angeles, London, 1981).

Kaula, David, 'Othello Possessed: Notes on Shakespeare's Use of Magic and Witchcraft', *Shakespeare Studies* 2 (1966), 112–32.

Kettle, Arnold, (ed.), *Shakespeare in a Changing World* (London, 1964).

Kirschbaum, Leo, 'Shakespeare's Stage Blood and its Critical Significance', *PMLA* 64 (1949), 517–29.

Knight, G. Wilson, *The Wheel of Fire* (London, 4th edn, 1949).

Knights, L.C., *'Hamlet' and other Shakespearean Essays* (Cambridge, 1979).

Knights, L.C., *Some Shakespearean Themes* (London, 1959).

Kott, Jan, *Shakespeare Our Contemporary*, trans. Boleslaw Taborski (London, 2nd edn, 1967).

Lenz, Carolyn R.S., Greene, Gayle and Neely, Carol T. (eds), *The Woman's Part: Feminist Criticism of Shakespeare* (Urbana, Illinois, 1980).

Lerner, Laurence (ed.), *Shakespeare's Tragedies: an Anthology of Modern Criticism* (Harmondsworth, 1963).

Lewis, C.S., *'Hamlet*: the Prince or the Poem', in L. Lerner (ed.), *Shakespeare's Tragedies: an Anthology of Modern Criticism* (Harmondsworth, 1963), pp. 65–77.

Locrine (London, 1595, repr. Tudor Facsimile Texts, Edinburgh and London, 1911).

Long, Michael, *The Unnatural Scene: a Study in Shakespearean Tragedy* (London, 1976).

Loughrey, Bryan and Taylor, Neil (eds), Thomas Middleton, *Five Plays* (London, 1988).

McAlindon, T. and Sacharoff, Mark, 'Language, Style and Meaning in Troilus and Cressida', *PMLA* 87 (1972), 90–9.

MacCallum, M.W., *Shakespeare's Roman Plays* (London, 1910).

McCluskie, Kathleen, 'The Patriarchal Bard: Feminist Criticism and Shakespeare: *King Lear* and *Measure for Measure*', in J. Dollimore and A. Sinfield (eds), *Political Shakespeare* (Manchester, 1985), pp. 88–108.

Mack, Maynard, *King Lear in Our Time* (Berkeley and Los Angeles, 1965).

Marienstras, Richard, *New Perspectives on the Shakespearean world*, trans. Janet Lloyd (Cambridge and Paris, 1985).

Markels, Julian, *The Pillar of the World* (Ohio, 1968).

Matthews, G.M., *'Othello* and the Dignity of Man', in A. Kettle (ed.), *Shakespeare in a Changing World*, pp. 123–45.

Mercer, Peter, *Hamlet and the Acting of Revenge* (London, 1987).
Muir, Kenneth (ed.), *King Lear* (London, 1950, repr. 1985).
Muir, Kenneth (ed.), *Macbeth* (London, 1951).
Muir, Kenneth (ed.), *Othello* (Harmondsworth, 1968).
Muir, Kenneth, *Shakespeare's Tragic Sequence* (Liverpool, 2nd edn, 1979).
Muir, Kenneth (ed.), *Troilus and Cressida* (Oxford, 1982).
Muir, Kenneth, and Edwards, Philip (eds), *Aspects of Othello* (Cambridge, 1977).
Murray, Gibert, *The Classical Tradition in Poetry* (Cambridge, Mass., 1927).
Nuttall, A.D., *Timon of Athens* (New York, London, etc., 1989).
Palmer, Kenneth (ed.), *Troilus and Cressida* (London, 1982).
Parker, Patricia and Hartman, Geoffrey (eds), *Shakespeare and the Question of Theory* (New York and London, 1985).
Paul, H.N., *The Royal Play of Macbeth* (New York, 1950).
Perrett, Wilfrid, *The Story of King Lear from Geoffrey of Monmouth to Shakespeare* (Berlin, 1904).
Phillips, J.E. Jr., *The State in Shakespeare's Greek and Roman Plays* (New York, 1940).
Poole, Adrian, *Coriolanus* (New York, London, etc., 1988).
Prosser, Eleanor, *Hamlet and Revenge* (Stanford, 1967).
Rabkin, Norman, *Shakespeare and the Common Understanding* (New York and London, 1967).
Raysor, Thomas Middleton (ed.), *Coleridge's Shakespeare Criticism* (London, 1930), 2 vols.
Reibetanz, John, *The Lear World* (Toronto, 1977).
Robinson, F.N. (ed.), *The Complete Works of Geoffrey Chaucer* (Oxford, 2nd edn, 1974).
Rose, Mark, 'Othello's Occupation: Shakespeare and the Romance of Chivalry', *English Literary Renaissance* 15 (1985), 293–311.
Rosenberg, Marvin, *The Masks of Macbeth* (Berkeley, Los Angeles, London, 1978).
Sanders, Norman (ed.), *Othello* (Cambridge, 1984).
Sanders, Wilbur, *The Dramatist and the Received Idea* (Cambridge, 1968).
Sanders, Wilbur and Jacobson, Howard, *Shakespeare's Magnanimity: Four Tragic Heroes, their Friends and Families* (London, 1978).
Schanzer, Ernest, *The Problem Plays of Shakespeare* (London, 1963).
Scragg, Leah, 'Iago – Vice or Devil?' in K. Muir and P. Edwards (eds), *Aspects of Othello* (Cambridge, 1977), pp. 48–59.
Sewell, Arthur, *Character and Society in Shakespeare* (Oxford, 1951).
Simmons, J.L., *Shakespeare's Pagan World: the Roman Tragedies* (Brighton, 1974).
Shaw, Bernard, *Collected Plays with their Prefaces* (London, 1970–4), 7 vols.
Smith, A.J. (ed.), *John Donne, The Complete English Poems* (Harmondsworth, 1971).
Smith, A.J., *Literary Love* (London, 1983).
Spivack, Bernard, *Shakespeare and the Allegory of Evil* (New York, 1958).
Stein, Arnold, 'The Image of Antony: Tragic and Lyric Imagination', *Kenyon Review* 21 (1959), 586–606.
Stirling, Brents, *Unity in Shakespearean Tragedy* (New York, 1956).

Stone, Lawrence, *The Family, Sex and Marriage in England 1500–1800* (London, 1977).

Sturgess, K. (ed.), *Arden of Faversham* (Harmondsworth, 1969).

Swanston, Hamish F.G., 'The Baroque Element in *Troilus and Cressida*', *Durham University Journal* XIX (N.S.) (1957–8), 14–23.

Thomas, Keith, *Religion and the Decline of Magic* (London, 1971).

Thomas, Vivian, *Shakespeare's Roman Worlds* (London and New York, 1989).

Thompson, Ann, *Shakespeare's Chaucer* (Liverpool, 1978).

Thompson, Ann, 'Who Sees Double in the Double Plot?', in M. Bradbury and D. Palmer (eds), *Shakespearian Tragedy*, Stratford-upon-Avon Studies, 20 (London, 1984), pp. 47–75.

Tillyard, E.M.W., *Shakespeare's History Plays* (London, 1944).

Turner, Frederick, *Shakespeare and the Nature of Time* (Oxford, 1971).

Velz, John W., 'Cracking Strong Curbs Asunder: Roman Destiny and the Roman Hero in *Coriolanus*', *English Literary Renaissance* 13 (1983), 58–69.

Wells, Stanley, (ed.), *Shakespeare*, Select Bibliographical Guides (Oxford, 1973).

Wells, Stanley and Taylor, Gary, (general eds), *William Shakespeare, The Complete Works: Compact Edition* (Oxford, 1988).

Wells, Stanley and Taylor, Gary, with Jowett, John and Montgomery, William, *William Shakespeare: a Textual Companion* (Oxford, 1987).

Wilders, John, *The Lost Garden* (London, 1978).

Wilson, John Dover, *The Essential Shakespeare* (Cambridge, 1932).

Wilson, John Dover, *What Happens in Hamlet* (Cambridge, 3rd edn, 1951).

Wimsatt, W.K. Jr (ed.), *Samuel Johnson on Shakespeare* (London, 1960).

Wymer, Rowland, *Suicide and Despair in the Jacobean Drama* (Brighton, 1986).

Index